THE SPANISH WEST

THE SPANISH WEST

By the Editors of

TIME-LIFE BOOKS

TIME-LIFE BOOKS / ALEXANDRIA, VIRGINIA

THE OLD WEST

EDITORIAL STAFF FOR "THE SPANISH WEST"
Editor: George G. Daniels
Picture Editor: Patricia Hunt
Text Editors: Valerie Moolman, Joan S. Reiter,
Gerald Simons
Designer: Bruce Blair
Staff Writers: Don Earnest, Frank Kappler,
Gerry Schremp, Rosalind Stubenberg
Chief Researcher: June O. Goldberg
Researchers: Jane Coughran, Loretta Britten,
Thomas Dickey, Terry Drucker, Harriet Heck,
Beatrice Hsia, Thomas Lashnits, Donna Lucey,
Mary Kay Moran, Fred Ritchin, Reiko Uyeshima
Design Assistants: Joan Hoffman, Deanna Lorenz

EDITORIAL PRODUCTION
Production Editor: Douglas B. Graham
Operations Manager: Gennaro C. Esposito
Assistant Production Editor: Feliciano Madrid
Quality Control: Robert L. Young (director),
James J. Cox (assistant), Michael G. Wight
(associate)
Art Coordinator: Anne B. Landry
Copy Staff: Susan B. Galloway (chief),
Barbara H. Fuller, Eleanore W. Karsten,
Susan Tribich, Florence Keith, Celia Beattie
Picture Department: Marianne Dowell
Traffic: Jeanne Potter

THE COVER: Proud and elegant, a California rancho owner of the 1830s rides out to inspect his domain in *Patrón* by James Walker. A grandee's sword, silver-buttoned raiments, and a steed with Arabian bloodlines bespeak his Spanish heritage. In the frontispiece photograph, four Santa Barbarans pay homage to their ancestry by performing a decorous Iberian folk dance at a party in the 1880s.

CORRESPONDENTS: Elisabeth Kraemer (Bonn); Margot Hapgood, Dorothy Bacon (London); Susan Jonas, Lucy T. Voulgaris (New York); Maria Vincenza Aloisi, Josephine du Brusle (Paris); Ann Natanson (Rome). Valuable assistance was also provided by: John Nielsen (Madrid); Bernard Diederich (Mexico City); Carolyn T. Chubet, Miriam Hsia (New York); Eva Stichova (Prague); Janet Zich (San Francisco); Villette Harris (Washington).

CONTENTS

Mounted Franciscan friars bearing crosses lead a procession forth from the California mission of San Carlos Borromeo in the early 1800s.

1 | "The best land in all these Indias"

When Cabeza de Vaca, a lost Spanish explorer, emerged from the wilderness in 1536 after eight years of wandering through parts of the vast country that was to become the American West, he reported, "It is, no doubt, the best land in all these Indias. Indeed, the land needs no circumstance to make it blessed." Later generations of Westerners could consider it twice-blessed—by the fruits of Spanish culture and labor as well as by natural endowment.

For 300 years the territory north of Mexico was part of a vast Spanish empire that, at one point, covered half the known world. The first adventurers to penetrate the region went there in search of gold and silver. Although these riches turned out to be only a glittering mirage, missionaries, ranchers and farmers later made their way into the wilderness, bringing with them their customs and laws, art and architecture, animals and agriculture. And when their Anglo-Saxon counterparts eventually arrived on the scene, they frequently found, as one observer put it, that "the backbreaking work of pioneering was already done for them. They came into an established community."

As dust rises from the milling herd, a *vaquero* lassos a corralled mustang before breaking it to the saddle. "For this business," wrote explorer Zebulon Pike in 1808, "there is no nation in the world superior to the Spaniards of Texas."

8

Indian converts round up horses and tend sheep at Mission Nuestra Señora de la Soledad, located in California's fertile Salinas Valley. Although it was one of the smaller California missions, Soledad by the 1820s was home to some 500 neophytes who cared for 15,000 head of livestock.

12

At seaside festivities near Santa Barbara, California, aristocratic rancheros and their families watch as a dauntless *vaquero* riding at full gallop swoops down to pull a partially buried rooster from the sand. Other popular horseback sports included throwing bulls by the tail and roping grizzly bears.

Cattle, poultry and goods heaped on two-wheeled ox-drawn *carretas* await sale or barter in San Antonio's Market Plaza, as traders from outlying ranchos pause for an alfresco repast. Town plazas continued to be centers of commerce in the Southwest long after Spanish rule had come to an end.

15

For God, for glory and for gold

Early in 1883, the citizens of Santa Fe, New Mexico, prepared to celebrate the 333rd anniversary of the founding of their city by the Spaniards. Actually, the exact date of the founding was then unclear; though the townspeople had some reason to believe that Santa Fe dated from 1550, Spanish documents uncovered years later proved that the first settlers had arrived at the site from Mexico in 1610. But the city fathers were willing to live with a bit of uncertainty, and they went ahead with plans for a long series of gala festivals. To cap these fiestas, civic leaders commissioned a poem commemorating the Spaniards' achievement, and they offered the assignment to no less a poet than Walt Whitman, the gray-bearded singer of American democracy and the common man.

Whitman replied in July from his home in Camden, New Jersey. He wrote, "Your kind invitation to visit you and deliver a poem reached me so late that I have to decline, with sincere regrets. But I will say a few words off hand."

The poet's remarks went well beyond polite praise for Santa Fe's rich Spanish heritage. "We Americans have yet to really appreciate our antecedents," he began. "Thus far, impress'd by New England writers and schoolmasters, we tacitly abandon ourselves to the notion that our United States have been fashion'd from the British Isles only, and essentially form a second England only—which is a very great mistake." On that point, no fair-minded man could disagree. The Eastern states had been melting pots even before they became states, and the trans-Mississippi region had been explored and settled by many "foreign" peoples. By

1883, every European nationality and several immigrant groups from Asia had thriving colonies in the Western part of the country.

Whitman then veered and headed into troubled waters. Echoing the flimsy racial theories of the times, he maintained that Anglo-Saxon Americans, with their aggressive practicality and their cultural chauvinism, "already threaten excess," and that "something outside of them, and to counterbalance them, is seriously needed." The poet declared that "character, literature, a society worthy the name, are yet to be establish'd, through a nationality of noblest spiritual, heroic, democratic attributes.

"To that composite American identity of the future," Whitman concluded, "Spanish character will supply some of the most needed parts. No stock shows a grander historical perspective—grander in religiousness and loyalty, or for patriotism, courage, decorum, gravity and honor. As to the Spanish stock of our Southwest, it is certain to me that we do not begin to appreciate the splendor and sterling value of its race element. Who knows but that element, like the course of some subterranean river, dipping invisibly for a hundred or two years, is now to emerge in broadest flow and permanent action?"

In spite of Whitman's well-intentioned tribute to the Spanish character, his letter undoubtedly dismayed many citizens of Santa Fe—Martinezes and Chavezes as well as Joneses and Johnsons. Neither ethnic group wished to be reminded of the differences—the distrust, cultural prejudices and conflicting ambitions—that had so long pitted Anglo-Americans and Spanish Americans against each other. Both groups wanted to forget the recent bitter past, especially Texas' bloody fight for independence from Mexico in 1836 and the far-flung war between Mexico and the United States a decade later. Spanish Americans were sensitive about those

Boasting superb stonework that made it a high point of Spanish architecture in the New World, San Antonio's Mission San José was 100 years old and badly neglected when this painting was made in 1878.

struggles because Mexico lost both, and they had cause to be offended by Whitman's clear implication that Spanish culture, that "subterranean river," was not a visible force.

Quite the opposite was true. In 1883, Spanish culture dominated a far larger part of the Western Hemisphere than Anglo-Saxon culture, and its vigor had been increasing steadily through the 19th Century as Spanish colonies staged their own American revolutions. Some 40 million people in the two Americas spoke Spanish, observed Spanish laws and worshipped in Spanish Catholic churches; and several million of these Spanish speakers lived as citizens of the United States. In fact, Spanish culture was far more pervasive in the United States than even many Spanish Americans realized.

Vast landholdings all across the West were still based on old Spanish grants. Spanish architecture—particularly the low, rambling thick-walled style of gracious country haciendas—was the rule throughout the Southwest, blending superbly with the austere landscape. Americans enjoyed Spanish cuisine, played the Spanish guitar, danced the Spanish fandango, and sang Spanish songs in translation (for example, the cowboy classic "The Streets of Laredo"). Even the most ardent Anglophile could hardly claim to be educated without at least some knowledge of Spanish literature.

The American vocabulary itself was much indebted to Spain. From the Spaniards came many words that had to do with horsemanship, at which they excelled: bronco, mustang, cinch, lariat or lasso, buckaroo, rodeo and stampede. No English terms could describe the Western land features quite so precisely as Spanish terms like canyon, arroyo and mesa. The special connotations of many Spanish or Spanish-derived words —grandee, *empresario,* savvy (from *saber,* to know), siesta and fiesta—could not be conveyed by their closest English synonyms. Spanish names had stuck to seven Western states or territories (Arizona, California, Colorado, Montana, Nevada, New Mexico and Texas), numerous rivers (Rio Grande, Brazos, Pecos, Sacramento and San Joaquin) and several mountain chains, among them the Sierra Nevada and the Sangre de Cristo Mountains.

While Spanish Americans had no reason to be defensive about their cultural present, they had plenty of cause for celebrating Spain's colonial past. It was an epic past—long, dramatic, crowded with saintly heroes and magnificent villains. For three full centuries, the Spaniards and their descendants were the glory of the New World, masterful and proud, often challenged but never seriously threatened—until they lost their northernmost lands to an aggressive and expansion-minded United States in 1846.

Those were centuries that saw spectacular Spanish achievement. By 1540, less than five decades after Christopher Columbus planted Spain's flag in the New World, small Spanish forces had overrun the high civilizations of Mexico's Aztecs and Peru's Incas, and had subjugated an estimated 11 million Indians to the Spanish crown. By 1600, Spain ruled about two thirds of the Western Hemisphere, and a century later the Spanish conquistadors had pushed their frontiers as far south as Buenos Aires and as far north as the Rio Grande. All this they accomplished with only meager manpower—the little that their homeland could spare from its interminable wars with England and France. Through much of this early period, Spanish soldiers numbered only a few thousand, and immigrants from Spain averaged no more than 1,000 a year.

Even before their hold on Mexico was secure, the Spaniards were boldly expanding to the north, and in the process they founded the first permanent settlements west of the Mississippi, beginning with Santa Fe in 1610. Then came Tucson around 1700, Albuquerque in 1706, San Antonio in 1718 and San Diego in 1769. (The earliest non-Spanish town west of the Mississippi was St. Louis, founded by the French in 1764—only to be immediately ceded to Spain, along with New Orleans and the rest of Louisiana.) Before long Spanish traders and explorers had plumbed the wilderness as far north as the regions later known as the Dakotas, Wyoming, Oregon, Washington and British Columbia.

In the meantime, Spanish colonists were making phenomenal progress behind their expanding frontiers. Almost as soon as they arrived in Mexico, the Spaniards discovered its enormous mineral wealth. In the mid-1500s, dozens of silver-mining towns mushroomed on Mexico's central plateau, producing great private fortunes as well as a flood of revenue to maintain Spain's power on the European continent. Affluent Spaniards established a university in Mexico City as early as 1551, exactly 85 years before the Massachusetts colony set up the New World's first English college, later named Harvard. Mexico City, with its seats of learning, government buildings and majestic cathedral rising from the ruins of the Aztec capital, quickly became a paragon of wealth and refinement —the Paris of the Western Hemisphere.

When Englishman Thomas Gage visited Mexico City in the 1630s, he wrote: "It is a byword that at Mexico there are four things fair, that is to say, the women, the apparel, the horses, and the streets. But to this I may add the beauty of some of the coaches of the Gentry, which do exceed the cost of the best of the Court of Madrid and other parts of Christendom, for they spare no Silver, nor Gold, nor the best silks from China to enrich them."

Although Mexico proved to be the world's richest silver-mining country, silver alone could not sustain it, and as the Spaniards diversified the economy, they inadvertently shaped the whole history of the American West. Aristocrats and common soldiers, rewarded for their conquests with great tracts of land, built estates along the northern frontier, and there they introduced into the West three invaluable animals: the beef cattle, the sheep and the horse. Commercial quantities of these animals began arriving from Europe as early as the 1520s, and all three species thrived and multiplied in regions whose semiarid climate and vegetation closely resembled Spain's. Centuries later, Spanish sheep and the free-roaming descendants of Spanish cattle formed the nucleus of huge Texas herds. Moreover, the Spanish *vaquero* was the prototype of the American cowboy—not just in the mechanics of his job, but also in his clothing, his foot-loose life style and his general attitude of stubborn self-reliance.

Historically, the most important of the three imported animals was the horse, whose speed, stamina and durability made it indispensable in the great open spaces of the West. Horses were introduced to Mexico by the earliest conquistadors in 1519, and horse-breeding followed the advancing line of Spanish settlement. By the early 1700s, Indian tribes along the Rio Grande had begun acquiring horses—by both trade and thievery—from the stock-raising haciendas. It was only a matter of decades before Spanish horses spread northward to such nomadic Plains tribes as the Comanches and the Sioux, and westward to more settled Indians such as the Nez Percés, who themselves became expert stock breeders.

The horse wrought powerful changes throughout the Indians' world, but nowhere more so than among the Comanches. Spanish horses transformed these tribesmen from foot-slogging hunters into swift, wide-ranging raiders; large war parties often swept deep into Mexico, making off with rich booty and still more Spanish horses—as many as 2,000 on a single foray. Yet the fierce Comanche horsemen were also unwitting allies of the Spaniards, for they effectively blocked the southward expansion of Spain's Canada-based rivals, the French and later the English.

The Spaniards themselves were paradoxical shapers of history. Although some of the conquistadors were cruel and greedy men, their constructive accomplishments placed them second only to the Americans as pioneers of the West. They were renowned for their skill and courage as soldiers—so much so that a 16th Century European who wished to compliment an enemy would say that he fought "like a Spaniard"; yet a conquistador might be just as adept at composing elegant love poems or melancholy odes. They were a haughty, race-proud, class-conscious breed of men who exploited the Indians as if they were mere animals; yet many Spanish soldiers married Indian women and treated them no better or worse than Spanish spouses. In matters of the law and religion, they were idealistic and strict; yet they could also be expedient and sometimes even cynical.

Ultimately these contradictory conquerors represented the last great flowering of Europe's feudal traditions. Like the armored knights of the Middle Ages, they were—by birth or aspiration—a warrior elite who lived according to an elaborate code of duty and honor. It was their duty to fight every enemy and endure every hardship to serve their king and propagate their faith; and by doing their duty with reckless abandon they fully expected to make themselves rich, famous and powerful. If these pious, ruthless men had had a motto, it might well have been "For glory, God and gold" —though not necessarily in that order. In any case, the world had not seen their like since the medieval crusaders, and it would never see their like again. ◉

A creative blend of native materials and Iberian flair

Spanish pioneers who pushed north and west from Mexico in the wake of the 16th Century explorations founded new styles in crafts and architecture even as they helped consolidate an empire. And to the former end, at least, they owed the Indians a major debt.

Unlike the Anglo-Saxons, who only rarely adapted tribal culture for themselves, the Spaniards found that native materials and such native tastes as a love of bright color could be felicitously joined to classic Iberian designs. For example, the doors of a *trastero (right)* —a massive cupboard used to store everything from jewelry to dishes— were often decorated with bold mineral paints used by the Indians. Most furniture was made from the soft, easily worked pines that covered the mountains, and even the simplest pieces usually bore gracious touches of carving.

The melding of cultures affected objects from shields to blankets, but it was especially evident in buildings. Except for the major churches and civic structures, architecture was the work of amateurs—padres and outpost commanders—whose designs were carried out by Indian workmen. The basic point of departure was the flat-roofed pueblo Indian building, whose walls of thick adobe brick kept out the blazing heat of summer and retained warmth in the cold months.

Expanding this straightforward style, the Spaniards designed their later missions around central patios inherited from the Arabs. On the perimeter of the patios they extended eaves to create covered arcades, which they supported with the rounded arch first brought to Spain by the Romans. And to the roofs they added heavy red tiles. This polygenous architecture, drawing on the ideas of several centuries and continents, came to be known as the California mission style and was one of the Spaniards' most distinguished contributions to the American West.

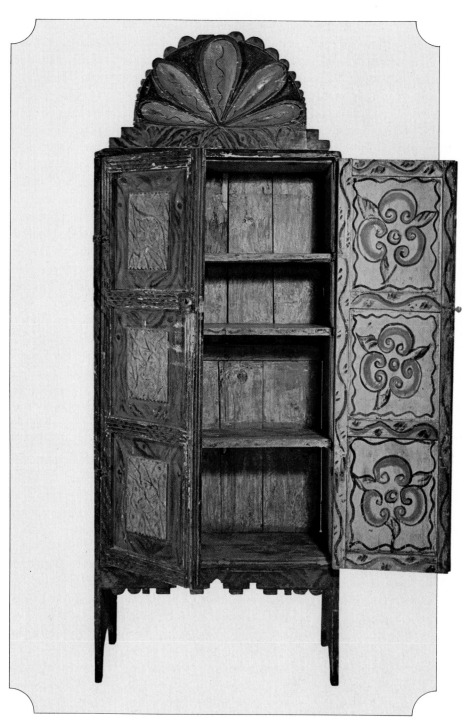

PAINTED PINE *TRASTERO*

PANELED PINE CHEST

CARVED CHEST ON REMOVABLE STAND

SANCTUARY BENCH

PINE CHAIR AND TABLE

WOODEN ST. BENEDICT IN NICHE,
CARMEL, CALIFORNIA

CARVED STONE WINDOW,
SAN ANTONIO, TEXAS

BELLS IN CAMPANARIO,
SAN JUAN CAPISTRANO, CALIFORNIA

22

ARCADE,
SAN FERNANDO, CALIFORNIA

DOUBLE-TIERED FOUNTAIN,
SAN FERNANDO

DOOR WITH STONE FACING,
SAN JUAN CAPISTRANO

ROWELED SPUR

CARVED-LEATHER SADDLE

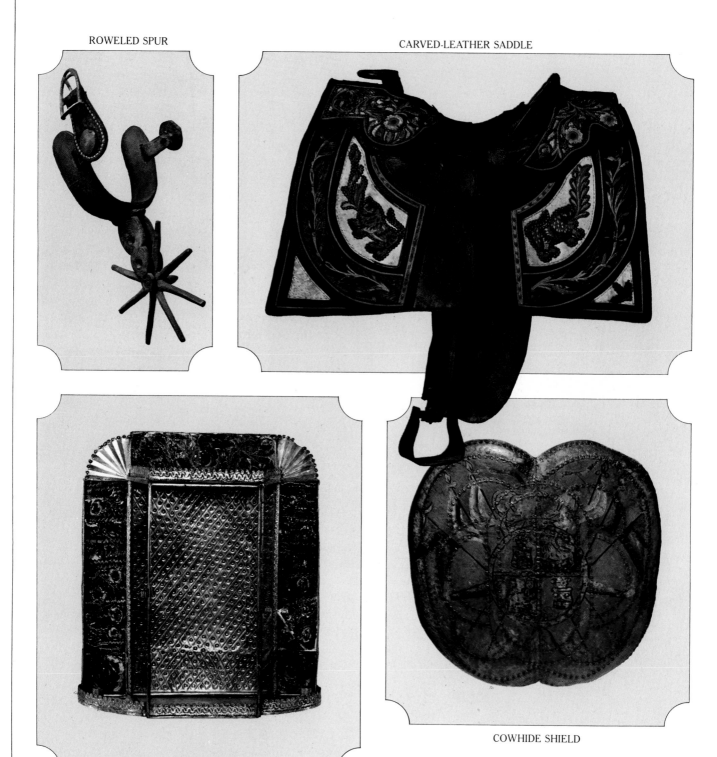

TIN AND GLASS SHRINE

COWHIDE SHIELD

RAWHIDE TRAVELING TRUNK

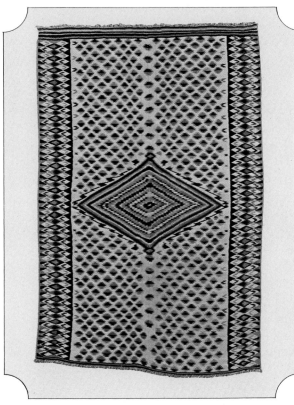

WOOLEN BLANKET

By the 1520s, the conquistadors had already set up the two colonies that would carry Spain's flag into the land that eventually became the American West. The first of these colonies was Cuba, established in 1511. The second was Mexico, then called New Spain, which had been invaded from Cuba in 1519 by some 500 soldiers led by the greatest of the conquistadors, Hernán Cortés (*pages 30-33*).

The governments of both Cuba and Mexico were authorized by the king to explore the vast unknown land mass between Florida and Baja (lower) California, whose shores had already been touched by Spanish captains. Theoretically, all the land claimed by any expedition was the private property of the king, but in practice the explorers themselves retained control as agents of the crown, which demanded only one fifth of the revenues produced by the new-found lands. So Cuba and Mexico became sibling rivals at exploration and conquest, and whichever government discovered rich territory might be expected to distribute land generously among its soldiers.

Naturally, plans to explore the mysterious continent attracted more and more would-be conquistadors to Cuba and Mexico, and at first their overriding ambition was to find gold. Gold was a form of wealth far easier than land to divide and spend. Furthermore, a whole body of legend promised the Spaniards gold, and the Aztec treasure Cortés shipped back to Spain convinced the soldiers that the legends were fact.

These legends spoke of seven dazzling cities of gold, all of them grander and richer than any metropolis in Europe. The events in the tales allegedly took place sometime between the Eighth and 12th centuries, when Spain and Portugal were occupied by the Moors. They involved seven Christian bishops who fled from Portugal to escape persecution by the infidels. The bishops, along with a handful of followers, sailed across the Sea of Darkness until they came to the Blessed Isles. Landing on an island they named Antilia, the refugees found streams that flowed over golden sand, and here they built seven gold cities, one for each bishop.

Though not a scintilla of evidence supported the tales, explorers and geographers persisted in naming a string of Caribbean islands the Antilles after the mythical Antilia. And when these islands proved largely devoid of gold, the Spaniards advanced new theories to

25

shore up the legends. Perhaps the seven cities were located on the mainland, in or near the Strait of Anian —an equally mythical waterway that supposedly cut through North America, joining the Atlantic and the Pacific? Or perhaps the seven cities were not cities at all but great golden caves located deep in the continental plateaus? Wherever the cities or caves might be, the Spaniards believed they would soon find them.

The first important expedition was launched from Cuba in 1528. Some 300 men under Pánfilo de Narváez landed on the west coast of Florida, struck out northward—and apparently vanished from the face of the earth. It was a sorry beginning, but the Spanish were not discouraged for long. In 1530, there was exciting news from Mexico. One Nuñez de Guzmán, an ambitious soldier who was the acting governor of a western province, had heard stories from the Indians of seven fabulous cities situated far beyond the wastes of northern Mexico. In that remote land, the streets were paved with gold, and the natives wore so much gem-studded jewelry that they moved about with great difficulty. It never occurred to Guzmán that the Indians had concocted the story because, understanding the Spaniards' lust for treasure, they hoped to send them on a wild goose chase—and the farther the better.

Guzmán eagerly swallowed the Indians' bait and started north with a band of soldiers. But the great adventure soon degenerated into a slave-hunting expedition. In taking captives for sale in Mexico, Guzmán knowingly broke the law; Indian slavery was forbidden by the Spanish crown and frowned on by the Spanish church. However it was clear to Guzmán, and to the authorities as well, that those humane, idealistic laws would have to be compromised. Most of the Spanish adventurers in the New World considered menial labor beneath their dignity, and unless Indians were impressed into service, Mexico's output of food and precious ores was bound to prove inadequate.

Having discovered a trade that was both lucrative and far less chancy than seeking treasure, Guzmán persisted in slave-hunting over the next several years, and it was during one of his expeditions to the north in 1536 that he accidentally learned of the fate of the Narváez party. A Guzmán lieutenant, reconnoitering for live merchandise along the Sinaloa River in western Mexico, came upon two strange outlanders. One,

tall and muscular, was obviously too dark to be an Indian. He was, in fact, a Moorish slave named Estéban who had accompanied his Spanish master on the Narváez expedition. The second man, clad in tattered deerskin, could have been mistaken for an Indian except for his heavy beard; his white skin had been burned by the sun to a reddish copper hue.

To the lieutenant's astonishment, the sunburned stranger spoke to him in perfect Castilian and began asking questions. Were they Spaniards? What captain did they serve? And where was their captain?

This peremptory individual was Alvar Nuñez Cabeza de Vaca, a hidalgo (landed aristocrat) and distinguished veteran of Spain's European wars. Cabeza de Vaca said that two more Spaniards were camped nearby with a band of friendly Indians; these four were the only survivors of the 300 men whom Narváez had landed in Florida almost exactly eight years ago.

Little by little, Cabeza de Vaca told of his wanderings—covering about 6,000 miles in all—and supplied the first authentic information about the American West. After crossing Florida, he explained, the expedition had set out on the Gulf of Mexico in a makeshift fleet of five horsehide boats. All of the flimsy craft save two were lost at sea; the remaining two, carrying about 100 men in all, ran aground on a large sandy island (probably Galveston Island) within easy swimming distance of the mainland. After crossing this gap, the hungry castaways were found by some Indians, who tried to be helpful. However the natives, emaciated themselves, could only supply the Spaniards with paltry amounts of fish and roots. One by one the explorers died of starvation, malnutrition, disease and exposure, until only four were left.

With their nomadic Indian companions, these four had roamed ceaselessly through the great wilderness expanses that would become known as Texas, Arizona and New Mexico. In desert regions, they consumed the exotic fruit of the prickly pear cactus, and on the grasslands they feasted upon buffalo and deer felled by Indian bowmen. The Spaniards traveled naked, as did their Indian escorts; the fierce Southwestern sun burned them so severely that, said one castaway, they shed their skins twice a year, like snakes.

Gradually the Spaniards found ways to improve their lot. Cabeza de Vaca discovered that he could profit as a trader, exchanging sea shells from the Gulf Coast for surplus food from inland Indians. All four of the explorers cloaked themselves in the powers of medicine men. Although they frequently served as slaves, they were also regarded as children of the sun and were believed to possess supernatural powers. They obliged the Indians by aping the rituals of native healers, blowing on their patients' wounds or aches and interminably chanting, Indian-fashion, their Catholic prayers. Apparently a respectable number of their patients recovered, because the Spaniards were presented with gourd rattles, the medicine man's status symbol, and were sometimes escorted ceremoniously from one Indian settlement to the next.

In the late stages of their tremendous journey, the Spaniards were treated with particular kindness by the Pima Indians of northwestern Mexico and southern Arizona. The Pimas gave them many gifts, including five ceremonial arrowheads made of a green stone that Cabeza de Vaca thought to be emerald, but which was probably malachite. When the Spaniards finally headed southward, they were accompanied by no less than 600 of the Pimas. The Indians were still with them when Guzmán's slave hunters turned up; however, Cabeza de Vaca warded off any intentions his rescuers may have had of enslaving them.

On their return to Mexico City, the four wanderers were welcomed as heroes. Cabeza de Vaca repeated his story for the most important man in Mexico: Antonio de Mendoza, who had arrived the year before as Mexico's first viceroy. Mendoza's rectitude had already earned him the nickname *El Bueno* — the good man; yet like every Spaniard he yearned for gold and dreamed of outdoing even the famed Cortés as a treasure finder. He questioned Cabeza de Vaca closely in the hope of finding clues to the seven cities of gold. The explorer told him only the ungilded truth — that the lands through which he had traveled were "remote and malign, devoid of resources." He allowed, however, that in the Sonora Valley a tribe of Indians had spoken of a rich, faraway people with whom they traded. Those distant Indians were city dwellers who lived in large houses and possessed marvelous wares — turquoises, emeralds, even cotton blankets. The Spaniards' Indian hosts said that the land of the wealthy tribe lay far to the north, beyond the deserts and mountains, and they pointed out the route they followed to reach those cities.

Cabeza de Vaca's secondhand report galvanized Mendoza's imagination. Here at last was evidence of those seven magnificent cities. The Viceroy made up his mind to launch a systematic exploration of the north. And for its leader he chose a man he could trust implicitly: Francisco Vásquez de Coronado, a young nobleman whom Mendoza had met at the Spanish court and brought to Mexico as his aide. The 27-year-old lord had soon proved his mettle by smashing an Indian revolt outside the capital. He had also acquired some powerful allies and a considerable fortune by marrying Beatríz de Estrada, the daughter of a royal treasurer. On top of these assets, Coronado routinely displayed the virtues of obedience to his superiors, diligence in tedious administrative chores and an almost childlike honesty that made it impossible for him to deceive or dissemble in any way.

To facilitate Coronado's new exploratory duties, Mendoza appointed him governor of New Galicia, a convenient northwesterly region from which the young hidalgo could oversee — and eventually lead — the various expeditions sent out to explore and conquer the rumored kingdoms beyond. Coronado soon was busy assisting a small party that Mendoza had ordered assembled for a preliminary reconnaissance.

This expedition was to be led by a distinguished Franciscan friar named Marcos de Niza, who had served with the conquistadors in Peru and Guatemala, and who was reputedly a skilled cartographer and a fearless explorer. Early in 1539, the expedition departed, with the Moor Estéban as its guide.

Coronado personally saw the friar off toward the frontier town of Culiacán and reviewed his written instructions from Viceroy Mendoza. Wherever the friar went, he was instructed to take note of "the people who are there, if they be many or few, and if they are scattered or live in communities; the quality and fertility of the soil, the temperature of the country, the trees and plants and domestic and feral animals which may be there; the rivers, if they are large or small, and the minerals or metals which are there." If the friar was able to take specimens of noteworthy findings, "bring them or send them, in order that his Majesty may be advised of everything." He was also to inquire about

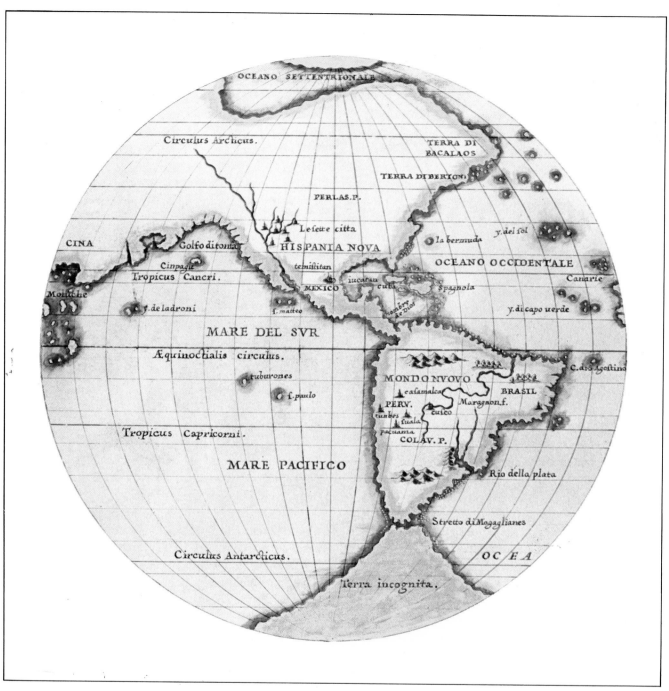

the coasts of the Atlantic and Pacific oceans "because some arm of the sea may enter the land beyond." Plainly the Viceroy was hoping to find the mythical Strait of Anián as well as the seven cities of gold.

On March 7, Fray Marcos left Culiacán behind him, and two weeks later he sent the Moor on ahead with some of their Indians. Estéban would keep Fray Marcos posted by sending back runners with crosses indicating the size of any settlements he discovered; the larger the cross, the bigger the community.

Estéban, puffed up with pride, swaggered north like some fantastic potentate. He wore long bright-colored robes, a plumed headdress and bracelets with jingling bells; and he carried a medicine man's decorated gourd that he sent ahead by an Indian emissary each time his party neared a settlement. The gourd seemed to guarantee him a respectful welcome, and his regal attire so impressed the natives that they showered him with gifts, including turquoise necklaces and young girls.

Four days after Estéban's departure, Fray Marcos spied the first of his messengers; the Indian was staggering under the weight of a man-sized cross, indicating that the Moor had discovered a major settlement. The messenger conveyed to the friar that Estéban had

In a 1550 map of the Western Hemisphere, an Italian cartographer confidently sprinkled the wilderness north of New Spain with seven cities, said by legend to hold riches rivaling those of the Aztecs.

learned of "the greatest country in the world." The Indian said that this country, which he himself had visited, lay a month's journey beyond Estéban's latest position. Its name was new to the Spaniards but it was soon to be a magic word throughout their empire: Cíbola. According to Fray Marcos, the Indian reported "seven very great cities, all under one lord," declaring that "the houses, of stone and lime, were very large" and had porches "worked with many designs of turquoises." The friar added: "Many other particulars he told me of these seven cities, as well as of other provinces farther away, each of which, he said, was greater than the seven cities."

Fired with visions of glory, Fray Marcos pushed on after the fast-moving Estéban. Other messengers confirmed the information about Cíbola and the even richer outlying provinces of Marata, Acus and Totonteac. As April gave way to May, Fray Marcos' party left the fertile Sonora Valley and entered a desert that stretched from northern Mexico into the region that would become New Mexico. They followed a trail well marked by campfire ashes, subsisting on rabbits and other small game.

In late May, the dream began to come apart. Two more of Estéban's Indians arrived from the north, both of them covered with wounds. They told the friar that as Estéban's party approached the first city of Cíbola, the Moor had sent his gourd ahead as a calling card. But the charm had lost its magic. The local chieftain had coldly imprisoned the invaders and then had executed them—all save the two messengers, who had been released to carry the grim news to Fray Marcos.

The good friar was stunned by word of the massacre but unshaken in his resolve to reach Cíbola. And in a few days, he spied in the distance what he took to be one of the fabled seven cities. To Fray Marcos' anxious eye, the far-off metropolis seemed "bigger than the city of Mexico." The friar said, "I was tempted to go to it, because I knew that I ventured only my life." But after an inner struggle he decided on a course of prudence, for it was his duty to bear witness to "the greatest and best of the discoveries."

The friar's party lingered long enough to erect a cross and a cairn of stones "in the name of Don Antonio de Mendoza, viceroy of New Spain, for the Emperor, our lord, in token possession of all the seven cities and of the kingdoms of Totonteac and of Acus and Marata." Then Fray Marcos and his little band of survivors turned their backs on Cíbola and started the long trek home.

Thus far, the friar had found no evidence of gold. But on his return trip he saw in the distance other cities. "I was informed," he declared, that in this realm "was much gold, and that the natives in it trade in vessels and jewels for the ears, and little plates with which they scrape themselves and remove the sweat."

Finally in August, six months after his departure from New Galicia, Fray Marcos reached Mexico City and composed his long-awaited report for the Viceroy. Though he faithfully reported the death of Estéban and the apparent hostility of the northern tribes, the real excitement lay in what he had seen of Cíbola and had learned of the rich surrounding provinces. The Spaniards were overjoyed. Fray Marcos was rewarded by promotion to post of father provincial—administrative head of all the Franciscans in Mexico. Viceroy Mendoza decided to go ahead with a full-scale expedition to Cíbola and sent orders for Coronado to begin preparations. Yet careful man that he was, the Viceroy decided on one final reconnaissance. Summoning Melchior Díaz, the trusted alcalde, or mayor, of the frontier town of Culiacán, the Viceroy ordered him to backtrack on Fray Marcos' trail, checking out travel time and other facets of his story. Díaz left for the north on November 17, 1539, with 15 mounted soldiers and a small body of Indians. In the next four months they would travel approximately 1,500 miles.

Meanwhile, Fray Marcos spoke of his trip with increasing embellishments. One of his servants quoted him on Cíbola: "The cities were surrounded with walls, with their gates guarded, and were very wealthy, having silversmiths; and that the women wore strings of gold beads and the men girdles of gold and white woolen dresses; and that they had sheep and cows and partridges and slaughterhouses and iron forges."

Throughout Mexico Spaniards scrambled to volunteer for Vásquez de Coronado's army. Some were elegant hidalgos and others were, in the words of one observer, "vicious young men with nothing to do." But rich or poor, famous or unknown, they all had one thing in common: a lust for adventure and for the fabulous treasures that seemed theirs for the taking. ◉

The stupendous conquests of Hernán Cortés

It was a testament to Spanish courage —or perhaps to arrogance—that the conquistadors embarked on prodigious enterprises with only the most meager manpower. Never was their disregard for unfavorable odds more brashly demonstrated than by Hernán Cortés.

In 1519, Cortés sailed from Cuba to the Mexican mainland with 508 soldiers, intending to conquer the Aztec empire—a highly civilized nation of 11 million Indians who ruled an area larger than all of Spain. Incredibly, it took him less than three years to destroy the Aztecs as a people, confiscate their wealth and turn their land into a bastion of Spanish power in the Americas.

In doing this, Cortés proved himself a cool and fearless fighter, a brilliant tactician and a master of diplomacy. But he was also blessed with astounding good fortune. The year 1519 was the very date for which Aztec priests had prophesied the return of their great blond god, Quetzalcoatl. According to legend, this deity had departed five centuries before, swearing to reappear one day out of the waters to the east. The arrival of fair-skinned, armor-clad men astride four-legged beasts seemed to herald the supernatural event and stirred deep unease in Aztec society.

By another stroke of luck, Cortés acquired a valuable Indian ally—a woman named Malinche. She was the daughter of an Aztec chief who had been enslaved by the Mayans of the Yucatan, where Cortés first landed. The Mayans presented her to Cortés as a peace offering. Since she was a noblewoman, "Doña Marina"—as he called her—understood the Aztec power structure. As Cortés' devoted mistress, she helped engineer his triumphs by translating conversations she overheard and by scheming to defeat her own people.

Cortés' first step toward conquest was to build the fortress seaport of Veracruz. He then launched a subtle campaign to undermine the Aztecs.

Through Marina, he saw that he was not dealing with a united nation, but rather with a collection of resentful vassal states that every year were forced to provide hundreds of their young warriors as sacrificial offerings to the Aztec gods. Cortés easily awakened a spirit of rebellion among these people.

Setting forth from Veracruz, Cortés won over the subjugated Totonacs and Tlaxcalans to his cause, and then defeated a third tribe, the Cholulans. Stunned by the Spaniards' successes, the Aztec emperor, Moctezuma, sent gold and jewels to Cortés with pious expressions of friendship. He then invited Cortés to enter the Aztec capital, Tenochtitlán, in peace and honor.

When the Spaniards approached the capital—built on islands in a lake—they were thunderstruck by its splendor. The spacious palaces, aromatic gardens and monumental temples prompted Cortés to murmur that he beheld "the most beautiful city in the world."

Moctezuma received his guests graciously and installed them in a grand palace adjacent to his own. Cortés accepted the sumptuous hospitality for a week. Then, accompanied by a few trusted men and the ever-faithful Marina, he forced his way into Moctezuma's quarters, took the ruler prisoner, and extorted from him treasure worth millions of ducats.

Suddenly trouble developed. Word came from the coast that more than 800 Spaniards had just landed at Veracruz. Cortés guessed that they must have been sent by the Governor of Cuba, long an enemy, and for only one purpose: to depose him and steal his plunder. Leaving a small force in Tenochtitlán, Cortés swooped down on Veracruz, routed his countrymen and then persuaded them to join his side. At this point, the conquistador had some 1,100 Spaniards under his banner. But when he led them back to Tenochtitlán, the city was wracked by

revolution. Cortés ordered Moctezuma to pacify the people. The hapless monarch tried to do his bidding, but was stoned to death by an enraged mob.

Cortés and his men had no choice but to flee. In the chaotic retreat, many of the Spaniards tried to swim across the city's canals and were dragged under by the weight of the chains of bullion they wore around their waists; in all, some 700 soldiers died. The indestructible Cortés, however, survived and spent the next year assembling a new army of Indian allies. Tlaxcala and the Totonac towns remained loyal to the Spanish, and other subject states, including populous Texcoco, threw in with the Europeans.

The final war for supremacy lasted almost four months, and cost about 150,000 Indian lives on both sides— though Spanish losses were slight. Cortés retook Tenochtitlán by a clever stratagem. He built 13 ships at Tlaxcala, disassembled them, carried the sections to the lake surrounding Tenochtitlán, and launched a waterborne attack. On August 13, 1521, the last of the Aztec resisters were killed—and the vengeful conquistador completed the destruction of Tenochtitlán block by block, razing it to the ground.

Cortés rebuilt the city as a Spanish metropolis. King Charles I confirmed his rule by naming him Governor of all New Spain. And when Cortés sailed triumphantly home in 1529 with a retinue of 40 Indian nobles, the King awarded him an estate in Mexico of 25,000 square miles and 100,000 subjects. But Charles was unwilling to let his New World empire remain for long under so formidable a man as Cortés. Royal officers began to erode his powers, and in 1535 Cortés was replaced by the first Viceroy of New Spain, Antonio de Mendoza. The great conquistador returned to his homeland, where he died, isolated and embittered, 12 years later, at the age of 62.

Working together, the Spanish and the Totonacs build the first European outpost in Mexico. Cortés named it Villa Rica de la Vera Cruz (Rich Town of the True Cross), and set an example by sharing manual labor with the Indians. It was a typical Spanish fortress town, with a plaza, an arsenal and a church — shown half-finished at right. This painting and those that follow were done in oil on mother-of-pearl by an artist named Miguel González in 1698.

The Spanish used both the sword and the cross to deal with the Indians of Mexico. In this painting, a priest baptizes converts at right, while a soldier at left cuts off the hands of an Indian spy. In the foreground, at right, a famished band of conquistadors is reduced to cooking a dog. The background scenes show military movements and a skirmish with the Tlaxcalans. At lower left center, the Indians cement their alliance with the Europeans at a banquet.

As pages blow trumpets, Cortés and his banner-carrying men enter Tenochtitlán, the Aztec capital, for the first time. In the background Indian nobles on barges wave green feathers and beat a welcoming drum. Cortés was wary of ambush, but at no point did he meet with anything but peace and friendship. The city itself was so astonishingly beautiful that one Spaniard exclaimed, "These great buildings rising from the water seemed like an enchanted vision."

Supported upon the shoulders of several lesser kings, the emperor of the Aztecs, Moctezuma, is brought forward to welcome Cortés. At the meeting, he presented the Spaniard with a pair of golden collars from which were suspended golden shrimp — the insignia of the long-lost god Quetzalcoatl. Subsequently the Indian ruler bowed his head to the conquistador and proclaimed: "You have come to your city, Mexico. You have come here to sit on your throne."

The captive Aztec ruler attempts to calm his rebellious subjects but is confronted with a hail of stones. The uprising, which took place six months after the arrival of the Spaniards in the city of Tenochtitlán, was prompted by the brutality of an officer, Pedro de Alvarado, who murdered 200 nobles and priests he suspected of hatching a conspiracy. During the disastrous retreat from the capital Cortés lost all of his treasure as well as the greater part of his army.

More than a year after being driven from the city of Tenochtitlán, a red-plumed Cortés recaptures the capital with the assistance of prefabricated boats. Following this, the victorious Spaniards toppled the idols of the Aztecs *(right, foreground)*. The last Aztec ruler to be brought before Cortés declared, "I have done my duty in defense of my city. Take that dagger and kill me." Instead, Cortés ordered that he be tortured — and ultimately had him hanged.

By February 1540, Coronado's provincial capital of Compostela was seething with activity. As the volunteers arrived, Coronado screened each and every man. For those who were promising but impecunious, he dug into his own purse and advanced money to buy horses, weapons and equipment. Before long, he had expended 50,000 ducats of his own on the enterprise.

Finally, Coronado scheduled a grand review and muster for Sunday, February 22. All through the preceding night, around campfires in the hills, his soldiers were busy oiling firearms, polishing armor, greasing saddles and boots. In the morning, 300 Spanish men-at-arms fell out for the journey: some 240 cavalrymen and 60 foot soldiers. This was not the entire army; one party, including Fray Marcos and several Franciscans, had gone on ahead to reconnoiter the route, and a few volunteers had yet to arrive. Nevertheless it was, according to Pedro de Castañeda, a foot soldier and chronicler of the expedition, "the most brilliant company ever assembled to go in search of new lands."

Along with the Spaniards, Coronado had gathered some 800 local Indian allies, armed with spears, bows and huge wooden swords edged with shards of flint or volcanic glass. In addition to the tribal warriors, there were hundreds of Indian servants and a few black slaves to tend to camp chores, handle the expedition's 1,000 pack animals and care for its traveling food supply — several hundred cattle, sheep and swine. All in all, the expedition gave the appearance of invincible size, strength and organization.

The army passed in review before the Viceroy; at its head was Coronado, wearing a plumed helmet and a suit of gilded armor whose golden sheen was to cause him grief in the days ahead. Next came the muster. With the sort of bureaucratic precision at which Spaniards excelled, the royal officials made comprehensive lists of the army's personnel and the equipment each man possessed. For example, one captain was catalogued thus: "Juan Gallego, seven horses, one coat of mail and breeches, one buckskin coat, one crossbow and other Castilian and native weapons."

After a mass was celebrated, Viceroy Mendoza addressed the men briefly, reminding them that they must render complete obedience to Coronado, and mentioning the great gains, moral as well as financial, that might reward their efforts. Each soldier was paid 30 pesos and all were promised rich grants of land in whatever territories they added to the Spanish realm.

The next day, February 23, the army departed Compostela, moving slowly northward through the mountain passes. The horses, fat from inactivity, sweated under their heavy loads. Livestock wandered off, and the army had to pause until the herders rounded up the strays.

Coronado received some cautionary news at the village of Chiametla, less than 200 miles north of Compostela. Melchior Díaz, the scout whom the Viceroy had dispatched four months earlier, stumbled into camp half starved and exhausted; during the bitter winter, several of his Indian bearers had died from exposure. Díaz verified portions of the friar's account, including the death of Estéban and his party, but his descriptions were much less enthusiastic, much less colorful. The Indians whom he had interrogated along the way were unable to tell him of any metal in Cíbola. "They have turquoises in quantity," he reported, "but not so many as the father provincial said."

That was not the end of Díaz' ill tidings. Although the scout had failed to reach any city he could recognize as Cíbola, he had received a message from the northern Indians: any white men who ventured into their territory would be attacked and killed. Díaz feared that many Indians south of Cíbola would also turn on the Spaniards, "because of the coolness with which they received us and the sour faces they have shown us." All this produced a marked change in the Spaniards' attitude toward Fray Marcos. When the army caught up with the friar's advance party, the soldiers regarded him with undisguised suspicion.

By April 1, the army had covered only 300 miles, and Coronado decided that more speed was essential. Leaving the main body to follow, he hurried on ahead with a vanguard of 75 horsemen, 25 foot soldiers and four Franciscans, including Fray Marcos. His route ran roughly parallel to Mexico's west coast for several hundred miles, most of it fertile plains crossed by rivers emanating from the Sierra Madre to the east. But when the vanguard left the Sonora Valley behind and moved into what was to become Arizona, the land turned sere and provisions grew scarce. Following the San Pedro River downstream, they reached Chichilticalli

— an Indian settlement — and there met a stunning surprise. Fray Marcos had described the place as a bustling town. But the community that met their eyes consisted of a single miserable hovel, made of red earth and lacking a roof.

The vanguard was now nearly exhausted, and its dwindling food supply could not be replenished locally. Coronado had no choice but to press doggedly ahead, marching about 150 miles northeast across desolate, uninhabited country. A number of horses collapsed and were left to perish. But then the vanguard crossed the Gila River and providentially began finding patches of pasture. Finally, on the night of July 6, they made camp in the Zuñi valley in present-day New Mexico, more than 1,000 miles northeast of their jumping off point at Compostela.

The next morning, Coronado and his men advanced toward the first of Fray Marcos' "cities of Cíbola." It lay on the side of a hill, and as it sharpened into focus, the soldiers' faces grew contorted with shock and disappointment. Here were no stately walls, no turquoise-studded portals, no silversmith shops, no sign of wealth. True, some of the houses were multistoried, as Fray Marcos had reported; but otherwise the alleged metropolis fell hopelessly short of Fray Marcos' favorable comparison to Mexico City. It was, in fact, the Zuñi pueblo of Hawikuh; the Spaniards judged it to hold perhaps 800 people. Chronicler Castañeda described it as "a little, crowded village, looking as if it had been crumpled all up together. There are haciendas in New Spain which make a better appearance at a distance." The soldiers turned angrily on the friar. "Such were the curses that some hurled at him," Castañeda said, "that I pray God may protect him from them."

Remaining at a distance from the village, Coronado attempted to negotiate with a band of armed Zuñis who came out to challenge the Spaniards. Through Indian interpreters, he called upon the Zuñis to submit peacefully and swear loyalty to the King of Spain. The answer came at once, in the form of a fusillade of arrows. Shouting their battle cry "Santiago" (St. James, the soldier saint of Spain), the soldiers charged to the attack, killing about a dozen Zuñis — the white man's first Indian victims in the war for the West — and driving the rest up the several ladders that led to the lofty pueblo. Coronado and his men followed hard on their heels, racing to the foot of the pueblo and scrambling up the ladders. Missiles rained down on them. Coronado's gilded armor marked him as a special target. Rocks and arrows clanged against his helmet and cuirass. Finally, a boulder knocked him from the ladder. He crashed to the ground and lay there unconscious.

A few soldiers rushed to Coronado's aid, and the others pressed their assault without him. Slowly, the heavily armed and armored Spaniards scaled the ladders and drove back the Zuñi defenders. They burst into the pueblo and ran through its narrow alleys, killing any Indian who dared to fight them. In less than an hour, the battle was over. The Zuñis, as one soldier reported, appealed to the Spaniards "not to hurt them any more, as they wished to leave the pueblo." The Spaniards told them they might remain in peace, "but they desired to leave, so they went away unharmed."

Coronado's own account of the victory, which he set down in a letter to the Viceroy after he regained consciousness, gave credit where it was due. He wrote that in the heat of battle his comrades "picked me up from the ground with two small wounds in my face and an arrow in my foot, and with many bruises on my arms and legs. I think if Don García López de Cárdenas had not come to my help by placing his body above mine I should have been in much greater danger than I was." In the same letter, Coronado passed stern judgment on the disgraced Fray Marcos. "I can assure you," he told Mendoza, "that in reality he has not told the truth in a single thing. The Seven Cities are seven little villages, all within a radius of five leagues."

Coronado put an end to the Fray Marcos matter by sending the friar back to Mexico City with the party he dispatched to carry his report to the Viceroy. The messengers were also to instruct the main body of Coronado's army to join him in Cíbola. While waiting for the main force to arrive, the vanguard pacified all the other cities of Cíbola with little difficulty. The spirits of the men revived as they feasted on the Indians' squash, maize and fowl — and rose still further when they heard from the surly Zuñis of a "rich" province that lay to the northwest. Suddenly, the dreams of gold were rekindled. In late July, Coronado sent 20 soldiers to investigate; he could not lead the mission himself since he was still recovering from his injuries. The party crossed about 75 miles of desert and came upon

Bold forays into the unknown

Over a period of almost three centuries, Spanish explorers blazed an awesome series of trails across the West and opened a wilderness nearly five times the size of Spain. The most prodigious of the journeys into these unknown lands was accomplished by gold seekers. In the early 16th Century, Cabeza de Vaca, a survivor of an ill-fated treasure expedition in Florida, traversed Texas, New Mexico and Arizona. Later, Francisco de Coronado and Juan de Oñate trekked as far north as the Kansas River in search of the chimerical treasures of a country the Indians called Quivira.

These initial thrusts paved the way for settlement, and soon a handful of lonely outposts in New Mexico and Texas asserted Spain's title against foreign interlopers. But large tracts of central and northern Mexico remained untamed, and for most of the 17th Century the Spaniards backtracked to colonize the neglected regions. The brunt of the work was borne by the missionaries, chief among them being Father Eusebio Kino, who tirelessly expanded the mission system into southern Arizona and Baja California.

Kino's labors for God set the stage for the last Spanish venture into the northern borderlands. In 1769, Gaspar de Portolá moved up the Pacific coast as far as San Francisco Bay. Five years later he was joined by Juan Baptista de Anza, who carved out an overland route from Arizona.

With the settlement of California, Spain's colonizing efforts were spent. Mexico soon assumed her territorial claims—but by 1846, Americans had overrun Texas, and Mexico held undisputed only the tinted area on the map.

Cabeza de Vaca 1528-1536

Francisco de Coronado 1540-1542

Explorations by Coronado's Lieutenants

Juan de Oñate 1596-1605

Padre Eusebio Kino 1687-1706

Gaspar de Portolá 1769

Juan de Anza 1774-1776

several villages of Hopi Indians. Again, the Spaniards were doomed to disappointment; there was no bright metal. But they did return with gifts of turquoises and skins and, more important, with news of a great river to the west of the Hopi lands.

Coronado immediately dispatched a party to search for this watercourse. A handful of soldiers under López de Cárdenas marched to the Hopi villages, where the Indians supplied them with food and guides. After 20 days of hard desert travel to the west, Cárdenas came to a sudden halt and stared downward in astonishment. There, before the explorers, was a colossal gash in the surface of the earth, and they saw far below, between almost vertical walls of stratified rock, a thin rivulet of water. That little stream was the mighty Colorado River, and the great crevice through which it ran was the Grand Canyon.

For three days, the soldiers prowled the rim of the canyon, searching for a path by which they could reach the bottom. "The three lightest and most agile men," reported Castañeda, "went down until those who were above were unable to keep sight of them. They returned about four o'clock in the afternoon. They said they had been down about a third of the way and that the river seemed very large."

While Cárdenas' party was exploring the Grand Canyon, a meeting of vast importance was taking place back in Cíbola. One day Coronado was visited by a delegation of curious Indians from Cicúye, a pueblo 200 miles to the east, beyond a land that the Indians called Tiguex. The ambassadors, using sign language, told Coronado that they had heard of "strange people, bold men," and had come to assure them they wanted only peace. "If we wanted to go through their country," Castañeda wrote, "they would consider us as their friends."

Still believing that great treasure must lie somewhere out in that immense wilderness, Coronado accepted the invitation with alacrity. He appointed a brave captain, Hernando de Alvarado, to escort the Indians back to Cicúye. The captain and 20 soldiers left Cíbola with the Indians on August 29, and five days later came to the towering mesa of Acoma (Acus, in Fray Marcos' secondhand report), atop which stood a small pueblo. At the party's approach, the men of the village swarmed down a stairway carved into the rock; they

37

were armed and made threatening gestures. But it was all a bluff. Seeing the Spaniards stand their ground, they became friendly and even subservient. The soldiers—laden with gifts of pine nuts, cornmeal and turkeys—resumed their journey.

On September 7, Alvarado's party reached Tiguex, a cluster of pueblos on both sides of the upper Rio Grande. The people poured out of their houses to welcome the ambassadors from Cicúye and their Spanish guests. "From twelve pueblos came chieftains and people in good order," wrote Alvarado. "They marched around our tent, playing flutes, and with an old man for a spokesman. In this manner they came inside the tent and presented me with food, cotton cloth, and skins which they had."

In return, Alvarado went from pueblo to pueblo distributing trinkets; the soldiers also erected large crosses and, reported Alvarado, "taught the natives to worship them." The captain was so pleased by the friendliness of the natives and the productivity of their land that in his dispatch he urged Coronado to leave Cíbola and set up winter headquarters in Tiguex. He then resumed the journey to Cicúye, traveling north along the Rio Grande, then east along the Pecos River. Five days from Tiguex, Alvarado reached Cicúye, a large well-built pueblo, and was warmly received by its inhabitants. One party member wrote: "Its houses are four and five stories high, some of them being very fine. These people neither plant cotton nor raise turkeys because it is close to the plains where the cattle roam."

The "cattle" were buffalo, which the Spaniards knew only by the huge, curly-haired hides that the Indians used as blankets. Alvarado was determined to see these wondrous beasts with his own eyes. For a guide, the Cicúye gave their guests a Pawnee captive, a native of the far north who knew the plains well. The Spaniards nicknamed him *El Turco* because they fancied he looked like a sinister Turk. And, as the Spaniards would learn to their dismay, *El Turco* was every bit as sinister as he looked.

With the captive confidently leading the way, Alvarado and his men continued following the Pecos River, then cut cross-country to the Canadian River, which took them still farther east. Within a few days, the Spaniards saw their first herd of buffalo, spread in black clusters over miles of plains. These animals, one

of the men wrote, were "the most monstrous beasts ever seen or read about"; and after shooting a few he added, "Their meat is as good as that of the cattle of Castile, and some said it was even better. The bulls are large and fierce. They killed several of our horses and wounded many others."

Alvarado's party was still proceeding along the Canadian River when one day, for no apparent reason, the Turk burst forth with a sensational story. Using sign language and the few words of Spanish he had picked up, he told the Spaniards of a fabulous land called Quivira and urged them to go there. He would lead the way. It was, he said, richer than any other land, "with gold, silver and fabrics, and abundant and fruitful in everything." The Turk even claimed that he had once owned a gold bracelet from Quivira, which the chiefs of Cicúye had taken away from him. Unbeknownst to the Spaniards, his sudden outburst had been caused by their arrival at a point where the trail to Quivira, and to his own homeland beyond it, swung northeast from the Canadian River. The crafty Pawnee undoubtedly hoped to improve his chances of making it back to his own people.

Though the tale of gold tempted Alvarado, there was not enough good autumn weather left for a long journey. However, the wary captain thought of a quick, easy way to learn whether Quivira really had gold. It was only necessary to return to Cicúye and ask the friendly chiefs about the Turk's golden bracelet. With that plan in mind, Alvarado began retracing his path.

Meanwhile, far to the west in Cíbola, Coronado had fully recovered from his battle injuries and was anxious to move on with his vanguard. Alvarado's message, suggesting that he winter at Tiguex, appealed to the general. Tiguex sounded like an ideal base for future explorations, and there he would finally be able to gather together his whole command, which was scattered through thousands of miles of terrain. When López de Cárdenas returned from the Grand Canyon, Coronado sent him ahead to prepare winter quarters for both the vanguard and the main army, now finally on its way north from Mexico.

Cárdenas hurried east with a small band of soldiers and a work force of Indian servants to put up a tent encampment. Shortly after reaching Tiguex, he was pleased to see Alvarado and his men arriving from the north. But he was less pleased to learn that Alvarado had with him, as prisoners, the two head chiefs of the friendly Cicúye pueblo. This could only mean trouble.

Alvarado felt that he was perfectly within his rights as a conquistador. When he had asked the Cicúye chiefs about the Turk's golden bracelet, they showed great surprise and "denied in all possible ways that they had any such ornament." Alvarado found their protestations suspicious. Therefore he politely requested that the head men accompany him, in order that Coronado himself might interrogate them further. The chiefs had haughtily refused. What else could a Spanish captain do but take them to Coronado, as captives in chains?

Meanwhile, Cárdenas had already contributed a blunder of his own to the worsening relations with the Indians. With the first cold weather, he concluded that his tent city would be far too uncomfortable for Spanish soldiers; so he ordered the people of a nearby pueblo to evacuate their homes, and also to leave behind the provisions they had stored away for the winter. The Indians, more stunned than outraged, complied, scattering to find quarters in other pueblos.

Such was the situation when Coronado arrived on the scene. Immediately, he was inundated by reports and special pleadings. Irritated by all the confusion, he acted with uncharacteristic arrogance, he summoned the head man of one pueblo and demanded 300 lengths of cotton for his soldiers' bedding; when the chief declared that he could not supply that much cloth, the harried commander construed his statement as open defiance. Coronado's natural restraint suddenly gave way. He sent squads of soldiers to the pueblos to obtain the desired goods — by force if need be.

Violence was almost inevitable, and the spark to ignite it was supplied by a lawless soldier who had spied a pretty woman as he approached one of the pueblos. Ordering an Indian man to hold his horse, he pursued the woman to the roof of her house and raped her. By a bitter irony, the Indian who was holding the rapist's horse turned out to be the victim's husband.

As news of the rape spread among the pueblos, a gathering of Indian leaders came to the Spaniards to appeal for justice. Assembling his men, the Spanish leader — either Coronado or Cárdenas according to different

accounts — asked the victim's husband to pick out the criminal. The Indian could not: all Spaniards looked alike to him, just as all Indians looked alike to the Spaniards. But the Indian said he could identify the rapist's horse and, on being taken to the Spaniards' corral, he did just that. The horse's owner denied the charge, and the Spaniards, unwilling to punish a soldier on the word of an Indian, let the matter drop.

The Indians did not. At dawn the next day, a band of men raided the Spaniards' corral, killed one of the allied Indian guards and drove off some 30 horses and mules. Naturally, the Spaniards retaliated. On orders from Coronado, López de Cárdenas led a troop of horsemen to the raiders' pueblo and attacked it, forcing the Indians into their kiva, an underground ceremonial center. The soldiers then battered a hole through the pueblo wall and lighted a fire inside, which soon smoked the Indians out. There were 200 of them, and they signaled a desire to surrender. It is unclear from the expedition journals what orders Coronado had given Cárdenas. In any case, the captain cold-bloodedly ordered all 200 Indians to be burned at the stake.

After the first few Indians died in the flames, all the others desperately attacked the Spaniards with their bare hands. About a hundred Indians were slaughtered before the rest collapsed and pleaded for mercy. One by one they were tied to stakes. Then, to the shrieks of their women and children, all were burned to death.

Coronado was now faced with the prospect of a full-scale Indian war, which he would have to conduct in the dead of winter a thousand miles from his nearest base in Mexico. He was vastly relieved when the main body of his army finally arrived shortly after the outbreak of hostilities to join his vanguard. Both forces had been reduced by attrition, courier duty and other special details; Coronado had at his disposal no more than three quarters of the 300-odd Spaniards and 800 Indian allies who had set out from Compostela 10 months before. The commander needed every fighting man he could get: the 12 pueblos of Tiguex had about 5,000 inhabitants, and all of them were deeply embittered enemies.

Moho, one of the pueblos on Coronado's side of the Rio Grande, was soon reported to be a center of resistance, and Coronado sent Cárdenas with a troop of horsemen to appraise the situation. The captain could

The English sailor the Spaniards called El Dragón

One of the chief prompters of Spanish expansion in the New World was, paradoxically, Spain's archenemy, the English patriot and pirate Francis Drake. The son of a farmer, Drake went to sea in 1566 when he was in his mid-twenties. He soon learned the nautical trade ferrying slaves between Africa and Spain's Caribbean colonies. Then, as England's relations with Spain faltered, he turned on his former customers. From Florida to Panama, he seized vessels or held entire towns for ransom, earning the name El Dragón in the process.

In 1577, with Queen Elizabeth's secret blessing, Drake sailed through the Strait of Magellan into the Pacific, which Spain considered a private sea, and plundered his way up the South American and Mexican coasts. One vessel, the *Cacafuego,* yielded eight million dollars in gold, silver and jewels.

Having filled his 100-ton *Golden Hind* with Spanish riches, Drake continued north in search of a safe haven to make repairs. On June 17, 1579, he anchored in a small harbor just north of San Francisco Bay, sweepingly claimed all of the surrounding land for Elizabeth, and named it Nova Albion: New England.

Drake returned home across the Pacific, thereby achieving the second circumnavigation of the globe. The Queen herself boarded the *Golden Hind* to accept the vast bulk of Spanish gold and then told her kneeling subject, "The King of Spain has demanded your head. I have here a gilded sword with which to strike it off." She touched the sword to Drake's

In a portrait made after his world trip, Drake is flanked by a globe and his coat of arms.

shoulder and he became a knight.

When Spain launched a 132-ship Armada against England in 1588, Sir Francis helped defeat it as a vice admiral commanding 30 war vessels. Afterward, he continued harassing Spain's Caribbean possessions until his death in 1596. Because of him, the Spanish could no longer take supremacy in the New World for granted. They bolstered their fortifications, built swifter vessels and, most importantly, were goaded into hurrying northward to colonize their outermost lands and thus nullify England's claim to the west coast of North America.

see from a distance that Moho had been fortified, and he was surprised when Indians atop the walls asked to talk peace. Cárdenas agreed; he advanced, alone, to meet with the chiefs. Almost at once, two Indians drew clubs from beneath their robes, knocked the hated captain to the ground and started dragging him toward the pueblo. The alert Spaniards rushed to his rescue and the troop hastily retreated.

Now it was Coronado's turn to be enraged. Grimly he marched his whole army to the offending pueblo. Beneath Moho's walls, he punctiliously recited the Spanish protocol, bidding the Indians to submit and swear fealty to the King of Spain. Receiving nothing but jeers for his trouble, Coronado gave the command that his soldiers yearned to hear: "Santiago!"

Charging the high walls with ladders they had brought along, the Spaniards swarmed upward, their iron shields ringing with the impact of arrows and rocks. Some 50 soldiers managed to top the wall and gain a foothold on the terraces just beyond. But five or six Spaniards were killed in vicious hand-to-hand fighting, and the rest were forced to withdraw. Coronado ordered his army to break off the assault and to take Moho by siege.

It was early January, 1541, when the Spaniards and their Indian allies surrounded the pueblo. The climate—dry and frigid at an altitude of 5,000 feet—was against them, but time was on their side. Coronado had learned, perhaps from the Turk, that the 400-odd Indians bottled up in Moho had plenty of food but only the little water they could get from a single well. The Indians started digging another well, but never hit water. Instead, the walls of the well collapsed, burying 30 diggers alive.

Then, to Coronado's dismay, the Moho defenders got a long reprieve. As one of his soldiers put it: "Just when he thought they must be soon forced to yield, a snowfall began and continued for several weeks, enabling the Indians to supply themselves during all that time by melting the snow."

The siege dragged on interminably. Every day, as constant as his morning prayers, Coronado enjoined the Indians to swear allegiance to the King. Every day his summons met with stony silence—until the middle of March, a week or two after the snow had stopped falling. Then the chiefs appealed for a parley. They told Coronado that they wished to surrender their thirsty women and children to spare them further suffering. The Spaniards admitted about a hundred women and children into their ranks. Many other women stayed behind to be with their men to the end.

For two more weeks, Moho pueblo continued to hold out. By then the well had gone dry and the defenders elected to attempt an escape. So strong was their hatred for the Spaniards that they burned everything they could not carry—food, blankets, spare clothing, hides, even jewelry.

In the dark just before dawn, the Indians filed stealthily from their pueblo and tried to slip through the Spanish lines. They were detected. Soldiers killed many of them—men and women alike—and captured most of the rest. Some Indians managed to reach the Rio Grande and tried to swim across. A few, dodging blocks of ice, actually reached the far side of the river—only to die there of wounds and exposure. The Spaniards made no official count of the casualties, but Castañeda estimated the toll at more than 200 dead.

Coronado was satisfied that Moho's fate, sealed at small cost to his army, had taught the Indians the folly of defying the Spaniards. Moho had indeed broken the back of Indian resistance. By early April, all Tiguex was pacified and, with spring in the air, Coronado was free to pursue a new enterprise that had long preyed on his mind: the search for Quivira.

All through the winter, the captive Pawnee had been tantalizing the Spaniards with ever-gaudier tales of Quivira and its gold. According to one report, the Turk declared that "There was so much gold there that they could load not only horses with it but wagons." Even the common folk of Quivira ate their meals off silver plates and drank from golden bowls. The King of Quivira traveled in a huge canoe with 40 golden oarlocks, one for each rower; and on this magnificent vessel he took pleasure cruises on a river five or six miles wide, which contained fish as large as the Spaniards' horses. Just in case all this was not wondrous enough, the Turk announced that beyond Quivira to the north lay an even richer realm called Harahey. He did not add that Harahey was the homeland of his own people, the Pawnees.

By the third week in April, Coronado had completed the necessary preparations for the journey to

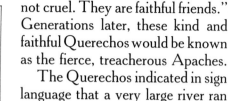

Quivira. He secured his rear areas by sending a troop of horsemen to subdue an Indian uprising in northern Mexico. To ensure peace in Tiguex itself, he assembled a large group of Indians to bring along as hostages. These captives, together with the Spaniards, their Indian allies and servants, added up to some 1,500 men; and 1,000 horses and uncounted mules packed enough maize to feed them all for about 30 days. In order that he could keep track of the exact distance they traveled, Coronado assigned an unnamed foot soldier the task of counting every step he took.

The army departed Tiguex on April 23, heading north along the Rio Grande, then veering east at the Pecos River to the pueblo of Cicúye. There, Coronado patched up relations with the Indians by releasing the two captive chiefs who had denied the Turk's story of the golden bracelet. When the army resumed its journey, the Cicúyans were seemingly well disposed toward the Spaniards. But as Coronado would later learn, the freed chiefs were still resentful of their abduction and had been plotting with the Turk to weaken the Spaniards by taking them on a roundabout journey to nowhere.

With the Pawnee leading the way eastward, the army reached the open plains in about two weeks. Coronado was overwhelmed by the size of the buffalo herds. "I found so many cattle," he later wrote, "that it would be impossible to estimate their number, for there was not a single day until my return that I lost sight of them."

On the journey across the plains, the Turk began leading the army southeast instead of northeast — 90 degrees off the course to Quivira. As they traveled, the soldiers met up with small bands of Indians who called themselves Querechos. These tall, athletic people were not settled farmers like the pueblo Indians but nomadic hunters who lived off buffalo, using every part of the animal they did not eat, making tipis and clothing of the hides, weapons and tools of the bone and sinew. Coronado thought that the Querechos had the finest physiques of all the natives he had encountered, and Castañeda observed, "They are a gentle people and not cruel. They are faithful friends." Generations later, these kind and faithful Querechos would be known as the fierce, treacherous Apaches.

The Querechos indicated in sign language that a very large river ran through the region to the east, and that there were many settlements along it, the first of which they called Haxa. Coronado sent out a party of mounted scouts. The horsemen found no river and no Haxa; they reported back to Coronado that they "saw nothing but cattle and sky." But new assurances by the Turk and the Querechos led the Spanish general farther to the southeast.

Coronado's arrival in the region that would become the Texas Panhandle was inauspicious from the first. At a tiny village in a deep gorge, greedy soldiers quarreled over the division of a gift from the Indians, a pile of buffalo hides. Then their encampment was hit by a tornado. The terrifying winds, driving fist-sized hailstones, leveled tents, dented armor and injured horses, and men might have been killed but for the sheltering walls of the chasm.

As Coronado penetrated deeper into this region, he grew suspicious at the startling change in the terrain: the high plains terminated abruptly in steep cliffs up to 1,000 feet high, with rugged badlands lying below them. From the local Indians, who called themselves Tewas, Coronado's interpreters learned that Quivira lay far to the north, even though the army had already covered about 600 miles. Moreover, the Tewas' description of Quivira differed radically from that given by the Turk. "These Indians," Coronado wrote grimly in a dispatch to the Viceroy, "described the houses there as being of grass and hides, and not of stone and several stories high."

On the night of May 26, the commander reached a momentous decision. To spare his ailing, slow-moving army, he would send a few swift, healthy soldiers north to make an unequivocal report on Quivira. For the expedition — which he would personally lead — the commander selected 30 of his best horsemen, six foot soldiers of superior stamina and a hardy priest named Fray Juan Padilla. On the off chance that the Turk might yet prove useful, Coronado decided to take that slippery creature along — but in chains to prevent any escape attempt. Sopete, another Plains Indian, replaced him as guide. The rest of the army would remain encamped for eight days, and if no messenger had come for them by then, they were to march back to Tiguex, now some 650 miles away.

On June 1, Coronado set out to the northeast, using as his compass a sliver of magnetized iron at the end of a silk thread. The party took a full month to emerge from the rough Panhandle country onto table-flat plains. The journey across the featureless landscape was a tranquil nightmare. Castañeda wrote: "Many fellows were lost at this time who went out hunting and did not get back for two or three days, wandering about the country as if they were crazy, in one direction or another, not knowing how to get back to where they started from." Every night the soldiers, after answering roll call to determine who was missing, "fired guns and blew trumpets and built great fires, but yet some of them went so far off that all this did not give them any help."

At last, on July 6, Coronado's party reached the first Quivira settlement, just below the great bend of the Arkansas River. The commander no longer expected to find anything remotely resembling the great cities of the Turk's tales; still, he was dismayed by what he found. The settlement was a small cluster of flimsy grass huts, and Coronado was received not by magnificent potentates but by yapping dogs, naked children, shy women and a few men in primitive ceremonial regalia. Coronado was heartsick with disappointment. But he dutifully recited his protocol and claimed still another realm for the King of Spain. As for the soldiers, they were raging for only one thing: the death of the treacherous Pawnee.

For 25 days, Coronado wandered through Quivira in a northerly direction. At one village after another he asked about precious metals. Everywhere Indians said they had none, and a few added that the land of Harahey, to the north, had none either. In a letter to the King, Coronado stated flatly, "There is not any gold nor any other metal — nothing but little villages."

But gradually, the Spaniards fell under the spell of another kind of wealth. With genuine enthusiasm, Coronado wrote to the King: "The country itself is the best I have ever seen for producing all the products of Spain, for besides the land being very fat and black, and being well watered by rivulets and springs and rivers, I found prunes and nuts and very good sweet grapes and mulberries." One of his soldiers wrote of "charming rivers with fine water," of plums "not exactly red, but shading off from reddish to green," of "a sort of flax growing wild in small clusters, with little heads of blue flowers."

Early in August, Coronado reached the northernmost point of his journey, a village called Tabas on the banks of a large muddy river — the Smoky Hill River in present-day Kansas. There he noticed that the Indians were begrudging his soldiers maize, and Sopete, the Turk's replacement as guide, explained that the Pawnee himself was the cause: he had been urging the local chiefs to give the Spaniards no more grain, saying that without it the horses would soon die, leaving the soldiers helpless and easy to kill.

Turning on the Turk, the Spaniards applied various tortures until they had extracted the whole truth from him. The Indian confessed that he had been lying all along about the gold, and that he had conspired with the two Cicúye chiefs to lead the Spaniards astray, so that even if they managed to return, they would be too weak to fight.

Without further ado, recounted Coronado's head groom, Juan de Contreras, "a soldier named Pérez, from behind, put a rope around Turco's neck, twisted it with a garrote, and choked him to death."

Coronado, alone among the Spaniards, felt a curious sense of loss at the Indian's death. He understood that the Turk, knowingly or not, had been truthful in speaking of Quivira's great wealth. The Indian had lied mainly in the matter of gold. The commander may even have realized that the Spaniards themselves, with their relentless questions about gold, were largely responsible for the Pawnee's lies. He was merely telling them what they demanded to hear.

In late August, the Spaniards began the long, disconsolate journey home. One man wrote, "We marched back — I do not know whether it was two days or three — to a place where we obtained a supply of green and dried maize for our return"; here the soldiers and Fray Padilla erected a large wooden cross, "at the foot of which some letters were cut with a chisel saying that

Francisco Vásquez de Coronado, general of the army, had reached this place."

With six Quivira Indians as guides, the party returned to Cicúye by a route 340 miles shorter than their misguided outward-bound journey. They were able to calculate this distance because the soldier assigned to count his every step had faithfully performed that brain-numbing task. Coronado wintered in Tiguex with the main body of his army. Discouragement and weariness showed clearly in every line of his letter to King Charles V of Spain. He had found "none of the things of which Fray Marcos had told," and declared apologetically, "I have done all that I could to serve Your Majesty and discover a country where God our Lord might be served and the royal patrimony of Your Majesty be increased."

In the spring of 1542, Coronado left Tiguex for the capital of New Spain—and watched his once-proud army melt away before his eyes. Several friars, including Fray Padilla, elected to stay behind to teach the Indians the true faith; they all died martyrs' deaths soon after the soldiers had moved on. Many soldiers, weary, disgruntled, fearing punishment for their misdeeds and failures, deserted on the way south. Fewer than a hundred of the original 300 Spaniards, tattered and exhausted, straggled into Mexico City with Coronado in the summer of 1542, two and a half years after their vainglorious departure for the land of gold.

For Spain, it made no great difference at first that Coronado had discovered vast fertile territories and staked the crown's claim to the whole southwestern quadrant of the North American continent. He had not found gold; he had not found silver; and that alone condemned his journey. Coronado himself was the biggest loser. He lost his reputation, not to mention his personal fortune; he soon faded from the public eye, to die in obscurity in Mexico City 12 years later at the age of 44. Viceroy Mendoza, who had also invested a fortune in the enterprise and lost, remained in his post for nine years, still striving to be "The Good Man" as the colonial world changed all around him.

The changes were spectacular and irreversible, and all of them turned the Spaniards' gaze back to the north. Many new silver mines were discovered in central Mexico, greatly increasing the need for laborers to wrench all that wealth from the bowels of the earth.

At the same time, however, the supply of Indians in New Spain was reduced by nearly half—from the estimated 11 million in the 1520s to about 6.5 million in the 1550s—by epidemics of cholera, measles and other European diseases against which the Indians had little resistance. Where were more slave laborers to be found? Obviously in the lands Coronado had discovered—Cíbola and Cicúye, Tiguex and Quivira.

Concurrently, other European powers—especially England—stepped up their explorations in the New World. In 1578, Sir Francis Drake in his *Golden Hind* landed on the California coast *(page 40)*. The Spanish feared that Drake or some other Englishman would find the mythical Strait of Anián, that English colonies would be planted along it, and English soldiers would descend upon Mexico from the north. If for no other reason than defense, Spanish outposts would have to be established along Mexico's northern frontier.

In the 1590s, a small party of soldiers and Spanish settlers under a general named Juan de Oñate took control of much of the territory on both sides of the Rio Grande, as far north as a place called Taos. But the few tiny outposts they planted were abandoned when the gold-bedazzled soldiers went gallivanting off to investigate the graveyard of Coronado's hopes, Quivira.

But in 1609, the Spanish crown decided to attempt once again to capture and to hold the lost conquests. An elegant hidalgo named Pedro de Peralta was dispatched to Mexico with orders to proceed north and to establish a capital city for a new Spanish kingdom to be called New Mexico. In the winter of 1609-1610, Don Pedro set forth with a contingent of soldiers and Spanish families. He selected for his capital a pleasant location on the fertile banks of a tributary to the upper Rio Grande, about 75 miles above Tiguex. There he laid out a splendid city, which he honored with the name of the Holy Faith—Santa Fe. Peralta marked out the center of his town with the usual *plaza de armas,* or parade ground, and ordered his Indian workers to construct, on the northern side of the open square, the *casas reales*—royal government buildings that would serve as his residence and as headquarters for the colonial militia. At first, Peralta's capital was simply a small cluster of low adobe buildings. But the founding of Santa Fe meant that Spaniards were now in and of the American West, and that they intended to stay.

Like a latter-day knight, a conquistador wore gleaming armor and bore a Toledo-steel sword and dagger at his side. A foot soldier fought with the single-shot matchlock and steel-tipped halberd, which could be used to spear or to hook the enemy.

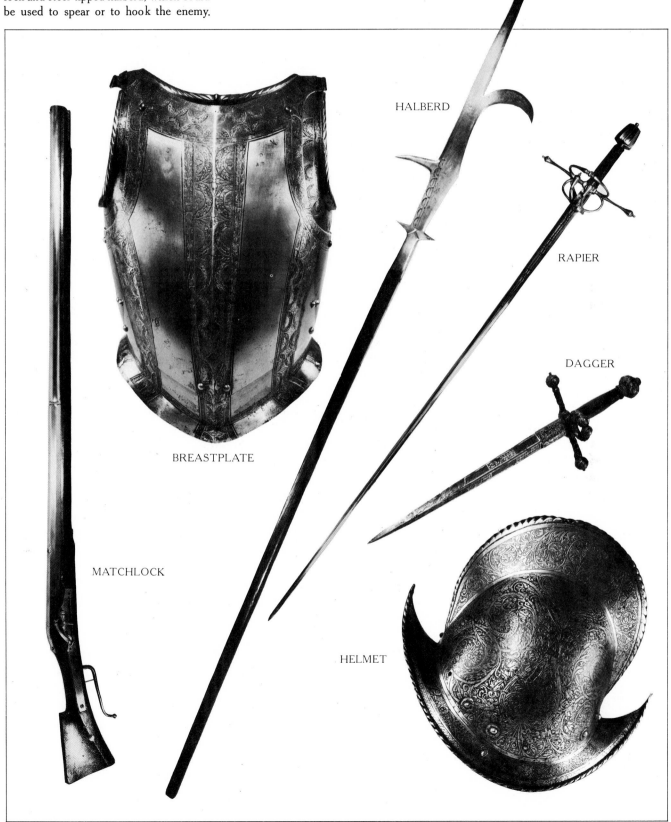

HALBERD

RAPIER

DAGGER

BREASTPLATE

MATCHLOCK

HELMET

2 | The cruel road to Empire

Of arms I sing and of the man heroic,
Of him whose endless, never-tiring
  patience,
Over an ocean of annoyance
  stretching,
Despite the fangs of foul, envenomed
  envy,
Brave deeds of prowess ever is
  achieving.

With this high-flown poem, an early 17th Century Spanish soldier saluted the fearless adventurer who trekked from Mexico to consolidate the gains of the first conquistadors. For the next 200 years, Spain competed with such empire builders as France and Britain to "search out all of the world yet hidden" — as the soldier-poet put it — and plant the Gospel among the natives.

At first, the Spanish colonizers appeared to make great strides in their God-given work. Either by persuasion or force, Indian groups were induced to help build missions across a frontier that eventually stretched from present-day California to East Texas. But Spanish greed and bungling combined to turn the Indians from their white mentors. Instead of earning gratitude and homage as saviors, the Spaniards came to be considered pernicious trespassers, as stiff and grim as the one- to three-foot-high representations at right.

Fifty feet up a sheer canyon wall and accessible only by a precarious ledge, this Navajo rock painting commemorates an actual army expedition moving through the countryside. The soldiers — including a member of the military order of St. James with a cross on his cloak — were sent to punish rebel tribesmen. They succeeded with a vengeance — trapping and killing 115 Navajos who had taken refuge in a cave. But on many another occasion, the Indians extracted an equally bloody price for Spanish attempts to settle their land.

Weapons ready, Spanish horsemen ride across the wall of the Canyon del Muerto in Arizona.

Pictographs of actual events were rare. Most Southwestern Indian rock paintings had the ceremonial purpose of assuring health and fertility.

Generations of turmoil along a 1,000-mile frontier

If the bold conquistador typified the first Spanish presence in the Old West, pursuing dreams of gold, planting the banner of His Spanish Majesty and the cross of the Catholic faith in regions whose extent he scarcely guessed at, it was the missionary friar who turned that first vainglorious claim into the fragile beginnings of reality. The missionary's zeal for souls was as fierce as any freebooter's lust for precious metals. But while the conquistador came to seize treasure, the mission friar came—by his lights—to bestow one. And to ensure that the blessings of Christianity took root and flourished, he was prepared to commit himself to the long process of civilizing the savage convert. The mission friar, even more than the soldier or the settler, was New Spain's greatest frontiersman and her foremost colonizing influence in the northern borderlands.

It was thanks to the Franciscan fathers that the Spaniards even bothered to establish Santa Fe in 1610 and thus to embark seriously on the colonizing process. After the failure of previous efforts to take control of the northern wilderness, the grandees in Madrid and Mexico City had doubted whether it was worth maintaining a settlement where prospects of material reward seemed almost nil. Furthermore, one motive force for colonization—the threat of incursion from England —had eased in 1604 when Spain negotiated the Treaty of London. But the Church had continued to urge Spanish dominion forward, so that it might reclaim for salvation the benighted aborigines.

Its manner of persuasion was most astute and timely. In 1608, just when the Spaniards were about to abandon New Mexico—as they called the vast area stretching north and west beyond El Paso—stunning news came from Franciscans in the field: the number of new Christians had jumped from 4,000 to almost double that figure within months. To King Philip III and his advisors, this was cause for genuine rejoicing—and for a sober reassessment. Could Spain turn her back on these souls so newly won to Christ? No, it was agreed, she could not. New Mexico should not only be held but turned into a royal province, its costs to be paid by the Crown rather than individuals.

This pious concern for the Indians' spiritual welfare was only half the picture in colonial Spain. Indians were also, in hard fact, an economic necessity without which neither this nor any other Spanish colony in the New World could survive. In a sense, the Indians *were* Spain's colonists. Instead of displacing them with Spaniards, the Empire simply incorporated them into its hierarchical system, as a bottommost social layer on whose labor and resources the upper classes subsisted. "I did not come to the New World to till the soil like any peasant," Hernán Cortés had angrily retorted when offered land in Cuba shortly after his arrival in 1511.

Harnessing the Indian to the Spanish yoke had been relatively easy in the early stages of Mexican settlement and exploration. The lesser tribes of the Mexican plateau, already subjugated by the mighty Aztecs, simply exchanged one master for another. Hispanicization became harder, however, as settlement pushed farther north; the Spaniards began to run out of tamed Indians. Pacifying had to start from scratch, and from that need developed the mission-presidio system, Spain's unique method of subduing a hostile wilderness.

The function of the mission—whether Franciscan, Jesuit or Dominican—was to persuade the wild Indians in its vicinity to gather there and adopt an agricultural way of life. They were instructed in the Catholic faith and taught arts and skills that would make them useful

Painting on a tanned buffalo hide around 1675, a mission-trained Indian artist faithfully copied the standard European pose for a sorrowing Madonna—but he endowed his subject with distinctly Indian features.

members of the community. Protection was supplied by the presidio, or garrison-fort, whose soldiery not only kept friars and converts safe from the unpacified, but rounded up any backsliders among the converts.

The Crown generally expected that at least 10 years would be needed to pacify and civilize a tribe. When it had been sufficiently "reduced," in the Spanish expression, the Crown would send in other Spaniards who would automatically become the middle class and the elite. In this system, the missionary's powers as teacher and inspirer made the crucial difference.

The Indians of New Mexico held promise of a particularly abundant harvest of souls. When the Spaniards arrived, perhaps 40,000 were scattered throughout the upper Rio Grande valley, as well as along the Little Colorado and Upper Zuñi rivers to the west. Though they were divided into four basic language groups and spoke dozens of dialects, all were settled agricultural people who lived in well-planned villages that the Spaniards called pueblos (pages 56-60).

These sophisticated Indians shared two enemies. Drought was the worse. Sometimes the dry periods lasted for years; and even in those villages where primitive irrigation systems had been devised, famine was a periodic menace. The other threat came from the region's war-loving nomadic tribes. These peoples, mostly from the north, had been preying on the Pueblo settlements for centuries before the white man reached the New World. The raids became more intense in drought years, since drought affected not only the crops cultivated by the Pueblos but the game sought by the nomads. Some of the wanderers called themselves *Diné,* or the People; the Indians of the pueblos referred to them as *apachu,* or enemy, and one group became known as *apachu nabahu,* or enemy of cultivated fields — hence the Apaches and the Navajo, who were to become as inimical to the Spaniards as they were to the Pueblo people.

Still, the settled natives of New Mexico had never been conquered and enslaved, as had so many of the peoples of old Mexico by the Aztecs. For the most part, they were peaceful and industrious, though as Coronado and others had learned to their cost, they could be aroused to awesome fury if their fields and pueblos were threatened. In any case, the conversions listed by the Franciscans in 1608 suggested that the Indians' re-

sistance to Spanish rule was softening. So the new governor of New Mexico, Pedro de Peralta, doubtless hoped as he journeyed north with his contingent of soldiers and settlers to take up his post and lay the foundations of Santa Fe in the winter of 1609-1610.

A year passed, and by the time the cottonwoods along the rivers began to turn green in the spring of 1611, Peralta could begin to appreciate some of the changes the Spanish had brought into an Indian world. From his newly built palace-fortress on the plaza, the Governor could watch horses, cattle, goats and sheep grazing on hillsides where only the Indian dog and the turkey had been seen before. New crops sprouted in the irrigated fields — oats, barley, wheat, onions, peas, melons and varieties of beans hitherto unknown to the Indians. Young fruit trees were blossoming.

From headquarters now established at Santo Domingo, some 30 miles southwest of Santa Fe, the Franciscans were pursuing their missionary labors with renewed vigor. There was still suspicion of the bearded white men, a legacy from Coronado's time. But the Pueblo people, who had always loved storytelling, were enchanted by the Biblical tales told them by the priests. And gradually they seemed to accept the faith. In addition to learning the teachings of the gospel, the Indian neophytes acquired such skills as carpentry and masonry, combining European tools and methods with native materials and techniques. Churches built by Indians under the supervision of the friars began to spring up everywhere. By 1630 the Franciscans could report to the King that 50 friars were at work in 90 villages, and that each village had its own church. Santa Fe and its environs contained about 1,000 persons, 250 of them garrison soldiers. The number of Spaniards farming and ranching along the Rio Grande amounted to another thousand.

But beneath the surface calm, a troublesome friction was developing between civil and religious officials. The governors were convinced of the supremacy of civil authority; the priests were sure that their divine mission among the Indians gave ultimate authority to them. In the power struggles that sprang from this rivalry, the Indians were the victims. Civil authorities tried to intimidate — with whippings and torture — Indians who supplied the priests with food, helped build churches or sang in the choir. In some cases, Indians were encouraged by Spanish civil authorities to return to their old religious practices. The priests retaliated by punishing the Indians for their reversion. Naturally, the Indians grew increasingly bitter.

In 1675, Governor Juan Francisco de Treviño tried to end the civil-clerical strife by siding with the clergy and campaigning against pagan observances. He strictly prohibited native rituals and the use of bizarre ceremonial masks to represent Indian gods. Acting on a tip from an informer, he raided a meeting at a northern pueblo and rounded up 47 Indians on the charge of practicing witchcraft. Four were accused of having tried to bewitch one of the local friars, and were hanged in the plaza at Santa Fe. The rest were publicly whipped, warned of further reprisals should they return to their evil ways and, after a spell of imprisonment, released. Among them was a middle-aged Indian named Popé, from the pueblo of Ohke, later renamed San Juan. All his life, Popé had both resented and resisted the friars' missionary work. He had long hoped to start a revolt against the Spaniards, and his public punishment was all the excuse he needed.

Popé began recruiting like-minded Indians, first in his own pueblo and then in others. His fiery words fell on receptive ears. For the past decade or so, a series of grievous troubles had plagued the New Mexican colony. An apparently endless drought had dried up crops, exhausted grain stores and killed people by the scores. Apache raids grew bolder, thinning the already lean herds of cattle, sheep and, particularly, horses, which the warrior tribes prized above all. Under the circumstances, the Spanish demands upon the natives for foodstuffs and forced labor, the restrictions of mission life, the viselike squeeze of Church and state, and above all the call of old religious loyalties combined to produce a swelling native discontent. Popé readily found allies. Never before had the Pueblo people been brought together by a single leader. Now they began to unite against the Spaniards.

Popé made his headquarters in a kiva, or ceremonial room, at the large Taos pueblo. There, to the awe of his growing band of followers, he received sage counsel from a black giant with yellow eyes. This terrifying being, it was said, was an agent of the Pueblo war god; actually he was an escaped mulatto slave from Mexico,

who had married a Taos woman and became a medicine man supposedly possessed of supernatural power. With the help of the black giant, Popé plotted a sudden, simultaneous attack on all white settlements in the province. It took long, careful preparation.

By midsummer of 1680, about 2,800 Spaniards were living in Santa Fe and in the little outlying hamlets and isolated estancias of the upper Rio Grande valley. Antonio de Otermín was governor. The colonists' dream of riches had withered. And, once settled, they were unable to leave the colony except by royal permission—a fiat as frustrating to them as the restrictions of Spanish rule were to the Indians. But they clung to the hope that conditions might somehow improve, and they tried not to read too much into the cold, sullen Indian faces they saw around them.

Setting the date of the revolt for August 13, Popé sent messengers to the chiefs of the pueblos. Each man bore a piece of knotted cord, the number of knots indicating the days remaining before the attack. Some chiefs, however, became uneasy, and on August 9 they sent word of the insurrection to Governor Otermín. The Governor's messengers rode posthaste to outlying settlements to warn of the attack. By nightfall Popé had heard that the secret was out. He advanced his strike date to the next day—Saturday, August 10.

At 7 o'clock that morning, Governor Otermín was on his way to church when a horseman galloped into Santa Fe shouting that the Indians of Tesuque, a mission north of Santa Fe, had donned warpaint, killed the priest at his altar, destroyed the holy images and burned the church. As Otermín sent soldiers to verify the report, other couriers raced in. The missionaries at San Ildefonso and Nambé had been slain. The church at San Juan was ablaze. Outlying haciendas had been attacked, and the toll was great: Doña Petronila de Salas and her 10 children—dead; the entire family of General Pedro de Leiva—dead; 38 persons at the Domínguez de Mendoza hacienda—dead.

All through the day reports flooded in. Pecos, Taos, Santa Cruz, San Marcos, San Cristóbal, Santo Domingo, Santa Clara, Picuris—all the pueblos in the area had risen, all the churches were being burned, all the priests killed. As far away as Ácoma and the Zuñi and Hopi villages to the west there was death and destruction. By the night of the 10th, all Spaniards in the

Santa Fe area had swarmed into the town. Survivors from the devastated areas to the north and west ran gauntlets of raiding parties to seek safety in Santa Fe.

On Tuesday, August 13, the original strike day, the cornfields outside town were seething with Indians, most armed with bows but some bearing looted Spanish firearms and swords, and some mounted on horses taken from Spanish corrals. Otermín aimed the town's two cannons at the Indians, but before firing he called for a parley. An Indian fluent in Spanish, who had always been thought of as a devout Christian, stepped forward bearing two crosses. One was white and one was red. Otermín, he said, must choose between them. White meant an immediate withdrawal of all Spaniards from New Mexico. Red meant war, a war that would not end until every Spaniard was dead.

Otermín tried to defuse the situation with chiding lectures, promises of leniency and, finally, threats of counterattack. The Indians' answer was a swift and savage onslaught. All day the 150-man Santa Fe garrison battled with the Indians in the fields around the town. But when 1,000 warriors arrived that evening from outlying pueblos, the Spanish had no choice but to retreat into the town and barricade themselves.

Overnight more Indians arrived, and the next day some 2,500 warriors encircled the capital. On the 16th of August they stormed it, and by nightfall they controlled everything except the plaza. On the following day, as an eyewitness recalled later, "the whole town became a torch." The Indians jeered in triumph as they watched the flames, and mockingly chanted Latin phrases from the Catholic liturgy. The previous day they had shut off Santa Fe's water supply by cutting the ditch that carried water to the town. Now intense thirst was added to the Spaniards' miseries.

The Indians' victory was so complete that they became careless. On Sunday the 18th, Otermín and about 100 of his soldiers — all who could still stand and wield a weapon — made a sudden counterattack. After attending mass together, they erupted from the palace and fell on the enemy in one last frenzy of effort. Taken by surprise, the Indians suffered grievous losses. Several hundreds were left dead in the smoking ruins, while only five Spaniards had fallen.

Yet Otermín knew that it was only a matter of time before he would be overwhelmed. The only salvation lay in swift retreat. The evacuation began on August 21. There were only two carts for the entire refugee party. Food was terrifyingly short. Otermín said later that they had not so much as a crust of bread or a grain of corn or wheat. There were, however, a few sheep, goats and cows — which would do as much to slow the procession as to stave off starvation. At the head of the stumbling column fluttered the old yellow silk banner that Spanish soldiers had carried into New Mexico the century before. The Indians stood on the hillsides above Santa Fe and watched the Spaniards leave. They did not attack. The departure was enough.

In October all the refugees from New Mexico — Otermín's party from Santa Fe and the survivors of other destroyed settlements — gathered at El Paso on the Rio Grande, where Franciscans had maintained a mission since 1659. There the gaunt and ragged survivors were welcomed by Fray Francisco de Ayeta, who had assembled supplies for the expected refugees. And there most of them stayed, to form the nucleus of a new civilian settlement. Of the 2,800 Spaniards who had lived among the Pueblo Indians, nearly 2,000 had reached El Paso. About half of the remainder were known dead; the rest were missing.

Spain had experienced other Indian rebellions during her almost two centuries in the New World, but never such a devastating outburst of Indian fury. For the Indians, however, the victory was no panacea. Having chafed under the domination of the Spaniards, they now suffered under the tyranny of one of their own. Popé, the hero of the revolt, declared himself the governor of all the pueblos. The autonomy and independence that had been traditional among the various communities was now wiped out. Each was forced to pay tribute in goods and services to Governor Popé, greeting him with the obsequiousness and ceremony that they had rendered the Spanish governors.

In other ways Popé moved to obliterate all traces of Spanish occupation. Churches and other Spanish buildings that survived the rebellion were destroyed, except the governor's palace; Popé wanted that for himself. Everyone who had been baptized was scrubbed with soapweed to erase the stigma. Christian marriages were dissolved. Horses, originally introduced by the explorer-colonist Oñate and now numbering in the thousands,

A Spanish horse bound for the New World is lowered onto a ship by pulleys *(above),* as shown in an 18th Century manual. Once aboard, the animals were often suspended in slings *(upper left)* to avert a fall in rough seas; still, as much as half of each shipload died on the voyage. In the Americas, the Spaniards ferried horses across inland waters in makeshift craft such as the dugouts lashed together at left.

The Mediterranean plow brought by the Spanish to the Rio Grande valley around 1600 raised the soil's output far above the level achieved by the Indians, who pushed seeds into the earth with sticks. Oxen or mules were yoked to the heavy shaft; the slender handle was used as a guide. Iron was scarce, so blacksmiths often beat wheel rims and broken swords into plowshares.

were traded to or stolen by Apaches—who in Popé's own time used their newly acquired mounts to raid the pueblos more mercilessly than ever. Pueblo after pueblo had to be abandoned. And although the native gods were once more propitiated in the kivas, drought continued to grip the land. By the time Popé died in 1688, his realm—the Pueblo realm—was weaker than it had ever been in the past.

Spain needed time to take advantage of this disarray, and the first sporadic attempts at reinvasion suffered from lack of manpower and strong leadership. Finally, in August of 1692, a military expedition led by Don Diego José de Vargas Zapata Luján Ponce de León y Contreras—usually known simply as Diego de Vargas—sallied forth from El Paso to begin the mission of reconquest. His force consisted of fewer than 200 men, only 60 of whom were Spanish soldiers. The rest were Indian allies, servants and friars. Yet Diego de Vargas was a charismatic leader whose commanding presence and absolute fearlessness more than made up for the shortcomings of his army.

Again symbolically bearing the yellow banner, the would-be reconqueror marched deep into New Mexico, passing one ruined pueblo after another. Finding the hacienda of Mejía abandoned but intact, Vargas fortified it as a rear base, then pushed north toward Santa Fe—about 66 miles distant—with only 40 soldiers, 50 Indians and three friars. Their route took them past Santo Domingo, 12 years earlier the missionary capital of New Mexico, now an empty ruin.

Before dawn on September 13, Vargas and his men approached the walls of Santa Fe. Those ramparts, at least, still stood, for the town was occupied by Pueblo Indians who had been driven from their homes by Apaches. Scouts reported that the governor's palace had been converted into a fort and that pueblo-type adobe dwellings had been built between the ruins of Spanish buildings. The town appeared to be asleep.

Vargas gave careful instructions. The town was to be surrounded, but no shots were to be fired unless he unsheathed his sword. His little band moved silently to the town walls and then, at a signal from Vargas, roared out in unison: "Glory be to the blessed sacrament of the altar!" Astonished Indians appeared on the walls. In the Spanish ranks a trumpet sounded and a drum rolled, and Vargas called upon the Indians to surrender. Instead they shouted defiance and began preparing for battle. Vargas made his preparations, too. Cannons were loaded and placed in position, charges of powder laid against the town walls, weapons cleaned, prayers offered.

At sunup, Vargas addressed the Indians again, urging them to yield peaceably and promising clemency. They demanded that he approach alone and take off his helmet so that they could see his face. With great coolness he did so, standing bareheaded below a line of Indians with drawn bows. He offered a full pardon to all the Indians within and told them that his friars would absolve them of their sins. They hesitated. Vargas withdrew a short distance, calmly ate his breakfast, waited. Late in the afternoon, something of a miracle occurred. The gates opened. Unarmed Indians came out to talk to Vargas, who greeted them with open arms. Two friars were permitted to enter town and offer blessings. Indians thronged out through the gates to meet the Spaniards. Vargas promised peace, "with great love," he later wrote, "embracing them, speaking to them with tender and loving words."

The next day, the Spaniards were invited into the town. Vargas stood in the plaza and announced that the Spanish King would forgive the people of the pueblos for the rebellion, for their apostasy and for the desecration of the churches if they would return to

Christianity and promise allegiance to the King. The Indians had suffered much since the revolt—the debilitating drought, the loss of morale under Pope's tyranny, anarchy following his fall and the increasing depredations of the Apaches. All these factors helped to confuse the Indians when Vargas came promising peace and forgiveness. Caught off balance, the Indians decided to take a chance. They agreed to his terms.

Vargas formally reclaimed Santa Fe for Spain. Mass was celebrated in the plaza, and the friars began baptizing children who had been born since the revolt. Delegations of Indians came from nearby pueblos within the next few days to volunteer their allegiance. Vargas himself traveled to distant pueblos with his message of forgiveness and peace. One after the other, the chiefs and their people came back into the Spanish fold.

By December 20, Vargas and his little troop were back in El Paso. It would take time before reconquest was assured and New Mexico recolonized. But in only four months Diego de Vargas had restored New Mexico to Spain and Catholicism. Not a life had been lost. As a contemporary Mexican scholar, Carlos Sigüenza y Góngora, enthusiastically described Vargas' achievement: "An entire realm was restored to the Majesty of our lord and king, Charles II, without wasting an ounce of powder, unsheathing a sword, or (what is most worthy of emphasis and appreciation) without costing the Royal Treasury a single copper."

One reason for the Spaniards' laggard interest in retaking New Mexico had been a sudden, frightening development on another part of the northern frontier. In 1685 rumors of French intrusion into eastern Texas began to filter back to Mexico City. The stories were all the more worrisome since the area was virtually unoccupied: the Spaniards had almost totally ignored this expanse of wilderness since Alonzo Alvarez de Pineda claimed it for the Crown in 1519.

As it happened, the rumors were solidly grounded in fact. Three years earlier, in 1682, the French explorer La Salle had canoed down the Mississippi River to the Gulf of Mexico. There he claimed the entire Mississippi valley for Louis XIV, in whose honor he named the region Louisiana.

Two years later La Salle returned to America from France with a small flotilla of vessels carrying soldiers, colonists and supplies to establish a permanent French settlement in Louisiana. But the expedition suffered one disaster after another. Navigational errors and the bewildering sameness of the coastline carried the party past the mouth of the Mississippi and on to Matagorda Bay on the Texas coast. There the dauntless La Salle built a little settlement on Garcitas Creek, a few miles from the Gulf, and called it Fort St. Louis. The venture was doomed, however: illness and starvation claimed many expedition members, and others fell to hostile Indians. When the colony's sole remaining ship slipped its moorings and broke up on a sand bar, La Salle made a last desperate gamble. With a party of the most able-bodied men, he set out on an overland march, hoping to reach Canada and get help for the colony. It was a journey he was destined never to complete: en route he was slain by his own mutinous companions. Behind, at Fort St. Louis, he had left a forlorn little band of 13 men and seven women—all that remained of the fort's 180 original settlers.

News of La Salle's establishment of a colony, meanwhile, had caused consternation in New Spain. A French stronghold on the Gulf of Mexico could not only furnish support for French pirates, who were already disrupting Spanish shipping in the area, but would be a threatening wedge in the unexplored territory Spain regarded as her own.

In 1686, the first of a series of forays into Texas was launched from Monterrey by Alonso de León, its purpose to find and destroy La Salle's colony. The Spaniards so lacked information that they did not even know the colony's location, much less its character and strength. Not until the fourth expedition, on which De León was accompanied by Franciscan friar Damián Massanet and 100 soldiers, was the search successful. In April 1689, the group stumbled on the ruins of La Salle's hapless effort on Garcitas Creek: five tiny houses plastered with mud and a small fort built of ship's timbers, with the date 1684 carved over its entrance. It was immediately clear that the French colony posed no threat to Spanish possession. "We found all the houses sacked," De León reported, "all the settlers' furniture broken. We found three bodies scattered over the plain. One of these, from the dress that still clung to the bones, appeared to be that of a woman. We took the bodies up, chanted Mass, and buried them." ◉

The sophisticated society of the pueblo

The Spaniards called the Indian settlements scattered across present-day Arizona and New Mexico "pueblos" —meaning"towns"or"villages" —and they regarded their 40,000 inhabitants as natural subjects for conversion to Christianity. And well they might. For generations, the residents of these compact, permanent communities had been the northern pioneers of civilization on the continent. Although their wealth did not remotely approach that of the mighty Aztecs of central Mexico, the pueblo dwellers were nonetheless sophisticated peoples compared with the rude nomadic tribes that surrounded and periodically preyed upon them.

When the Spanish arrived in the 16th Century, they met dozens of pueblo groups, each one of which regarded itself as distinct from its neighbors. The fragmented populace did, however, fall into four basic linguistic divisions that were identified with particular locales. The Tano and Keres groups were concentrated along the Rio Grande and its tributaries in New Mexico; the Hopi were clustered far to the west, above the Little Colorado River; and the Zuñis lived mainly along the Upper Zuñi River, on the western edge of New Mexico.

All told, Spanish explorers discovered no fewer than 70 inhabited pueblos in the Southwest, some of them containing apartments for more than 1,000 people, but usually holding a population of around 400. Depending on the materials available at the sites, the apartment complexes were variously constructed of sun-baked adobe bricks, quarried sandstone or volcanic *tufa* rock. Many were multisto-

ried, with their upper levels successively set back to provide families with terraces. As a defense against raiders, the lower stories often had neither doors nor windows in their walls; the residents entered a rooftop hatchway by means of ladders, which could then be drawn inside.

Skilled weavers, potters and tillers of the soil, the pueblo Indians were industrious and singularly provident. The storerooms at the back of their homes were filled with dried corn, beans and squash—sometimes more than a year's supply. They showed equal diligence in attending to the spiritual dimension of their lives. Their apartments were often arranged in a rectangular pattern, facing on an open square, where the villagers frequently met to offer prayers to the supernatural forces believed to control the universe.

Ceremonies were performed to ensure successful crops, achieve social harmony, thwart enemies, ward off illness and bring good fortune in the pueblo Indians' periodic hunts for antelope, bear and other game. In one of their rites, the participants wore hideous masks to frighten and purify disobedient children; at other times ceremonial participants appeared in magnificent embroidered cotton robes of various colors, white moccasins or boots, and shell and turquoise jewelry.

Such rites were naturally frowned upon by the Spanish missionaries. But even though the pueblo tribes paid nominal obeisance to the Roman Catholic religion their conquerors imposed upon them, they never, in all the years of Spanish rule, dismissed their old gods and became true Christians.

This Zuñi pueblo, exhibiting modern additions in a 19th Century photograph, was one of the cities of Cíbola whose rumored riches lured the Spanish up from Mexico.

Zuñis load burros on a pueblo street. The hardy pack animals — along with horses, cattle and sheep — were quickly adopted by the agrarian pueblo tribes after the Spaniards introduced them into the Southwest.

To distance themselves from Spanish influence, Hopis who had originally occupied lowland villages constructed the pueblos of Mishongnovi (*right*) and Walpi (*below*) on lofty mesas in northeast Arizona.

Corn and chili peppers dry in the sun at the Tano pueblo of Ohke. Though corn had always been a staple of pueblo diet, peppers were unknown until the Spaniards brought them to the area from Mexico.

The Keres' pueblo of Ácoma sits atop a 357-foot-high mesa in western New Mexico. Oldest of the communities discovered by Coronado's soldiers, it was built on the easily defended site around 1,000 A.D.

Hopi priests wearing feathered shields representing the sun god — the most powerful of all their dieties — bless a spring that supplied water for their pueblo. The benediction was preliminary to a 16-day summer ritual by which the Indians hoped to guarantee rain for a second corn planting.

Everything suggested an Indian massacre, though the identity of the attackers would never be known. Happily, the Indians De León's party met seemed hospitable enough. These were Caddo people of the Hasinai confederacy, who became collectively known to the Spanish as Tejas, from the Hasinai word *tayshas*—meaning "allies," or "friends." Hence the name Tejas, or Texas, given to the area. De León saw in the Tejas a golden opportunity. In a nice mingling of the pious and the practical, he wrote in his official report: "Certainly it is a pity that people so rational should have no one to teach them the Gospel, especially when the province of Texas is so large and so fertile and has so fine a climate."

Taking his own cue, De León set out the next year with Fray Massanet on a fifth venture, this time to establish a mission among the Hasinai. The Spanish flag was raised over San Francisco de los Tejas, near the Neches River, in May 1690. It was Spain's first outpost in Texas. Three Franciscan friars and three soldiers were left there to convert the natives and resist further encroachment by the French. A second mission was founded nearby later that year. But further missionary efforts were hampered by disease and crop failures, and in 1693 the heretofore friendly Indians —perhaps irritated by the unruly behavior of the soldiers—ordered the Spaniards to leave. Hearing this, and convinced by now that the French threat had vanished with La Salle, the viceroy in Mexico ordered the missions abandoned. Fray Massanet buried the religious paraphernalia, burned the mission buildings and sadly departed. For the next two decades Texas once more lay unoccupied, a Spanish province in name only.

Yet the French threat did not conveniently disappear. In 1699, La Salle's dream of a Louisiana colony began to come true when the French founded a settlement at Biloxi, commanding the mouth of the Mississippi, and followed it in 1702 with a fort at Mobile. In 1713, the military commander at Biloxi, a French-Canadian named Louis Juchereau de St. Denis, set out on a bold reconnoitering sweep into the territory beyond the Mississippi. One of the assignments given him by the Louisiana authorities was to set up a trading post on the Red River for marketing goods to Indians. St. Denis found an ideal site in what is today the western sector of Louisiana. The base he built,

Natchitoches, was to become that state's oldest town.

Again the Spaniards were stung into action. Natchitoches stood on the very doorsill of their northeastern Texas border, and the idea of the French dealing amicably with "their" natives was intolerable. Again friars and soldiers made the long trek north to build mission stations in Tejas country near the Neches; one outpost, San Miguel de los Adaes, they boldly positioned near the Red River, only 15 miles from Natchitoches. To guard the route between Mexico and these fragile new seedlings, New Spain decided in 1718 to do something about a promising site Father Massanet had noted in south-central Texas, where a river fed a fertile land inhabited by complaisant Indians. The presidio-mission of San Antonio, founded by 72 settler-soldiers and priests, and equipped with 548 horses, 200 cows, 1,000 sheep and 200 oxen, took firm root and grew into early Texas' most important settlement. The mission's first chapel later became popularly known as the Alamo, after the cottonwood, or poplar (in Spanish, *álamo*), trees that grew nearby.

Soon afterward, the struggling frontiersmen in East Texas were overwhelmed by international events. On January 9, 1719, France declared war on Spain. Five months later, when the news washed up in the New World, the French force at Natchitoches sallied forth to carry the King's war to the enemy — in this case, the little settlement at nearby San Miguel. The invaders consisted of seven armed men, but it massively outnumbered the complement at the isolated Spanish outpost: one lay brother and one soldier. The latter, at the instant war struck, was not only unarmed but unclad.

The French seized the vessels and ornaments from the church and attempted to capture a flock of chickens. However, the indignant chickens made so much noise that the French commander's horse bucked in alarm and threw its rider to the ground. In the ensuing confusion, the lay brother managed to escape, carrying word of the assault to other Spanish settlements. The French, he reported breathlessly, intended to drive all Spaniards out of Texas and had already dispatched a major expeditionary force from Mobile. Thoroughly panicked, the settlers of East Texas beat a hasty retreat cross-country to the shelter of San Antonio.

The comic-opera "chicken war," as it came to be called, did yield an immensely valuable by-product: it brought to Texas the second Marquis of San Miguel de Aguayo, one of the most impressive figures of the Spanish American frontier. Aguayo was the wealthy and capable soldier-governor of Coahuila, the Mexican province adjacent to Texas, and to him fell the duty of organizing a force to meet the French threat. On the underpopulated frontier, this was no easy task. When he had raised a cavalry company of 84 men and sent them to reinforce the San Antonio garrison, he had nearly exhausted the available manpower. Almost a year elapsed before he managed to find and equip an additional 500 soldiers. At last Aguayo reached San Antonio on April 4, 1721, found that bastion secure, and used it as his base for sweeps through Texas.

Reports of a French invasion turned out to have been greatly exaggerated. Aguayo caught not a glimpse of a Frenchman as he probed north and east. Only when he reached the Neches River was he met by French captain St. Denis, founder of Natchitoches. St. Denis told him that France and Spain were, for the time being, at peace, and that he was willing to observe the truce if Aguayo was. Moreover, he would return the church vessels taken at San Miguel. Aguayo agreed, but stipulated that the French withdraw to Natchitoches and thus vacate all land to which Spain had laid claim. It was easy for St. Denis to accept: he *was* the French in Texas. Seldom has international diplomacy produced such swift and satisfying results.

Aguayo now moved vigorously to consolidate and extend the Spanish presence. When he retired to Coahuila in 1722 he left behind him in Texas 10 missions where there had been only two, four presidios instead of one, and a permanent military establishment of 268 soldiers, compared to 50 previously.

Spanish Texas was to be comparatively secure for more than a century. But despite the Crown's efforts to stimulate population and economic development, growth was painfully slow. Two decades after Aguayo's expedition, the Spaniards numbered only 1,500. The chief reason was the more or less constant hostility of the Indians — not the peaceful Tejas, but the tribes that had acquired the horse from the Spaniards in New Mexico. With these warlike nomads the Spanish method of colonization proved utterly ineffectual.

First the eastern, or Lipan, branch of the Apaches began terrorizing the frontier. Traditional foes of the

Tejas, the Apaches had extended their enmity to the Tejas' mentors and protectors, the Spaniards. And with the founding of San Antonio, the Apaches had a convenient target for their hostility. They made repeated raids, driving away horses and cattle on which the young community depended and often capturing or killing mission Indians who were in charge of the herds.

From the outset, mission priests and presidio soldiers differed sharply on how to deal with these warlike Indians. The Franciscans clung to the belief that they would cajole the horsemen into a settled existence as mission farmers. The soldiers were convinced that only punitive counterattacks would solve the problem. But neither the friars' gifts nor the soldiers' muskets made any lasting impression. The raids went on.

Then, in 1749, a delegation of Lipans appeared at San Antonio with an astonishing request: they wanted a mission in their country. The Franciscans were jubilant. Eventually a site was chosen on the San Sabá River, not far from the present-day town of Menard.

What the good friars did not discover until later was that the Lipans had begun to suffer from the depredations of their own enemies, the Comanches, many of whom were equipped with guns obtained from French traders. The Comanches had erupted south out of Wyoming around 1700, and by acquiring Spain's great gift to the nomad—the horse—had transformed their culture almost overnight. Incredibly skilled riders and hunters, unmatched for ferocity, they were becoming the scourge of the Plains. The Lipan Apaches' conciliatory gesture to the missionaries was nothing but a stratagem—a calculated ploy to lure one enemy, the Spaniards, within range of another, the Comanches, in the hope that the two would destroy each other.

Unaware of all this, the Franciscans were mystified and disappointed when their newly established mission at San Sabá failed to attract converts. The few Indians who came left hastily after accepting the friars' gifts, and none would agree to settle. Determined to be patient, the Franciscans still had not recognized the true state of affairs when disaster struck on March 16, 1758. Two thousand mounted Comanches and allied Wichitas, their faces bedaubed with war paint, assaulted the mission and destroyed it (pages 74-75).

The attack caused dismay in San Antonio and anger in Mexico. A punitive force of 600 men with two

El Señor D.º Diego de Bargas Zapata, Lujan, Ponze de Leon, Marques de la Naba de Barcinas, del Orden de S.ᵗⁱᵃᵍᵒ Governador, Conquistador, Pacificador, y Capitan General del Nuebo Mejico, perdió la Vida en Campaña Rasa por libertar los Vasallos Sublevados en el Sitio de Bernalillo año de MDCCIV

Este cuadro, que el Instituto de Cultura Hispánica ofrece al Museo de Nuebo Mejico, es copia del verdadero retrato de D. Diego Bargas Zapata, de la Casa de los Vargas, cuyo original se conserva en la capilla de San Isidro sita en el Pueil de Santisteban de Madrid.

field guns and a long supply train was assembled at San Antonio to teach the Comanches a lesson. By Spanish standards it was a major effort: Cortés had conquered all Mexico with an army no larger. Alas, a still greater and more humiliating outrage lay in store.

When the expedition finally tracked the marauders to the Red River on October 7, 1759, they found a contingent of several thousand Comanches, Wichitas and other Plains Indians waiting to meet them behind well-built defensive breastworks; the Indians were flourishing French firearms, and actually flying a French flag. The four-hour siege that followed turned into a debacle for the Spaniards, who could neither breach the Indians' defenses nor find shelter from their gunfire. In confusion they fell back to the San Sabá River, abandoning their cannon and losing the supply train along the way. It was one of the greatest military defeats the Spanish suffered in the Americas — not in terms of lives lost, for only 19 had been killed and 14 wounded, but in its psychological effect. The rout at Red River forced the Spanish to recognize that in Texas their methods no longer worked. From now on, the bloodthirsty Comanches would keep the Texas settlements in a permanent state of siege.

Not many of the Spaniards who came to America in the 16th Century knew how to read. But many of them had heard a chivalric romance called *The Exploits of Esplandian*. The story dealt with an attack by pagan forces on the medieval Christians holding Constantinople. At a crucial point the pagans were aided by a warrior queen, Calafía, who came from a place "at the right hand of the Indies, an island named California, very close to that part of the Terrestrial Paradise, which is inhabited by black women, without a single man among them, and they lived in the manner of Amazons. They were robust of body, with strong and passionate hearts and great virtues. Their weapons were all made of gold. The island everywhere abounds with gold and precious stones, and upon it no other metal was found." Furthermore, on this island, "there are many griffins. In no other part of the world can they be found."

When Hernán Cortés was pushing his conquest to the west coast of Mexico, he heard from the natives of a land across the water. Cortés suspected that it might be where the Amazons and the gold could be found. He built ships, sent out expeditions, and in 1535 established a short-lived colony about where La Paz, Baja California, now stands. There proved to be no gold, no griffins and no Amazons; it was a very poor country indeed, both in terms of natives and resources. Nevertheless, in time, the name California became attached to it. It was thought to be an island, possibly separated from Asia by the legendary Strait of Anián, somewhere in the mysterious north.

Knowledge of California advanced so haltingly that not until 1705 did there appear a map that showed the reality: California was not an island but a peninsula — Baja California — directly attached to the land mass above it, called Alta, or Upper, California.

The remarkable cartographer who drew this map (it would remain the most reliable for a century to come) was Father Eusebio Francisco Kino, a Jesuit missionary whose character and skills were to help shape the future of both Californias. A devout priest and inspiring leader, he was also a mathematician, an astronomer, and a tireless explorer. His first mission, founded among the Pima Indians on Mexico's San Miguel River, was followed by a chain of missions farther north, along the Altar and Magdalena rivers in what is today the Mexican state of Sonora. In 1700, he founded San Xavier del Bac, near the present Tucson, and thereafter six other missions in what is now Arizona.

Thanks to Kino's labors, a stable and productive series of outposts existed on New Spain's northwest frontier, an essential factor in the subsequent colonization of California. In addition, his personal enthusiasm was largely responsible for the Jesuit order's building a string of missions in forbidding Baja California *(pages 78-83)*. The Baja missions, each one an oasis in a desert wilderness, could not have survived their infancy had not Kino kept up a steady stream of supplies from his thriving missions in Sonora. Shipment of such goods across the Gulf of California was always risky, however, because of the fierce currents and frequent storms. It was Kino's need for a better supply route to Baja that prompted his explorations northward, until repeated trips along the Gila and Colorado rivers to the head of the gulf convinced him, as he wrote triumphantly to Jesuit officials in Mexico in 1702, that *"California no es isla, sino penisla!"* His subsequent map showed that both Alta and Baja California should, in theory, be reachable from Mexico by land.

But no land route was blazed to the Californias in his time. When Kino died in 1711, there was no one of his caliber to follow up his lead. Like Texas, California lay forgotten until foreign threats prodded the Spaniards into action. In the 1760s, Spain became alarmed by reports of English and Russian shipping ac-

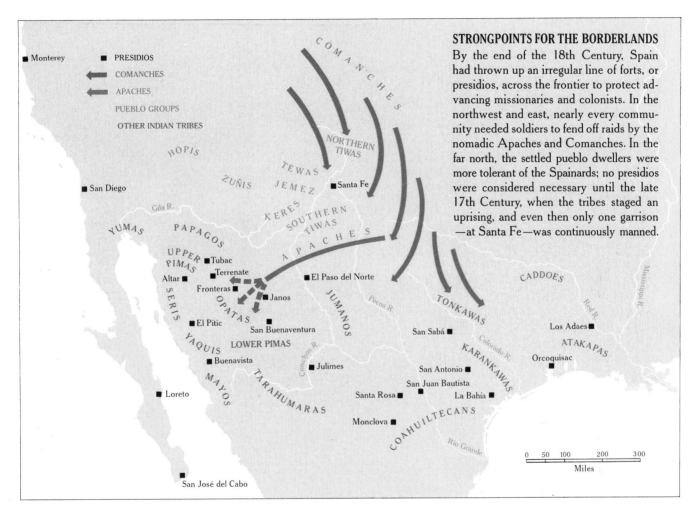

STRONGPOINTS FOR THE BORDERLANDS
By the end of the 18th Century, Spain had thrown up an irregular line of forts, or presidios, across the frontier to protect advancing missionaries and colonists. In the northwest and east, nearly every community needed soldiers to fend off raids by the nomadic Apaches and Comanches. In the far north, the settled pueblo dwellers were more tolerant of the Spainards; no presidios were considered necessary until the late 17th Century, when the tribes staged an uprising, and even then only one garrison —at Santa Fe—was continuously manned.

tivities near the west coast of North America; especially distressing was Russia's declared intention to establish settlements on the North American coast. Obviously, Spain must occupy and secure her neglected Pacific frontier — particularly Alta California, which was unexplored except for the few places along its coast where mariners had briefly landed. Virtually all the Spaniards knew was that there were two promising bays: San Diego, discovered in 1542, and Monterey to the north, first sighted in 1602. The founding of mission colonies in these and adjacent areas would presumably discourage foreign intruders.

A man of vision and vigor, Don José de Gálvez, arrived in Mexico from the Spanish court in 1765. As *visitador,* or visitor-general, his primary function was to oversee royal revenues and government operations in Mexico, but he was also charged with protecting Spain's possessions to the north. It did not take him long to see the urgent need to settle Alta California. When Charles III sent his approval in 1768, Gálvez quickly began organizing an expedition of exploration and colonization, with parties to proceed by both land and sea. Two small ships, loaded with supplies, soldiers, artisans and a few Franciscan priests, were to leave from La Paz in southern Baja, round the tip of the peninsula and sail up the coast to San Diego. Meanwhile, two groups would travel overland from the Baja missions of Velicatá and Loreto, heading north for a rendezvous with the ships at San Diego.

Gálvez named Gaspar de Portolá, the newly appointed governor of Baja California, to command land operations and coordinate the expedition. Fray Junípero Serra, father-president of the Franciscan friars who had recently taken over the work of the Jesuits

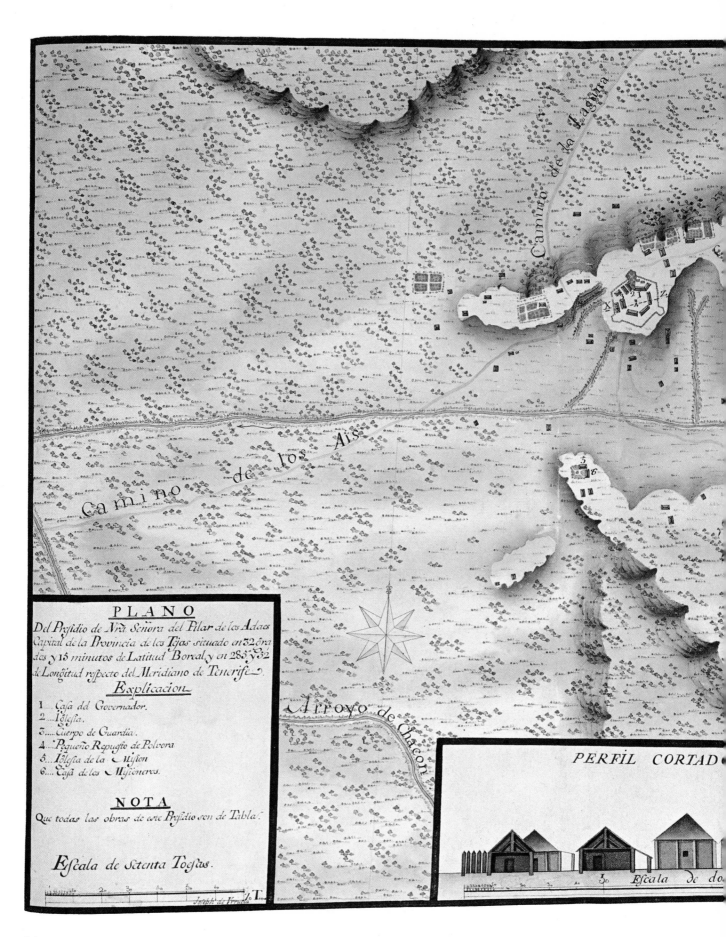

PLANO

Del Presidio de Nrã Señora del Pilar de los Adaes
Capital de la Provincia de los Tejas situado en 32 gra
dos y 15 minutos de Latitud Boreal, y en 285° y 52
de Longitud respecto del Meridiano de Tenerife

Explicacion

1 ... Casa del Governador.
2 ... Iglesia.
3 ... Cuerpo de Guardia.
4 ... Pequeño Repuesto de Polvora
5 ... Iglesia de la Mision
6 ... Casa de los Misioneros.

NOTA

Que todas las obras de este Presidio son de Tabla.

Escala de Setenta Toesas.

Joseph de Urrutia

Camino de la Laguna

Camino de los Ais

Arroyo de Chacon

PERFIL CORTADO

Escala de do

66

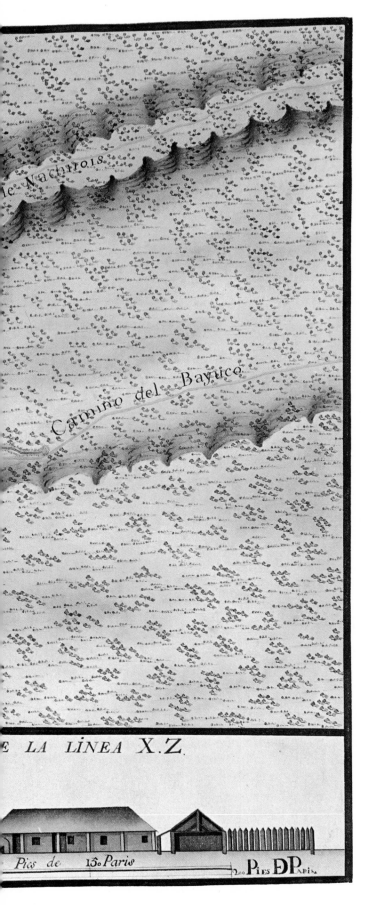

Pies de 15º Paris

Pies D'P.

in Baja California, was to serve as spiritual leader.

The two ships, carrying the bulk of the supplies, set sail in January and February 1769, on what was to be a cruelly difficult voyage. The *San Antonio* sailed too far north and reached San Diego only after 54 days at sea. The *San Carlos* made even more serious errors in navigation and took 110 days for the trip. A third vessel, the *San José,* which sailed in June to join the others, never did arrive; it simply disappeared.

Meanwhile an advance land party of 25 leather-armored soldiers, three muleteers, and 42 Indians armed with axes, picks and shovels headed north to break trail. Traveling through hundreds of miles of mountains and deserts, the company reached San Diego on May 14, 1769. Six weeks later, Portolá and Serra arrived with their party: 10 soldiers, two servants and 49 Baja California natives. Between them, the land expeditions had used almost all the supplies of the Jesuit missions along their route; many of the overland travelers had fallen by the wayside — hungry, ill and discouraged. One thing was clear: the Baja missions did not have the productive capacity to support the would-be colonists of Alta California.

When the survivors met in San Diego on July 1, the outlook was grim. All but two crew members of the *San Carlos* had died of scurvy, and everyone else on board was incapacitated by scurvy and dehydration. Among the few healthy survivors were Don Pedro Fages, a fiery Catalan infantry officer, and some of his soldiers. Eight men of the *San Antonio* complement were dead, and nearly all of those still alive were ill. Nevertheless, on July 3 a hopeful salute was fired; Father Serra raised a cross, said mass and led in the singing of the *Te Deum.* Soon afterward he began con-

THE LAYOUT OF A WILDERNESS BASTION

Drafted in 1767 by an inspecting engineer of New Spain's army, this delicately hued chart provided the general staff with a plan of the remote Presidio of Los Adaes in eastern Texas. The hexagonal stockade, at center, contained a guardhouse, chapel, powder shed, barracks for the troops and the provincial governor's house — the largest structure in the cross-sectional view of the presidio, at bottom. Homes and gardens of settlers surround the fort, while on a jutting promontory across the gully stands a mission. Built in 1721, Los Adaes was the capital of Texas and Coahuila until 1770, when the government was moved to San Antonio.

A fully equipped cavalryman of New Spain, as indicated in this 17th Century drawing, was a mounted armory, with broadsword, lance, musket, pistols, shield and *cuera*, or coat of arrowproof leather.

struction of the mission, San Diego de Alcalá. It was the first of 21 missions the Franciscans were to build in Alta California, nine of them under Serra's supervision. These Franciscan outposts were the foundations on which California would grow.

Father Serra, born Miguel José Serra in Majorca, had adopted the name Junípero from the friend and counselor of St. Francis of Assisi. Serra was a man who had accustomed himself to hardship. In his pulpit in Mexico City he had sometimes punished his own flesh with burning tapers and chains to atone for the sins of his flock. No longer young when he reached California, he still pursued his goal of soul-saving with dedication and energy. Spying a group of Indians, he would strike a bell to attract their attention, and urge them to love God and adopt a Christian way of life.

While Serra was busy finishing the San Diego mission, Portolá headed north to find the second of the Spaniards' two immediate objectives in California: the

harbor of Monterey. With him he took about 60 men, including the Catalan, Pedro Fages, and his soldiers.

Traveling slowly northward, the Portolá party reached the point where they expected to find Monterey. But the broad bay they gazed upon—though in fact it was Monterey—did not seem to match the descriptions of early mariners. They pushed onward. Many days and many miles later, they reached a magnificent body of water, a great sheltered bay that sailors had so far failed to discover because of its narrow entrance. Portolá knew that by now they were far north of Monterey and, because his men were weary and hungry, he did not explore it to any extent. He mistakenly assumed it was part of a vaguely known bay to the northwest that, nearly two centuries earlier, a friar aboard a Spanish galleon had named for St. Francis. And so Portolá alluded to it as San Francisco Bay, a name that stuck even after his error was discovered.

On the return march to San Diego, his men were

forced to kill one mule from their train each day in order to survive. When they reached their destination on January 24, 1770, Portolá reported later, they smelled strongly of mule. At that, they were in better condition than those left behind. The infant colony was near starvation, and most of the men were ill. All were anxiously awaiting the return of the *San Antonio,* which had been sent back to Mexico to fetch badly needed provisions and medicine. Two more harrowing months dragged by before its sails were sighted on the horizon. In the nick of time, San Diego was saved.

Portolá determined to make one more search for Monterey. Late in May he and his men returned to the place they had first found; a more thorough investigation convinced them it was Monterey. On May 31 the *San Antonio* arrived bearing Father Serra and supplies. Three days later, Serra and Portolá inaugurated the settlement of Monterey and the mission of San Carlos Borromeo. His assignment ended, Portolá turned

command over to Pedro Fages and sailed for Mexico.

He could not report on the California colonies with any great optimism. The "unhappy Spaniards" whom he had left there were, he said, enduring great discomforts. "The mines of gold and silver and other rich products foretold to us in advance advices we never saw nor found, as our first care was to hunt for meat to keep from starving." The colonies could not support themselves, nor was there any truly effective way of supplying them, since the proved hazards of navigation made shipping unpredictable. Portolá concluded that "it was impossible to send aid to Monterey by sea, and still more so by land, unless it was proposed to sacrifice thousands of men and huge sums of money."

There was one ray of light in an otherwise dismal scene: "The natives of California are so gentle that we never had to defend ourselves," Portolá wrote. Yet even this boon had its drawbacks, as the colonists soon discovered. These gentle Indians, it turned out, were

69

not very industrious. A few along the Santa Barbara Channel were skilled artisans who fashioned seaworthy canoes with primitive tools. Some fished. But most of the California Indians had little interest in the agricultural labor so essential to the Spaniards in developing their colonies. The staple of their diet was acorns, which the women gathered and ground into meal. Unlike Indian tribes in other parts of the West, they had no fields of corn, beans and squash with which to support the colonists. Time would be needed to coax — or coerce — them into learning to grow crops.

By 1773, five missions had sprung up; from south to north, they were San Diego, San Gabriel, San Luís Obispo, San Antonio de Padua and San Carlos. But "colonies" existed in little more than name. In all of Alta California there were only 61 soldiers and 11 priests. There were no artisans, no doctors, no skilled farmers and no white laborers. Nor were there any white women. Some 600 head of livestock were divided among the five missions, but they had to be kept as breeding stock and supplied no food other than milk. No supplies were available from Baja California, and supply ships from Mexico were few. Near-starvation became a way of life.

Supply problems increasingly vexed the viceroy of New Spain, Antonio María Bucareli, who had been ordered to maintain a strong Spanish posture in California. He was therefore gratified to receive a letter from Don Juan Bautista de Anza, the energetic and frontier-wise commandant of the presidio at Tubac in present-day Arizona. Anza was well known to King and Viceroy: both his father and grandfather had been distinguished frontier commanders. But the enterprising Juan Bautista III would shed even more luster on the family name. As soldier, explorer and provincial governor, he was to prove one of the most intelligent and able men ever to serve Spain in the New World.

"The fervent desire which at all times moves me to serve his Majesty and advance his conquests," Anza wrote, "impels me to beg of your Excellency permission to make the necessary efforts to see if we can open communication between the port of Monterey and the province of Sonora. This has always been considered as impossible or very difficult, but without the best foundation, for in this region no examination has ever been made sufficiently exact to justify such an opinion. Indeed, there are today plenty of indications that it might be effected at slight cost, although with some effort on our part."

Anza had good reason for optimism. At the mission of San Xavier del Bac, not far from Tubac, was a certain Fray Francisco Garcés, a venturesome explorer who had spent much time rambling up and down the Gila and Colorado rivers. On the most recent of his trips he had crossed the Colorado and journeyed north, where he had seen a range of blue mountains with what seemed to be at least one or perhaps two passes. Indians told him that beyond and to the west were white men. These, he theorized, must be members of the Portolá-Serra expedition — the men who were so desperately in need of supplies.

Anza immediately recognized the significance of Garcés' discovery. Until then it had always been assumed that the land beyond the Colorado was an endless desert. But mountains meant water, and travel through such country might not be impossible after all. To Viceroy Bucareli, Anza now proposed to lead an exploratory expedition to and — with luck — through the mountains. Thanks to Bucareli's endorsement, the proposal easily won royal approval. Early in January 1774, Anza and Fray Garcés set off with a band of 20 volunteers, and 65 head of cattle as a food supply.

Garcés and Anza knew that the Yuma Indian settlements at the junction of the Gila and Colorado would be a key point on the route to Monterey, and the party approached them cautiously. They need not have feared. The principal chief, known in his own tongue as Olleyquotequiebe, and hastily renamed Salvador Palma by the Spaniards, proved friendly beyond Anza's hopes and unhesitatingly acknowledged the primacy of the Christian God and the Spanish King. Anza bestowed upon him a medal bearing the likeness of Charles III, which filled the Yuma chief with awe and pride. Later Anza distributed baubles and tobacco to Palma's people. The Spaniards could not fail to notice that the Yumas' fields, enriched by river silt from the annual flooding of the Colorado, grew excellent corn, squash, beans, pumpkins and melons — "all in such abundance that we marveled," Anza reported.

Anza's party had to ford both the Gila and the Colorado. Though both streams were low at this season, the crossing was still a major undertaking that required the Indians' help. The livestock were driven across, while the Yumas swam over with supplies on their heads when the footing was too dangerous for mules. The Spaniards got across on horseback—except for Fray Garcés, who did not trust his horse, could not swim, and had to be carried by Yumas.

The next stage of the journey consisted of a nightmarish month of wandering through desert, dune and volcanic rock. Finally, to their immense relief, the travelers sighted Fray Garcés' "blue mountains" and headed for the gap he indicated. At about the same time, they found the first of several springs of sweet water. The gap was indeed a pass that led them through the mountain wall and on March 22, nearly three months after setting out, the weary band trudged into the San Gabriel mission. They were not expected, and food was short, but the discomforts of a lean larder were trifling compared to the exhilaration of having blazed a trail from Mexico to the California colonies.

In Monterey, where Anza hurried next, he was greeted by a surprised and delighted Pedro Fages, whose ingenuity and courage had kept the settlements going. For months the men at the presidios and missions had lived mainly on dried bear meat, the result of a hunt that Fages had organized and led.

Anza did not tarry long in California. Accompanied by six of Fages' soldiers to help mark the trail, he hurried back to Mexico City to report to Viceroy Bucareli. Plans were immediately made for a much larger expedition, one that would include settlers—women as well as men—and enough livestock and supplies to make the California colonies self-sustaining. This time the ultimate goal was the northern Bay of San Francisco, where a new, major outpost was planned.

Anza recruited emigrants from impoverished settlements in western Mexico, promising a richer life in California. The government proposed to outfit them completely, from undergarments to guns and leather jackets for the men, from chemises to hair ribbons for the women. There were to be bolts of cloth; tents for shelter on the trail; kettles, pots and pans for cabin kitchens. The settlers would be given enough cattle to build the herds in California and also allow one animal to be killed each day for food on the march; also three barrels of brandy and one of wine, 30 loads of flour, 60 bushels of beans, and modest amounts of ham, sau-

sages, biscuits, cheese, spices, oil and vinegar. And, of course, a flag with the royal Spanish arms.

When the expedition assembled at Tubac in October 1775, it counted 240 persons (the majority of them women and children), 695 horses and mules, and 355 head of cattle. Thus began the most impressive migration yet undertaken on the continent by the Spaniards. With it went three friars: the veteran Garcés, Tomás Eixarch and Pedro Font, the latter serving as diarist of the journey and official astronomer.

The size of the party slowed progress, but it reached the Yuma settlements with no great difficulty. Chief Palma welcomed them and seemed delighted with Anza's gift—a costume that included a blue cape trimmed in gold braid and, in Father Font's words, "a black velvet cap adorned with imitation jewels and a crest like a palm." Again the Yuma chief helped them cross the river. This time they headed toward dunes west of the Colorado, where scouts had learned that water could be found by digging. Anza split his party into three groups, to proceed at specified intervals so that the waterholes would have time to refill. He led the first group to a site known today as Harper's Well, where he found a spring and decided to make camp.

The weather was bitterly cold, but there was brushwood for fires as Anza's group waited. Slowly the other parties straggled in. Some of the livestock had died along the way, but the colonists were in surprisingly good health. When everyone was on hand, they held an ecstatic reunion. Father Font wrote disapprovingly: "At night with joy at the arrival of all the people they held a fandango. It was somewhat discordant, and a very bold widow sang some verses which were not at all nice, applauded and cheered by all the crowd." Apparently this was California's first fandango—a characteristically Spanish display of high spirits in the form of a drinking-dancing-singing bout.

Soon the sobersided Father Font had more cause for complaint. The weather continued cold, water and forage were scarce, and many horses and cattle died as the party pressed ahead. But on Christmas Eve, Anza distributed liquor rations to the footsore marchers, and the quiet of the night was shattered by the sounds of celebration. Father Font commented in his journal: "The people were very noisy, singing and dancing from the effects of the liquor, not caring that we were in so

A disastrous expedition against "heretical Huguenots"

Next to hostile Indians, the Spanish regarded the French as their worst enemies in the New World during the early 18th Century. And any suspicion of a joint campaign by the two was sure to send waves of fear and anger through Spanish officialdom. In late 1719, word reached Mexico City of what appeared to be a deadly menace: French-armed-and-led warriors had reportedly attacked peaceful Indian allies northeast of Santa Fe. Spain and France were fighting a continental war at the time; now it appeared that the French were about to invade the Spanish overseas empire.

Orders went out for Don Antonio Valverde, governor of New Mexico, to make a reconnaissance from the Santa Fe provincial capital. Declining to lead the party himself, Valverde appointed as commander Pedro de Villasur, his militarily inexperienced lieutenant governor. For the mission, Villasur assembled a detachment of 42 soldiers — nearly one half of the Santa Fe garrison — together with 60 pueblo Indians, three civilians, one chaplain and a French turncoat to act as interpreter.

The expedition left Santa Fe in June, and by August had reconnoitered as far as present-day eastern Nebraska. On August 9, Villasur's scouts reported a sizable body of Pawnees about 25 miles away. Con-

vinced that he had found the French-Indian force, Villasur marched on until he spied the Pawnee camp on an island in the Platte River.

At that point, he ordered a halt and spent several days attempting to establish contact with the supposed French leaders of the Pawnees. He demanded to know their intentions, and even sent ink, quill and paper to the island to facilitate their reply. When no response came — and the Pawnees' actions grew increasingly threatening — Villasur was persuaded by his soldiers to withdraw nearly 30 miles to a position across another river. During the night sentinels reported the sounds of men fording the riv-

The catastrophe that befell the Villasur expedition is vividly — if inaccurately — reconstructed in this 19-foot-long contemporary painting on

72

er, but no intruders were discovered.

The Pawnees attacked at dawn, just as the Spaniards were breaking camp. The Indians stampeded the horses, surrounded the Spaniards and their pueblo allies, and poured volleys of murderous musket fire into their panic-stricken ranks. Villasur was among the first to fall; before it was over, 34 of his soldiers and civilians were killed. Only 14 Spaniards escaped the carnage.

Did Frenchmen participate in the massacre? The Pawnees undoubtedly got their firearms from French traders. But there was never any evidence that Frenchmen had actually accompanied the attackers, or that the Spaniards had encountered anything more than a roaming party of Indians spoiling for a fight. However, Don Antonio Valverde, who bore heavy responsibility for the debacle, fervently insisted that Frenchmen were present.

The vast hide painting below depicts the battle much as Valverde reported it to the Viceroy in Mexico City. Though the work's origins are obscure, the Governor himself may well have commissioned it as a deliberate piece of propaganda to buttress his contention that the French were responsible. In any case, it shows more than three dozen French soldiers in tricornered hats or conical helmets fighting alongside the Pawnees. The major action takes place at center, by the blue tipi. There, a ring of Frenchmen and naked, war-painted Indians has surrounded the gallant little band of Spaniards. Villasur, in a rust-colored tunic, lies dead, just to the left of the main body of Spaniards. To the right, the expedition's chaplain —gripping a crucifix in one hand and holding his blue cassock over his head with the other, perhaps to disguise himself—rushes to succor the wounded. He, too, died in the battle— though probably not at the hands of those Governor Valverde blamed in his letter to the Viceroy: "The heretical Huguenots did not even spare the innocence of the priest."

hides. The artist was probably a mission Indian, working with mineral and plant dyes that have stood up remarkably well over the centuries.

bad a mountain in the rain, and so delayed with the saddle animals and the tired and dead cattle." It was not only Christmas they celebrated: they had completed the hardest part of their journey. And that night in camp, one of the soldiers' wives gave birth to a son, the third child to be born since they left Tubac.

The year 1776 was four days old when Anza brought his tattered column to the San Gabriel mission. In March he delivered the group to Monterey, then hastened on with Father Font to select locations for presidio, mission and dwelling places on the San Francisco Bay site. In September of 1776 — about two months after a new American nation far to the east announced its birth with the Declaration of Independence — the Presidio of San Francisco was formally dedicated.

By then Anza was back in Mexico. On his return journey, he had found the Colorado flooded and made the crossing with difficulty. He could not have made it at all without the Yumas who guided his rafts across the turbulent rivers. "If the peoples who dwell along this great river are attached to us," Anza noted, "we shall effect its passage without excessive labor. And if they are not, it will be almost impossible to do so." He decided that bonds of friendship could best be forged by establishing Spanish settlements among the Yumas.

Chief Palma found the idea attractive and readily consented to accompany Anza to Mexico City. There the Yuma chieftain was accorded a royal welcome by Viceroy Bucareli, then baptized with great solemnity in the capital's imposing cathedral. Palma returned to his own land full of pride and loyalty to the King of

THE MARTYRED PADRES OF SAN SABÁ

Among the worst disasters to befall Spanish colonization in Texas was the 1758 massacre at San Sabá, in which two missionaries and half a dozen settlers and mission Indians were killed. In this contemporary depiction by an unknown artist, the martyred priests — Fray Terreros (left) and Fray Santiestéban (right) — have been resurrected in attitudes of Christian forgiveness. The massacre is shown sequentially. First, Comanche and Wichita raiders enter at lower right, led by a chief in a red French uniform and carrying a white "parley" flag. The chief next appears before the stockade at left, then is seen on the far side, where he dupes the friars into opening the gates. The raiders swarm in and slay Fray Santiestéban by the church; Fray Terreros dies on the hillside at upper left. The scrolls at bottom extol the friars' virtues, while the central block describes the awful event.

OLEGIOS DE PROPAGANDA FIDE, B.LA S.ᵃ CRUZ B.QUERETARO, YF . . . B.S.
e promovio la nueva Reduc. y Conquista de los Indios Apaches, el d. de 57. se p. . . planta, con el resguardo de el
llas de su Rio: fue el promotor el R.P.F.ᵉ Alonso Giraldo de Tierreros, Aiudado de la nunca aplaudida determinaci,ᵒ
ᵈ. Pedro Tierreros, de la Órden d Calatrava, quien à costa de su hacienda, funda todas las Missiones ã se puedan poné
en, aun en medio d la Invasion, y perdida considerable presiste en el Zelo de los d̄s. Indios; D.ᵖ la Mi-
sericordia le aiuda à tan S.ᵃ Empressa.

...ᵒ à su Abecedario.	Sale el P.P.ᵉ cõ vn Soldado acõpañado p.ᵃ el Presidio	Vn Soldado veleroso ã cõ la Espada en la mano se de-
. . .uanicion d cien Solad.ˢ	cõ la chusma d̄ Barbaros Indios las ã prevenidos cõ	fendio d̄ el chos̄ disi . . . ando much.ˢ Ind.ˢ fue atravesa-
a la Mission.	sus armas ê mano, quando à poc.ˢ pasos ã anda	do p.ᵉ el Pecho cõ una Lanza desnudolo p̄ muerto y desñ.
. . .el Presidio.	disparara . . .el P.P.ᵉ da halua . . . ê el pecho, y d el Soldado	y recobrado como lal à la Miss.ⁿ donde fue echado en la Igl.ᵃ
. . . acad. Ig.ᵃ y la cales.	le dieron otro halaso . . .y cayeron d los Cavall.ˢ d̄ el Sus̄	solo d̄ el milagrosamente y se Cõcluió para morir.
. . .barbaros p la Mission	dando sus Almas al Criador, y no satisfe-	Detrás de los españoles desde los lexetos mẽtando su . . .
. . .cito ã pasaron à Mil.	su Ravia le metieron vna lanza y cõ su mismo Ba-	Incendio de la Mission.
	culo le atraviesan el Pecho y le quitaron el Cerquillo	Muerte d̄ el P. Santestevan lo apeleteavã y corta . . .
. . . de Amor y parla cõ ell.	de la Cab.ᵃ y los desnudaron; y desnudarõ à el Soldado	la Cabeza y le dieron muchos Golpes.
. . .P.P. Mig. Molina, y	Choy ẽtre l Espai, el codan en el Camino d̄ el Presid.	Vistã ã yle pares d̄ ã vuerõ ro las S.ᵃ Y así, y destrosos de
. . .duleta halaria pide Paz	donde quedaron muertos tres y los demás huieron	la d̄ el Priu. J.ˢ S.ᵃ d̄ el R.ᵐˢ Pat.ᵉˢ y P. cõ ch.ᵃ d la Mi.
. . . cõ ellos d̄ el Presidio.	p.ᵃ el Presidio y mal eridos.	Funeral p̄ escapar, indignarõ. los Sol.ˢ y quedarõ y la Mis.
		y no hal . . . p̄ ã mueño d la chusma pasaron aun à v̄ vista . . .
		La muerte d̄ el mayordomo loaron los Ojos Vivo y le desnuvarõ . . .
		dispando y lo infestaõ el . . .rõ ã . . .

Spain. No difficulty seemed to stand in the way of implanting missions on Yuma soil and consolidating the essential link to California. Anza himself hoped to be assigned to the Yuma presidio when it was established.

But Anza's hopes were not realized. Late in 1776, after a change in Spanish colonial administration, he was assigned to put down an Indian rebellion in Sonora; next he was appointed governor of New Mexico, again to deal with menacing Indians. The new authorities, busy with other matters, could spare little time for the Yumas or the needs of the California settlers. Only in 1780, after repeated solicitations by Chief Palma, was it decided to go ahead with two outposts on the Colorado near its junction with the Gila. Trapped by an administrative passion for economy —penny-wise and pound-foolish, as it turned out—each little settlement had to subsist on an austerity budget and with a minimal staff.

During the long delay, the Yumas had grown impatient, and they gave a cool welcome to the small contingents that finally turned up. They had formed the opinion that Christianity was a kind of economic transaction in which one exchanged conversion for gifts. When the new settlers arrived nearly empty-handed, the Indians were annoyed. Chief Palma's influence waned noticeably. The Indians' disillusion deepened when the colonists built their two settlements on land that the Yumas used for farming; moreover, the newcomers' livestock trampled Indian crops. When the Spaniards tried to buy foodstuffs from the Yumas and the Indians demanded exorbitant prices, it was the settlers' turn to get angry.

Then, in June of 1781, a contingent of Spaniards arrived—colonists bound for Alta California to found Los Angeles, and led by Fernando Rivera y Moncada, a veteran of the Portolá-Serra expedition. They, too, were short of gifts, confirming Indian suspicions that the niggardliness was to be permanent; worse, their cattle herd chewed its way through groves of mesquite and screwbeans that were essential food for the natives. Even Chief Palma was disgruntled.

Finally, on July 17, Yuma indignation exploded into violence. The commandant of the two outposts was leaving the church at the upper settlement after early mass when the Yuma warriors attacked, clubbing to death him and his companions, among them the Indians' old friend, Fray Garcés. Simultaneously, at the downstream settlement, 18 men, including two friars, were killed and the little church and houses set ablaze.

Across the river, Rivera had sent most of the Los Angeles party ahead while he and a few of his men remained to refresh their livestock. Apparently they were unaware of the settlements' plight, and on the 18th a band of Yumas surprised Rivera and his men and annihilated them. Altogether, at least 55 Spaniards died in the massacre. Another five soldiers, four male settlers and some 67 women and children were taken captive and forced into labor at the Yuma settlements.

It was a crushing blow, as devastating as had been the Pueblo revolt in New Mexico a century before or the rout on the Red River two decades earlier. That autumn, Pedro Fages led a foray into Yuma territory and managed to ransom some of the captives; and in the following year, a much larger force returned and killed some 200 of the rebellious Indians. But for all practical purposes the overland route to California so heroically pioneered by Anza and Garcés was lost. Still obsessed with economy, the authorities declined to restore the ruined settlements among the Yumas. Of what use were they? If it were absolutely necessary to get to California overland, they argued, 30 soldiers could always be dispatched to force a passage through the hostile tribe and across the Colorado.

No such aggressive reopening of the overland route ever occurred. California was thenceforth virtually isolated from both Mexico and Spain, her colonists dependent on themselves. Superficially, the colony seemed well able to survive on its own terms. Protected on the east by its Sierra barrier, blessed with a mild climate, rich soil and Indians to do the hard work, California in the coming decades indeed developed a seductively charming pastoral existence. But the long-term consequences of isolation were disastrous, first for Spain and later for the Republic of Mexico. Without a constant infusion of new colonists from Mexico, California could not people its huge area adequately. And without sources of supply, it lacked manufactured goods. Into these twin vacuums of population and commerce, foreign traders and foreign emigrants — especially the Americans — would eventually rush in overwhelming numbers. New Mexico seemed a far more urgent concern than California in the late 18th Century: the

Spanish saw that province as an essential buffer protecting the rich Mexican heartland from the marauding tribes of the American plains.

As governor of New Mexico, the capable Anza would manage by force of arms, diplomatic skill and simple kindness to win a surcease from Indian raiders that lasted a generation. Yet after the Louisiana Purchase of 1803, the expansionist new American nation was positioned next door, and venturesome traders soon came swarming in over the Santa Fe Trail.

It was only a matter of time until further American pressure would seal New Mexico's destiny. Before New Mexico's hour of reckoning arrived, the Anglo-Americans cast covetous eyes on Texas. Geographically it was the most immediate target; and by endowment, a savory lure for land-hungry frontiersmen from the East. Its vast area was still populated with only a few Spanish desperately struggling against the fierce Comanches; they would become all the more vulnerable when revolution against Spanish rule in Mexico left the disordered capital unable to cope with enemies in the northernmost provinces. Texas had been the first part of the American West that Spain had seen and claimed for its own. It would also be the first lost.

Vivid mementos of mission life in Baja

"Nearly everywhere we found good land for sowing, many streams, charming valleys and plains, lagoons of water beautifully fresh, very big trees, prickly figs, many deer and hares."

Thus did Father Eusebio Kino describe Baja California in 1683. The Jesuit priest, who later founded missions in Mexico and present-day Arizona, had landed with about 100 men near the tip of the peninsula jutting south from the mainland. Intent upon setting up a permanent colony and saving a fresh complement of Indian souls, he had allowed zeal to color his vision.

Actually, Baja was a forbidding land peopled with primitive, often hostile tribes. The mission that Kino went on to establish lasted less than two years before drought and disease forced its abandonment. But little more than a decade later, other Jesuits landed on the peninsula and, in time, built a chain of 17 outposts of God and Spain.

In 1768, a missionary who had labored five years in Baja, Father Ignacio Tirsch, returned to Spain with a portfolio of drawings. As those reproduced here show, Father Tirsch was a gifted amateur artist with a simple style, and he created an intimate record of both mission life and the flora and fauna in a harsh corner of the Spanish Empire.

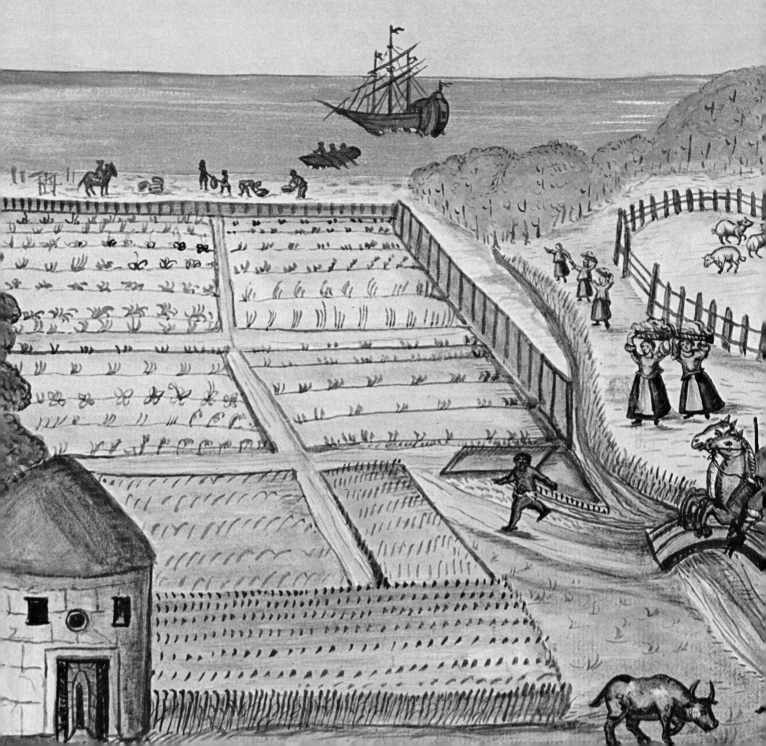

A bright red sun sets over the bustling Mission San José del Cabo, on the southern tip of Baja California, as a galleon from the Philippines puts in for provisions. The settlement was blessed by one of the arid land's rare springs, which the friars tapped to irrigate their fields of grain and vegetables.

79

A bird that Father Ignacio Tirsch called the *catalinta* — possibly a sparrow hawk — clings to a twig of the *granadilla de China,* or passion fruit of China, at left. The pair of birds perched on top of the apricot-like *mamey* fruit at right are unidentified but appear to be members of the oriole family.

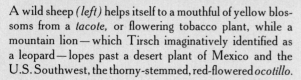

A wild sheep *(left)* helps itself to a mouthful of yellow blossoms from a *tacote,* or flowering tobacco plant, while a mountain lion — which Tirsch imaginatively identified as a leopard — lopes past a desert plant of Mexico and the U.S. Southwest, the thorny-stemmed, red-flowered *ocotillo.*

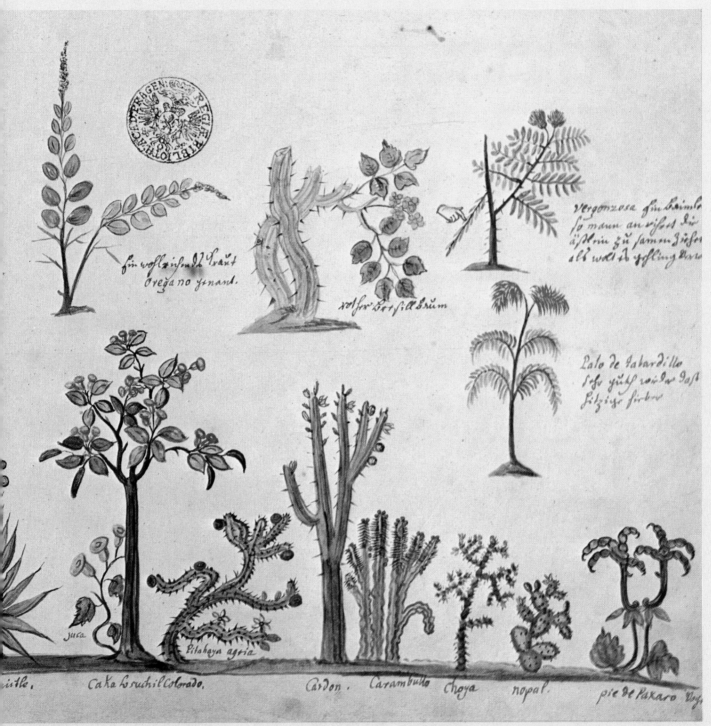

fin wolfrifindtes kraut
oregano gonant.

Köstlich bersill ßraum

vergonzosa fin baimle
so mann an rifset die
äftlein zu samm zühet
als wolt sie gsling sterbe

Palo de labardillo
sehr guth roidar das
fitzigs fiebar

Juca

Pitahaya agria

ustle.   CaKa lo ruchil Colorado.   Cardon.   Carambullo   Choya   nopal.   pie de Paxaro vg.

Drawings of plants include *(top, left to right)* a wild pepper tree, oregano, a red Brazil tree, and a mimosa — "a little tree," noted Tirsch, "which when touched, shrinks as if it is wilting." Below that is a type of calliandra — "good against a high fever." Desert shrubs and trees are at bottom.

81

Father Tirsch's caption for this lighthearted drawing of life on the peninsula reads, "This is my little farm which I received as a bequest from the Mission of Santiago." Like all church property, it passed to his successor when he left.

A settler family plays outside a cabin in southeast Texas. These frame dwellings were roofed with reeds from a nearby river.

3 | Pioneers in the farthest borderlands

The Spaniards who carved out a life in Texas were forever a frontier people. Concentrated in the eastern half of the sprawling province, they were more than a thousand miles from Mexico City, and they understood that they had to sustain themselves without much help from the outside, even after Mexico won independence in 1821. Many occupied rude cabins like the one below and were required by law to be armed whenever they ventured abroad. No place settled by children of Spain, however, could be entirely without amenity. Dances, horseraces and cockfights were staged in every community. By the time the French artist Theodore Gentilz arrived in the 1840s to create the views of Texas shown here and on the next pages, Anglo-Saxon culture was emerging. Yet the imprint of the Spaniards was so strong that much of what he saw still looked like the wilderness province of old.

Carrying lighted candles and making music with a violin and a guitar, nine gallant *caballeros* ride up to a San Antonio doorway to invite the belle of the house to a dance. Their *calzoneras* — fitted trousers whose bottoms flared out when unbuttoned — lent themselves to both riding and dancing.

Gentilz

On a hill-rimmed stretch of plain near the western border of Texas, a group of rancheros halts to inspect a faint track. Settlers often ventured a hundred miles or more in search of game or mustangs, or in pursuit of marauding Indians.

A solitary fiddler provides the music for a fandango in a San Antonio mansion that had been a governor's palace. As the couples perform a slow, decorous dance with candles, one celebrating stag swigs something more powerful than the usual coffee, and another fires his pistol into the ceiling.

Embattled Texas–an arena of hate and violence

In October of 1783, General Felipe de Neve, the Spanish commandant responsible for Mexico's northern frontier, received a prophetic warning from one Jean Gasiot, a French frontiersman whom he employed as an Indian agent. Gasiot anticipated trouble from a surprising source: the infant republic of the United States, which had just emerged in exhausted disarray from its war for independence from England.

"It is necessary to keep in mind," Gasiot wrote, "that a new independent power exists now on this continent. It has been founded by an active, industrious, aggressive people. Their development will constantly menace the dominion of Spain in America and it would be an unpardonable error not to take all necessary steps to check their territorial advance."

This blunt-spoken prophecy sketched out the shape of things to come for the next six decades and more. The Spaniards would do all they could to thwart their new nemesis, but the birth of the United States sounded the death knell of Spain's empire in the West. The Spaniards themselves would never reach a showdown with the Americans; the final acts would be played out after a violent revolution had ousted them from Mexico. Their Mexican successors in turn would be driven from the frontier provinces in a series of further revolutions and bloody wars.

As the easternmost province of the Spanish West, Texas was, in the words of one Spanish general, "the key to all New Spain." But as the Spaniards had learned to their terrible sorrow, it was a key they could not own. Ever since their rout at the hands of Co-

manche warriors in the Battle of Red River in 1759, the Spaniards had been forced to acknowledge that the Indians were the real masters of the Texas interior.

With war-painted savages roaming at will through Texas, Mexico City found it impossible to build up the province's population. Only three classes of people went willingly to Texas: missionary priests, eager to teach the faith and ready to die a martyr's death; reckless young army officers, out to make a quick reputation; and a few independent-minded ranchers, who realized that Texas' prairie lands were ideal for stock raising and who felt that the chance to escape from Mexico's bureaucratic controls more than offset the Indian peril. At no time in the 18th Century was Texas inhabited by more than a few thousand Spanish settlers, most of them concentrated around the towns of San Antonio and La Bahía, later known as Goliad. The entire eastern half of the province lay unoccupied, and it was into this vacuum that the Americans were irresistibly drawn.

Spain's first direct political contact with the Americans came in 1777, shortly after the outbreak of revolt against England. Rebel requests for aid put the Spaniards squarely on the spot. As a colonial power, Spain could ill afford to endorse the principle of revolution, yet it thoroughly approved of this particular revolution, which was bound to weaken England, its mortal enemy.

After long and sober consideration, the Spanish Crown followed the lead of its pro-American ally, France, and declared war on England. But the Spaniards had no real enthusiasm for the Anglo-Saxon family quarrel, and did little to help the Americans win their revolution in 1783.

Soon after, the Spaniards began to realize that the Americans were far more inimical to their interests in

Lithographed views of San Antonio—including its battered presidio, the Alamo (*right side, top*)—decorate stationery popular in Texas after Mexican rule was overthrown. This sheet was used to inscribe a song honoring a departing French dignitary.

The mission church, like Nuestra Señora de Guadalupe in El Paso del Norte, was the cornerstone of Spanish settlement in the northern provinces of New Spain. However, of some 30 missions established in Texas, more than half were quickly abandoned because of the regional tribes' deep — and frequently violent — distaste for sedentary living.

the New World than even the British. Suddenly hordes of Americans began pouring into Spanish Louisiana with casual disregard for laws prohibiting foreign immigration. By the year 1797, American squatters made up nearly half of Louisiana's population of roughly 50,000 and Spain abandoned hope of holding the territory. By a secret treaty signed in 1800, Spain ceded Louisiana back to France, which was then resurgent under Napoleon, with the proviso that the territory would never be allowed to fall into the hands of an English-speaking government. But Napoleon, hard pressed for cash to finance his European conquests, broke his word three years later and sold Louisiana to the United States for $15 million.

Texas immediately became the Americans' next target, and it seemed to lure the dregs of their society: deserters from the U.S. Army, runaway slaves, debtors with fugitive warrants out for their arrest back home. By 1805, conditions were so chaotic along the Texas border that Spanish and American authorities sought to bring order by establishing a so-called "Neutral Ground" from which citizens of both nations were barred. This broad buffer zone lay between the Sabine River in the west and the Arroyo Hondo, a tributary of the Red River in the east, but since the Spanish could not police it and the Americans did not choose to, it continued to be a haven for swarms of outlaws and a spawning ground for conflict.

The worst of the troubles dated from September 1810, when events in Mexico sent Spanish and Mexican refugees streaming across Texas into the Neutral Ground to join the Americans already there. This new crisis had been caused in Mexico by a protest movement that grew willy-nilly into a full-scale social revolution. The leader was a country priest named Miguel Hidalgo y Costilla, and at first he had hoped for nothing more than just reforms that would relieve the plight of Mexico's great mass of downtrodden peasants. His impassioned oratory produced such an outpouring of support that Hidalgo soon began calling for war against the haughty, callous Spanish-born aristocracy.

Before he knew it, the padre was at the head of a militant mob of 50,000 rebels marching on Mexico City. The peasants knew so little about fighting that they tried to muzzle the government artillery by holding sombreros over the cannon mouths. But they pushed back the royal army through sheer weight of numbers, and by October, now 80,000 strong, they were at the gates of the capital.

Suddenly, on the verge of victory, Hidalgo realized that his unmanageable rabble would only bring Mexico anarchy rather than reform. Instead of seizing Mexico City, he ordered his people to retreat. And as the confused rebels turned northward, the royal army started after them. The rebels suffered a crushing defeat in Guadalajara. Hidalgo himself fled into the frontier province of Coahuila, where he was captured, tried and executed; his head was put on public display as an object lesson for all malcontents.

To all appearances, the Hidalgo revolution had been crushed. Yet the violence it had triggered was not yet spent. In August 1812, a motley horde of 2,000 diehard Hidalgo rebels and American adventurers joined forces in the Neutral Ground and swept down on Texas. They quickly captured La Bahía and San Antonio, but their victories turned to ashes. Acting to liquidate the Texas aberration, Mexico City dispatched a royal army of 2,000 men under General Joaquín de Arredondo. It reached the Medina River just west of San Antonio on August 18, 1813. A rebel force of 850 men swarmed out of town—and blundered straight into a trap laid by Arredondo. Surrounded, the rebels broke ranks and the royal troops methodically slaughtered them. Only 93 survived.

In his report to the Viceroy of Mexico, General Arredondo commended 81 of his officers for gallantry in the Medina battle. Among the heroes was a 19-year-old lieutenant who would become a major figure in the future of Texas and who was to dominate politics in Mexico for nearly a half century. He was Lieutenant Santa Anna—his full name being Antonio López de Santa Anna Pérez de Lebrón. As time would tell, Santa Anna was a liar, a thief, a compulsive gambler, a notorious womanizer, and a corrupt and ruthless self-seeker. For his consummate villainy and exquisite cruelty, he was universally feared by his countrymen, who gave him the nickname Don Demonio—Sir Devil.

Nevertheless, Santa Anna was endowed with all the skills essential for leadership in his anarchic world. He had an uncanny ability to anticipate shifts in the political winds. He knew enough about military tactics to win textbook battles and had a genius for making his de-

feats seem like personal triumphs. He was a gifted demagogue who could rally popular support no matter how often or how flagrantly he misused the people.

Santa Anna also had a keen sense of historical perspective. He realized early, as Hidalgo finally did, that the Mexican masses lacked the political experience to govern themselves; he once put it unpleasantly, "A hundred years to come, my people will not be fit for liberty. A despotism is the proper government for them." And he fully intended to be Mexico's despot.

Santa Anna had embarked on the road to power at 16, when he managed to escape from his family's bourgeois station in life. The boy's father, a modest mortgage broker, had apprenticed him to a merchant in their home town in Veracruz province. But Santa Anna pleaded and won his parents' permission to join the army, which offered unimportant young men their best chance for advancement in Mexico's stratified society.

The Hidalgo revolution erupted while Santa Anna was taking his cadet training. He missed the campaign against the rebellious padre but graduated in time for the Texas expedition. His actions there were revealing. Although he served under General Arredondo with vigor and courage, he displayed a dangerous weakness for snap judgments; for example, the smashing victory over the rebels convinced him that regular army troops could never be defeated by irregulars. He also displayed a casual indifference to morality. To pay off some gambling debts, he forged Arredondo's name to a draft on the company funds. He was caught, and his uniforms and cavalry saber were sold to replace the pur-

GOVERNOR CABELLO'S RIGOROUS CENSUS

A census of Texas drawn up by Governor Domingo Cabello for the year 1783 lists a total population of 2,819, breaking the total down, from left to right, into numbers of men, women, boys, girls, and male and female slaves, and specifying in the horizontal panels where they live *(top)*, their race *(center)* and their marital status. San Antonio was the most populous area, followed by the Presidio of Bahía and finally by the small town of Nacogdoches. Overall, the adult population declined by 21 from the previous year, while births and deaths among the children apparently canceled each other out exactly. Spaniards outnumbered other races, though there were surprising numbers of mission Indians and people of mixed blood. Eight priests and three secular ecclesiasts tended to this flock of 655 married couples, 183 widowed and 208 single parishioners.

Provincia de los Texas.

Estado que Manifiesta el Numero de Vasallos, y Habitantes q.e tiene el Rey en Esta Probincia, con distincion de Clases, Estados, y Castas de todas las Personas de Ambos Sexos Ynclusos los Parbulos.

Nombres de las Poblaciones.	Ombres.	Mugeres.	Niños.	Niñas.	Esclabos.	Esclabas.
Pres.do de San Antonio de Bexar, y Villa de S.n Fern.do	331.	311.	321.	264.	8.	13.
Mision de Sñr San Jose	41.	31.	26.	25.		
Ydem de San Juan Capistrano	53.	26.	13.	7.		
Ydem de San Francisco de la Espada	32.	28.	30.	6.		
Ydem de Nuestra Sra de la Concepcion	32.	27.	18.	8.		
Ydem de San Antonio Balero	43.	35.	36.	27.		
Présidio de la Bahia del Spîu Sto	193.	147.	68.	45.	1.	
Mision del Spîu Sto	75.	66.	33.	40.		
Ydem de Nuestra Srâ del Rosario						
Pueblo de Nrâ Srâ del Pilar delos Nacodoches	129.	104.	52.	50.	8.	6.
Totales del Presente Año	935.	777.	597.	474.	17.	19.
Totales del Año Anterior	947.	786.	597.	474.	17.	19.
Diminucion	12.	9.				
Resumen Grâl de Españoles	488.	373.	376.	340.		
Ydem de Yndios	290.	241.	70.	76.		
Ydem de Mestizos	43.	38.	32.	12.		
Ydem de Color Quebrado	114.	125.	119.	46.		
Ydem de Esclabos					17.	19.
Totales	935.	777.	597.	474.	17.	19.
Resumen Grâl de Eclesiasticos Seculares	3.					
Ydem de Regulares	8.					
Ydem de Casados	655.	655.				
Ydem de Viudos	61.	122.				
Ydem de Solteros	208.					
Totales	935.	777.	597.	474.	17.	19.

Real Pres.o de San Antonio de Bexar, y Dir.e 31. de 1783.

Dom.o Cabello

loined pesos. But the disgrace was only temporary, and it taught him nothing.

In 1814, Santa Anna was reassigned to Veracruz. There, for several years, he fought rebels operating as robber bands. Thanks in no small part to his boastful reports, he won a reputation for leading "terrible excursions" against the heirs of Hidalgo's revolution. But as the weakly organized peasants succumbed to royal troops, the revolution passed into the hands of the *criollo* elite, who possessed the resources to succeed.

The native-born Mexican upper classes—military leaders, high clergymen and landed aristocrats—had deep-seated reasons for rebelling against Spanish rule. For three centuries, they had been disqualified from holding the top posts in their own government; they remained frustrated underlings to arrogant and very often incompetent royal officials sent over from Spain. Recently, onerous taxes further eroded their loyalty: by 1820 they were seething with rage. All they needed was a leader who could unite their jealous factions.

That leader came forward in February 1821. He was Colonel Agustín de Iturbide, a flamboyant opportunist who had secretly been building up a corps of troops loyal to himself instead of to Spain. At just the right moment, Iturbide published a highly appealing three-point revolutionary credo. The first point was independence from Spain, which everyone wanted. Second, to win over the peasantry, Iturbide promised full equality. And to the clergy, whose wealth he needed to finance his revolution, he guaranteed the Church's traditional rights as the state religion of Mexico. Iturbide's platform attracted followers all over Mexico, forming a patriot force that he grandly dubbed "The Army of the Three Guarantees."

To Santa Anna, these developments were unimpressive at first. Cordially obeying his orders from the royal commandant of Veracruz province, he moved his troops into position to chastise some rebels in the town of Orizaba. At 4 a.m. on March 29, he launched a surprise attack and won a modest victory. But within a few hours, the rebels received enough reinforcements to prompt the young officer, now a captain, to reconsider the situation. The upshot was that Santa Anna switched sides. He later claimed that "I wished to aid in the great work of our political regeneration." But his main interest had been in personal gain:

the rebels made him a colonel for joining their ranks.

Santa Anna immediately began fighting for the rebel cause just as effectively as he had fought for Spain. And in June of 1821, when the royal high command realized that Mexico was lost, it was Colonel Santa Anna who arranged for the last Spanish viceroy, General Juan O'Donojú, to discuss peace terms with Iturbide. During their talks, O'Donojú sized up Santa Anna and said of him acidly, "This young man will cause all Mexico to weep."

The gist of the peace treaty signed on June 30 was that Spain officially recognized Mexico's independence. Celebrations were staged in one province after another as each departing Spanish governor relinquished authority to Mexicans. In Texas, civic and military leaders assembled in San Antonio, and in a formal ceremony they swore allegiance to the new republican government. But nothing else had changed. The province was still beset by Indian raiders and American squatters from Louisiana. The citizens could only hope that their home-grown leaders would do more than the Spaniards to relieve their plight.

Alas for Texas, the *criollo* factions fell to quarreling as soon as their patriotic euphoria flagged. General Iturbide and other influential conservatives demanded a strong central government, whereas various liberal elements favored a loose federation of largely autonomous states. As the federalist-centralist battle raged on the floor of the brand-new Congress, Mexico slipped closer and closer to chaos. At last, in May 1822, Iturbide dissolved his fractious Congress and proclaimed himself Emperor Agustín I.

Letters of congratulation poured in. Santa Anna, now a brigadier general in command of a regiment in Veracruz, kept plying "my always beloved monarch" with unctuous flattery and shameless requests for preferment. And on his first visit to Mexico City, he vigorously courted Iturbide's maiden sister, who happened to be 60 years old. This absurd performance earned the 28-year-old Santa Anna a sharp rebuke from the emperor, who advised him to stick to his soldiering.

Clearly, Iturbide saw Santa Anna as a potential rival. And when Santa Anna realized that he had nothing to gain as Iturbide's minion, he became his overt enemy. On December 1, 1822, at the head of some 400 soldiers personally loyal to him, Santa Anna rode through the streets of Veracruz, proclaiming a Mexican republic and calling for a revolution to overthrow Iturbide's centralist "empire."

This unlikely revolt immediately produced widespread ripples. Two liberal generals—rare birds in the military—hurried down from Mexico City to plot with the newly revealed champion of the federalist cause. By February 1823, the revolution had such strength that the emperor was forced to flee into exile.

Now it was the liberals' turn to discover Mexico's heritage of nearly insurmountable problems: widespread poverty, illiteracy, prejudice and political inexperience. But by a tremendous effort, sustained through 1823 and into 1824, the reconvened Congress hammered out a national constitution. Borrowing heavily from the much-admired constitution of the much-feared United States, it set up machinery for a viable government and guaranteed every citizen equal justice and a better life.

Frequently during these years, Mexico City was reminded of poor, bleeding, long-neglected Texas. The reminders came from a young American visitor named Stephen F. Austin, who was patiently petitioning for Mexican confirmation of a Spanish land grant in Texas. The background of his case was well known in the capital. During the last months of Spanish rule, the royal government had launched a desperate experiment in Texas: responsible Americans would be admitted and awarded large land grants in the hope that they would defend the province from illegal Americans and predatory Indians alike. Austin's father became the first American to benefit from this bold policy; and Austin had inherited the grant on his father's death in 1821.

Young Austin's tact and persistence persuaded the Mexican Congress to act favorably on his requests. As a contractor, or *empresario,* he was awarded a huge grant in east Texas, with the right to settle 300 American families. All the Americans were to become Mexican citizens and Roman Catholics.

The door to Texas was opened officially in April 1823, and in the next 12 years nearly 28,000 Americans poured through it. Most of them came legally, under the auspices of Austin and other *empresarios.* But more and more of the newcomers belonged to that illegal breed of squatters and fugitives who had infested the Neutral Ground. And soon, even the respon-

sible Americans began causing Mexico grave concern.

These ambitious colonists demanded American-style public services such as roads, post offices and schools—which the Mexicans could not afford even in their home states. The Americans complained especially about the justice system, which they found interminably slow. Soon, most Mexicans perceived the Americans as boorish ingrates. And as relations soured, the government adopted repressive measures that made enemies of the most tractable Americans.

While the Texas tinderbox approached the combustion point, Santa Anna was busily adding to his fame, wealth and power. In 1829, Santa Anna benefited from an unexpected piece of good luck. Resurgent imperialists in Spain launched a foolhardy attempt to reconquer Mexico, and that August an invasion force of 3,000 men landed at the port of Tampico. Santa Anna charged up to wage war. The Spanish army, hungry, fever-ridden and ill-equipped, was easily routed in what Santa Anna described as an epic victory. He called himself the "Hero of Tampico," and soon expanded that to "Napoleon of the West."

It remained only for Santa Anna to make himself master of Mexico. In 1833, following a series of Byzantine maneuvers that involved one revolution and several monumental double crosses, Santa Anna was elected to the presidency on the liberal ticket. But within 10 months of his election, he had betrayed his liberal supporters, forced his civilian vice president into exile, dismissed the liberal Congress and replaced it with a body of hand-picked conservatives. His new government then moved to destroy federalism completely, dissolving the few remaining state legislatures and ousting troublesome governors.

The president-general was sojourning at Manga de Clavo, his estate in Veracruz, when his dictatorial policies touched off a chain of rebellions in eight states. In April 1835, some 5,000 federalists revolted in Zacatecas, and Santa Anna himself led 3,500 troops to an easy victory. Then another revolt broke out in Coahuila. And by the fall of 1835, when the Coahuila mess had been mopped up, the momentum toward revolution in Texas was irreversible.

In October of 1835, an ad hoc group of Americans, meeting in Stephen Austin's colonial capital, San Felipe de Austin, declared themselves indepen-

The gracious life on a baronial hacienda

The Spaniards who trekked north to the Texas frontier hoped to re-create the good life they had observed on Mexico's great haciendas. But these claimants to a warrior-infested wilderness could hardly have had a less realistic goal, for Mexican ranches boasted one of the most extravagant life styles imaginable.

Back in the provinces of Guanajuato or Querétaro the huge whitewashed house of a landowner usually dominated a village of huts where hundreds of Indian laborers lived. Such an estate often sprawled over many miles, and boasted great herds of livestock. The owner pursued the noble pleasures of hunting, while managers handled the day-to-day supervision of his livestock and crops.

Yet life on a hacienda could be lonely. Visitors were assured a princely welcome and were often urged to stay for days. When an English traveler dropped in on a hacienda near Cuernavaca one day in the 1820s, he and his companions were seated at a Gargantuan feast. "The dishes," he recalled, "followed each other in such numbers that I am almost afraid to mention them—they were not less than a dozen, besides auxiliaries; and everything was excellent."

After the meal the Englishman sauntered onto the terrace and joined an assortment of aristocrats, lawyers, soldiers and priests—most of whom had also come uninvited and unexpected. In the evening, after yet another handsome repast, the guests set out for a nearby village, where they strolled through the streets, played billiards and attended the tiny provincial theater. As the English visitor loftily observed, "The stage was a crazy platform, measuring about six feet by three; the scene paintings were only two in number," and the play itself a tale of woe, "for the heroine dies, the lover kills himself, and the parents break their hearts."

The local theater might have been amateur, but the visitor could only marvel at the entertainments staged at the hacienda—among them, an impromptu bullfight, a steer-throwing contest and a cockfight. In a gentler vein, his host also organized picnics in the fields, where the guests were serenaded by minstrels playing guitars and marimbas. Such outings, declared the blissful traveler, produced "a powerful impression of cheerfulness and gaiety, inspired by a beautiful sky and clear atmosphere, and the pleasing serenity of every object around me."

A wealthy hacienda owner in southeastern Mexico in the 1830s rides out with his daughter to consult with his estate manager.

Cigarette-smoking belles adorned in brightly colored cotton skirts flirt with a *vaquero* turned out in his best sombrero and serape.

Strolling through a provincial Mexican town, ladies in lace mantillas chat with a gentleman as a peasant couple huddles on a bench.

dent of Mexico on the ground that Santa Anna "and other military chieftains have by force of arms overthrown the federal constitution."

In reply, Santa Anna sent a force of veteran soldiers under his brother-in-law, General Martín Perfecto de Cós, to show the sword to the incipient rebels. However, General Cós soon found himself besieged in San Antonio, and by December 1835 he had found it necessary to surrender. Cós and his troops were sent home on his false pledge never to resume hostilities against Texas. This mortifying indignity to Mexican arms demanded the personal revenge of the Napoleon of the West. Santa Anna sent out orders for an army to be marshaled at San Luis Potosí. The war for—and against—Texas independence was about to be joined.

Full of confident bombast, Santa Anna by early February 1836 was at Monclova, within striking distance of Texas. He commanded a complete army—infantry, cavalry, artillery and a battalion of sappers, the *Zapadores*. Yet its size, 6,000 strong against a Texas force that never exceeded 900 men, was deceptive.

In fact, it had serious problems. It had been bled white by endless revolution and now consisted mainly of raw recruits led by an officer corps that was experienced but jaded and often lax. Santa Anna's second-in-command, General Vicente Filisola, observed later that many men were firing their weapons for the first time when they met the Texans in combat.

These new troops were largely conscripts, often taken by force from their families and their farms, and naturally the desertion rate was high. Some were felons released from prison on a promise to fight. Their equipment and supplies were poor and their food was worse, the men subsisting on hardtack and a handful of beans issued daily. Filisola reported that many soldiers lacked even footwear as they started to march hundreds of miles over hard winter ground. Their muskets were relics of the Spanish period and hurled a ball only 70 yards and inaccurately at that, while they faced Texan rifles that were deadly at 200 yards.

José Enrique de la Peña, a lieutenant colonel of the sappers, the only outfit that could remotely be considered elite, observed that, until now, Mexican fighting had all been internal. But in Texas, "our soldiers would be dealing with men of a different language and a different religion, men whose character and habits were likewise different. All was new in this war."

The Texans whom the unwilling Mexican troops would face were untrained as soldiers, but they were proficient frontiersmen who were used to living out-of-doors and feeding themselves with their rifles. The Mexicans sometimes called them *soldados god dammes* for their language habits and often addressed individual Texans as "Señor God Damn." Describing his capture at a later point, a Mexican officer wrote of the formidable Texans: "You should have seen these men converted into moving armories; some wore two, three and even four braces of pistols, a cloth bag filled with bullets, a powder horn, a saber or bowie knife, besides a rifle, musket or carbine."

On February 8, 1836, the first of Santa Anna's main force of 4,000 left Monclova. An advance column of 1,500 under General Joaquín Ramírez y Sesma was on the Rio Grande. At Matamoros, General José Urrea had 600 men preparing to drive up the coastal plain of Texas toward Goliad.

The mild weather changed as Santa Anna broke camp. The wind swung to the north, the sky darkened, and snow blew in. By morning, it was a foot deep and drifting. After five days of march, the army was still only a few miles from Monclova. Santa Anna, always oblivious to his troops, tired of the slow pace and struck out for the advance guard on the Rio Grande.

His army lurched along in agony, its men hungry and freezing. Rain followed snow and the streams rose. Hardtack, gunpowder and most other supplies were lashed to the pack animals in gunny sacks, and much of it was soaked and ruined. Away from streams, the men ran short of water; as troops in the rear approached water holes, they found them fouled by the men who had been there first. Dysentery swept the ranks.

Sesma's advance guard left the Rio Grande on the 15th of February, and Santa Anna caught up on the 17th. He then ordered a forced march to San Antonio, where he hoped to catch the Texans by surprise. The army groaned and increased its pace.

The Texans, meanwhile, were in equal disorder. The provisional government that had declared independence in October had collapsed, and nothing could be done about replacing it until a new convention met in March. The fighting men were scattered about. Some 400 were at Goliad under James W. Fannin, who had briefly entertained a mad plan to invade Mexico but had abandoned it. About 150 were in San Antonio under William B. Travis, planning to defend the Alamo, a thick-walled old mission which, though in disrepair, still was the most imposing fortress in Texas.

Sam Houston, the only real soldier among the Texans, was in nominal command but had no actual power. He knew that the only way the outnumbered Texans could fight was to fall back, draw in the Mexican columns until they were vulnerable, and then lash out at them if and when the opportunity arose. He ordered Fannin to withdraw from Goliad and the men at the Alamo to pull down its walls and fall back. Fannin ignored him, and so did the men at the Alamo.

Texans were obsessed with the Alamo. Travis shared the widely held belief that only the Alamo stood between the Mexicans and the defenseless eastern settlements. In fact, the Mexicans could have bypassed it and gone straight east to settle matters at once.

But Santa Anna also was obsessed with the Alamo, undoubtedly because taking it would solidify support in Mexico City. His own men thought the trek to San Antonio was foolish. General Filisola later observed that San Antonio was "almost insignificant," and Lieutenant Colonel de la Peña said, "We should have attacked the enemy at the heart instead of weakening ourselves by going to a garrison without any political or military importance." But, he added, "General Santa Anna becomes irritable with discussions."

On February 22, Santa Anna and his troops were on the hills overlooking San Antonio and the Alamo. Soon Santa Anna's red banner flapped from a bell tower in town. It signified that no quarter would be given, no prisoners taken. Some of his officers protested, but Santa Anna quoted the remark of a commander under whom he had served: "If you execute your enemies, it saves you the trouble of having to forgive them." When the Texans sent out a man to parley, Santa Anna dismissed him: unconditional surrender was the only option. As the Texans prepared the Alamo for battle, Santa Anna settled down to bombard the walls with his light artillery, while awaiting his heaviest pieces. To entertain himself, he dressed a sergeant as a priest and had him perform a mock marriage with a young San Antonio woman, so that he might enjoy her favors with her family's approval.

As the siege went on, the Texans sent letters calling for help. At the last moment a small force from Gonzales arrived, and the Texans then faced the Mexicans with 183 men. They could have escaped. De la Peña noted that Mexican security was slack and that any night the Texans easily could have slipped away.

On March 4, Santa Anna tired of waiting for his heavy artillery. He told his officers that he intended to go over the walls. His officers pleaded with him to hold off until the big guns arrived: the steady cannonading had already weakened the Alamo, and a few more hours of saturation fire with the siege weapons on the way would surely crumble the walls for assault troops. At one point, a rumor raced through the Mexican ranks that the Texans in the Alamo had forced Travis to agree to surrender on the 6th if no help came. Santa Anna outwardly scoffed at it, but his officers believed that it was this potential loss of a glorious victory that led him to order the charge at daybreak on the 6th.

Santa Anna planned to send four columns against the Alamo, with a fifth held in reserve. "Santa Anna assigned General Cós to the post of honor, of greatest danger, as the leader of the assault," Colonel Juan Almonte noted in his diary. "To himself he assigned the post of greatest safety, to command the reserve."

At 1 a.m., the men started for their positions, and by 4 a.m. they were in place, lying on the chill ground. At dawn, Santa Anna signaled the go-ahead with a nod. A trumpeter sounded what de la Peña called "that terrible bugle call of death." Then they were on their feet, running in the soft gloom. They began to fire their muskets while still out of range of the Alamo.

The Texans appeared on the walls, seizing rifles

and ramming charges into the mouths of cannons. On the ground, the Mexicans were screaming — *Viva Mexico! Viva Santa Anna!* And then the cannon belched sheets of flame, and shot slashed through their ranks. Men grunted and screamed as it struck. Whole rows of them fell, and those behind jumped over their bodies and ran forward. "A single cannon volley did away with half the company of light cavalry from Toluca," de la Peña said. The Texas rifles opened up, and the troops wavered and stumbled. Their officers saber-whipped them forward into the guns again, and the fire from above increased. The mass of men raged along the walls, tormented by the fire from above and came to a redoubt of earth and timber that had been raised in front of a break in the wall. They started up it.

De la Peña was with the sappers, waiting in reserve. He described what he saw: "The first to climb were thrown down by bayonets or by pistol fire, but others hurried to occupy their places, climbing over their bleeding bodies. The sharp reports of the rifles, the whistling of bullets, the groans of the wounded, the sighs and anguished cries of the dying, the arrogant harangues of the officers, the inordinate shouts of the attackers bewildered all." And, he added, "The shouting of those being attacked was no less loud and from the beginning had pierced our ears with desperate, terrible cries of alarm in a language we did not understand."

As the Mexicans came over the walls, the Texans fell back toward barricades in buildings inside the compound. Texas gunners still on the walls turned their cannon and raked the yard. Soon the Mexican dead were stacked in windrows. But the Mexicans outside were now free to swarm up the walls; they bayoneted the gunners, took the cannon and began to blow apart the Texans' barricades. "Blind with fury and smoke," recalled de la Peña, "men fired their shots against friends and enemies alike." De la Peña urged Cós to stop the firing, but "the bugler blew in vain, for the fire did not stop until there was no one left to kill."

Afterward, five Texans were found hiding. Santa Anna signaled for them to be bayoneted on the spot. He then had the dead — Mexican and American alike — burned in a huge pyre. "The enemy could be identified by their whiteness, by their robust and bulky shapes," said de la Peña.

All 183 of the Alamo's defenders were dead. In his

Crying "Death to the Spaniards!" Miguel Hidalgo, a village priest, rallied 80,000 peasants in Mexico's first revolutionary army in 1810. But 10 months later, the revolt was crushed and Hidalgo executed.

Viva Agustín I. General Agustín de Iturbi[de ?] [made him]self Emperor of Mexico in May 1822, after [Spain. The high point of his 10-month reign] [was his] July coronation, modeled on that of a [more authentic] emperor, Napoleon Bonaparte.

reports, Santa Anna claimed 600 enemy dead, presumably to offset his own fearsome losses. When the Mexican army realized that the Alamo had cost something like 1,600 casualties, dead and wounded, morale fell still further. In later years, Santa Anna himself admitted that the attack had not been strictly necessary. "A siege of a few days would have caused its surrender," he said, "but it was not fit that the entire army should be detained before an irregular fortification hardly worthy of the name."

Santa Anna's sickened officers saw it another way. Second-in-command Filisola said the assault was ordered "for the mere gratification of the inconsiderate, puerile and guilty vanity of reconquering San Antonio by force of arms and through a bloody contest." Even if the Texans would not have surrendered—and Filisola thought they would have—"what could the wretches do, being surrounded by 5,000 men?" And he put his finger on the real significance of the Alamo when he added, "The massacres of the Alamo convinced the rebels that no peaceable settlement could be expected, and that they must conquer or die."

On March 18, Santa Anna set out for the east. He divided his big army, with one arm moving north toward the town of Bastrop and an advance force under Sesma hurrying forward after Houston, who now was retreating swiftly toward the flooding Colorado River. Santa Anna followed with another force and left Filisola to bring up the rear with artillery and supplies.

To the south, Urrea was to continue his successful sweep up the Texas coast. He defeated two small Texas contingents and then caught up with James Fannin, who was still lingering near the town of Goliad. Fannin had started to retreat after the Alamo fell, but Urrea was too close. The Mexicans trapped the Texans in an open field. They fought all day, and Urrea, low on ammunition, was wondering if he could hold out when Fannin surrendered. Urrea moved on, leaving Fannin and some 400 prisoners under guard.

Santa Anna's orders—death to all prisoners—were still in force, and he insisted that Fannin and his men be executed. His officers fought the order for reasons both humane and tactical. But Santa Anna was sure that the act would destroy the Texans' will to resist, and he sent written orders in triplicate to be sure they were received. Fannin's men were doomed. When they

were marched out of Goliad at dawn on March 26, they believed that they were going to Matamoros, where there would be food and medical attention. Near a swamp, they were broken into small groups. Their captors fired on them at point blank range. Only about 25 of the 400 fled through the swamp and escaped.

It was a bitter time in Texas, for terror struck the whole countryside as Houston fell back and back. Stories of the coming hordes that put fire and bayonet to all they encountered went ahead of the Mexicans, and the settlers fled after Houston's retreating army.

The pursuing Mexican soldiers were moving from the familiar desert into a new kind of country—rolling, wooded, well-watered and green. De la Peña described the "inexhaustible paradises" of woods and the "meadows carpeted with a great variety of exquisite flowers that seduce the eye and intoxicate the soul." Ducks and chickens, pigs "as big as a five or six month's calf," and cattle "so domesticated that they rushed up to anyone coming near the house" met the invading troops. "The stock was beautiful and the meat had an exquisite taste," said de la Peña. Again and again, he and other diarists returned to praise the achievements of the Texans. The solid frame houses, the well-made utensils, the strong barns and cotton gins, the split-rail fences all showed how much the Texans had made of this country in their few years there.

But this countryside aroused darker feelings, too. The rain thundered down, the roads turned to mud, wagons and cannon sank, streams roared out of their banks and had to be forded with barges. And always the Texans were a step ahead in a country that increasingly came to seem huge and lonely. As they marched ever farther from home, some of the Mexicans began to perceive Texas with horror. This was evident in the later remark of a captured officer when he described the Texans' fear that he might escape: "The fools! Where could we go in this vast country, unknown to us, intersected by large rivers and forests, where wild beasts and hunger lurked, and where they themselves would destroy us."

Indeed, Mexican morale was desperately low. Livestock along their line of march would not feed an army —though it did grace the officers' mess—and the men were always hungry. "Frequently they are seen begging for a tortilla," de la Peña said, adding that his

A French pirate in league with the Americans

One of the most fascinating rogues to influence history in the New World was a Texas-based buccaneer who had as many images as a house of mirrors. Jean Laffite appeared by turns gallant, guileful, heroic and treacherous. During his career, he bedeviled the Spanish, frustrated the British and finally so annoyed the Americans that they banned him from U.S. waters.

Laffite was probably born around 1780 in Bayonne, France. At 17, he turned up on the Caribbean island of Martinique, where, according to legend, he eloped with the ward of a Spanish official—only to have that worthy annul the marriage and send him to prison. Laffite's distraught bride committed suicide, and when the young man emerged from jail he swore revenge on the Spanish.

Arriving in New Orleans around 1804, he joined the Barataria company, a notorious band of smugglers and pirates who preyed mainly on Spanish galleons in the Gulf of Mexico. During the War of 1812, the British offered him a commission in the Royal Navy if he would aid in the attack on New Orleans. But the wily Laffite informed the Louisiana governor of the impending invasion. In the battle, Laffite's freebooters fought so splendidly for the United States that they were pardoned for all past crimes by President Madison.

Shortly afterward, an unrepentant Laffite set up base on Galveston Island off the coast of Texas. In three years, his cruisers seized hundreds of Spanish galleons, virtually sweeping Spain from the Gulf. Laffite also prospered at slave-smuggling.

Over the years, Laffite maintained an uneasy truce with the U.S. government, which claimed Galveston Island. But in January 1821, a warship put into Galveston harbor with orders to oust Laffite. He was given 60 days to leave. When the ship returned, Laffite hosted a sumptuous banquet for the Americans, declaring, "I am at peace with the world, except Spain." His men then set fire to their town, and Laffite sailed to Yucatán, where he disappeared into the mists of time. Historians suspect that he died there five years later—having no doubt caused his old enemy continued misery in the interim.

Jean Laffite founded a pirate lair on Galveston Island in 1817; by the 1850s, when this drawing was made, Galveston had become the chief seaport of the state of Texas.

soldiers were "the most long-suffering in the universe."

Another cruel shortage, the lack of hospitals and doctors to care for the wounded, also depressed morale. Many of the men wounded at the Alamo died for want of care, and one of the few surgeons reported that there were "neither bandages nor material for making them, nor gauze for the initial dressings. The bandages finally given were of cotton material which is noxious to wounds." It enraged him that Santa Anna and other high officers would not spare so much as a thread of their linen garments to bind the men's wounds.

Despite the ebbing of its strength, the Mexican army continued to pursue Sam Houston's small band across Texas. The advance guard paused at the swollen Colorado until Santa Anna caught up. Scouts reported that Houston had moved on to San Felipe on the Brazos and thence to the plantation of one Jared Groce. When sharpshooters kept the Mexicans from crossing at San Felipe, Santa Anna impatiently took 800 troops and swung south toward the crossing at Fort Bend. He had learned from intercepted messages that the new rebel government was at Harrisburg, firing off angry demands that Houston stand and fight.

On April 14, Santa Anna crossed the Brazos and the next night personally led a party of dragoons into Harrisburg. The government was gone, fled to New Washington, a town on Galveston Bay only 20 miles distant by land. Santa Anna also learned that Houston expected to take a ferry across the San Jacinto River just north of New Washington, the only route to the east. There would be time, Santa Anna decided, to strike New Washington and then double back to catch Houston at the San Jacinto crossing. He hurried on to New Washington, missed capturing the Texas government by minutes and settled down for a couple of days at a place called Morgan's Plantation, where a pretty young slave named Emily had caught his eye. On the 20th, he burned New Washington and set out for the ferry crossing. He took Emily with him.

Houston, meanwhile, had captured Mexican couriers and discovered Santa Anna's plans. He drove his men a distance of 55 miles in two days through rain that never slackened, reaching Harrisburg on the 18th. The next day, he marched for the ferry, and at dawn on the 20th he seized it and posted his men in the woods overlooking a grassy, open swale. There, on the

plains of San Jacinto, the Mexican army found them.

Santa Anna was angry that morning. He had rushed far ahead of his army with only 800 men and was feeling suddenly vulnerable. At the moment when word of Houston's presence came, the Mexican troops were strung along a narrow path in the woods approaching the San Jacinto River. Upon hearing the report, Colonel Pedro Delgado wrote later, Santa Anna "leaped on his horse and galloped off at full speed for the lane, which being crowded with men and mules, did not afford him as prompt an exit as he wished. However, knocking down one and riding over another, he overcame the obstacles, shouting at the top of his voice, 'The enemy are coming! The enemy are coming!' The excitement of the General-in-chief had such a terrifying effect on the troops that every man thought of flight or finding a hiding place, and gave up all idea of fighting."

From that beginning, the Mexicans met the Texans in an inconclusive skirmish, then withdrew about a mile from the Texas position to a grove of live oaks strung with Spanish moss. Santa Anna chose a dubious position at best. It was on the edge of the open prairie, with a lake behind it and a swamp on its right. Retreat would be possible only to its left. "Any youngster," Delgado commented, "would have done better." He protested to another officer, General Manuel Castrillón, and quoted him as answering, "What can I do, my friend? You know that nothing avails here against the caprice, arbitrary will and ignorance of that man."

Santa Anna was sure the Texans would attack at dawn on the 21st. He spent the night erecting a flimsy barricade of pack saddles and supply cases. At first light, the Mexicans stood to their weapons, but the Texans did not come.

Gradually the Mexicans relaxed. General Cós arrived with 550 reinforcements, and Santa Anna's confidence returned. Cós' men had marched all night and were exhausted. Santa Anna told them to eat and sleep. His own men were weary from working on the barricade. They, too, ate and rested. Santa Anna retired to his silken tent, taking Emily with him. After all, as he explained later, "my duties as general-in-chief did not forbid my resting."

Inexplicably, the Mexicans failed to post a single sentry. No one gave the alarm that afternoon at 4 when the Texans first appeared out of the haze, walking qui-

etly across the open field. Houston never explained why he chose that unlikely hour to attack. Some Mexican officers later believed that a black slave had slipped out of their camp and gone over to the Texans with word that Santa Anna's army was sleeping.

And it was—so soundly that the enemy was within 200 yards before anyone noticed them. Then a soldier shouted and a bugle called and the Texans came running and firing and screaming, "Remember the Alamo!" It was those yells, the Mexicans said later, that were most of all unnerving. The Texans struck the barricade and ran up and over it, shooting as they came, and the Mexicans broke and ran.

"Upon awakening," remembered Santa Anna, "I saw with astonishment that the enemy had completely surprised our camp." All was turmoil. Delgado recalled that "General Castrillón shouted on one side; on another Colonel Almonte was giving orders; some cried out to commence firing; others to lie down to avoid grapeshot. Among the latter was His Excellency. Then, already, I saw our men flying in small groups, terrified, and sheltering themselves behind large trees. I endeavored to force some of them to fight, but all efforts were in vain—the evil was beyond remedy; they were a bewildered and panic-stricken herd. The enemy kept up a brisk crossfire on the woods. Meeting no resistance, they dashed lightning-like upon our deserted camp."

"It is a known fact," Delgado said, "that Mexican

An 1836 cartoon depicts Sam Houston humbling defeated Santa Anna and General Cós after San Jacinto. Actually, Santa Anna said that Houston "addressed me courteously and offered his hand."

soldiers, once demoralized, cannot be controlled." These soldiers dropped their weapons and fled, most running to the swamp on the right. Delgado ran with them. "Unfortunately," he later wrote, "we met on our way to an obstacle difficult to overcome. It was a bayou, not very wide but rather deep." The troops huddled at the water's edge and were cut down as though by a scythe. Delgado mounted his horse and leaped the bayou, but the horse bogged on the far side and Delgado abandoned him, losing his boots in the muck.

It was a rout, a most incredible rout. Santa Anna, dictator of Mexico and general of all its armies, had marched clear across Texas, scattering death and destruction in his path. And finally, on the banks of an obscure river, the Texans had turned on him and smashed him like a bug. Now, as Santa Anna himself fled, the slaughter went on and on. It lasted for more than an

hour, and when the Texans were finished, they had lost two men while killing more than 600 Mexicans. Virtually all the rest, 750 men, were prisoners.

Santa Anna's secretary, who fled with him, said that the general in chief was one of the first to go, mounted on a big black stallion he had taken from a nearby farm. When Santa Anna found that the bridge across the Brazos had been burned by Houston's men, he abandoned the horse and spent the night in rushes. He was afraid to try swimming across the rain-swollen river — and the war may have turned on that fear, for he had an army of 4,000 men, fresh and well armed, barely 20 miles away. The next day, dressed in stolen slave's clothing, he was captured by Texas soldiers. They did not recognize him, but when they turned him in to a prisoner compound, his soldiers identified him.

Houston was lying on the ground in an agony of

pain from a bullet-shattered leg when the captured general was brought before him. Santa Anna pleaded with Houston to be a "generous" victor, and Houston, obviously aware that he had defeated only a fraction of the Mexican army, was prepared to go along. He pointed out to Santa Anna the importance—to protect the lives of the Mexican prisoners—of avoiding further combat between the two armies. "This," Santa Anna wrote later, "was as a ray of light to a lost traveler in a tempestuous night by which he finds his way." Quickly he and Houston cut a deal: he would order his armies to retreat immediately from Texas, and the Texans would spare him and his men.

Santa Anna drafted the orders, and a Texas scout who spoke Spanish set out to find the Mexican forces, now under the command of Filisola. The scout reached the army and delivered the message on April 27. Later, Filisola said that he carried out the retreat to save Santa Anna's life. In fact, believing that all Mexicans had perished at San Jacinto save the few who had brought word of the defeat, he had ordered the retreat two days before Santa Anna's message arrived.

The first news of the debacle at San Jacinto had reached Filisola's force at Fort Bend on the 23rd. Had he marched that same day, he could have attacked the Texans on the 25th and undoubtedly changed the outcome of the war. Instead, fearful that the Texans would attack him, he spent two days ferrying his artillery back to defensive positions across the Brazos. He then called a conference at which he decided to retreat to Mexico, and await new orders from the national government. When he received Santa Anna's instructions, the rationale for the retreat simply changed.

The Mexican officer corps was outraged. De la Peña said that the army "was routed in a shameful retreat as precipitate as it was unnecessary." They marched in silence, he said, shamed. They still had some 4,000 troops untouched and ample munitions. The general they had lost was now hated and ridiculed. There was nothing to keep them from attacking an army barely a quarter of their size—except a failure of nerve at the command level. De la Peña and others later noted bitterly that Filisola was not a native-born Mexican anyway, but an Italian, one of several foreign-born generals who "abandoned their own country to adopt ours."

The retreat of the Mexicans was just as brutal as

the advance had been, with Filisola driving the men along the muddy roads in frantic haste. The units lost all order and were strung out for miles along the road. The wounded hobbled on crutches or rode in wagons that often spilled them into the mud when a wheel collapsed. Rain beat in the faces of men too weak to lift their hands to ward it off.

But most unbearable of all was the sense of an army unbeaten, unmarked by combat, fleeing home in defeat. De la Peña wrote, "Never has General Santa Anna performed a more contemptible deed than in selling out his country by relinquishing Texas' delightful territory, as if he were the sole arbiter of the Republic."

A white-hot rage for revenge gripped Mexico City in the aftermath of Santa Anna's humiliating rout at San Jacinto. On May 20, 1836, the Mexican Congress disavowed Santa Anna's deals with his Texan captors—and when the dictator was released months later, he was driven into retirement. More important, Congress ordered the army to resume the war against the Texans. By June, when the last remnants of Santa Anna's legions straggled back into Mexico, fresh troops were being mobilized to reconquer Texas. Their grim motto: "Extermination as far as the Sabine."

It was not to be. In 1837, Mexico was denied its revenge by the first of a series of debilitating rebellions in the provinces. But Mexico's intransigent pride also denied Texas the final fruit of victory—recognition of its independence. In terms of international law, Texas would remain Mexican until Mexico finally was forced to cede all its rights. It would take nearly 10 years and an international war to accomplish that.

In the meantime, Texas and Mexico found themselves locked in a frustrating pattern of vicious border clashes. Whenever Mexico's resolve for revenge began to sag, the Texans would bolster it with some arrogant act. In September 1836, the Texans brazenly voted to seek annexation to the United States. Three months later, the Texas Congress decreed that the Rio Grande River marked the Texas-Mexico border, thereby claiming parts of four Mexican states. Next, the Texas government began encouraging sea captains to commit piracy on Mexican shipping. And the Texans constantly added insult to injury, making ethnic slurs of the most infuriating sort. Typically, a Texas official referred to Mexico as that "imbecile nation," and a Texas newspaper called Mexicans "the abject race, whom, like the mosquito, it is easier to kill than to tolerate its annoying buzzing."

At the same time, Mexican animosity toward the United States was on a steady rise. Though the American government charily declined to act on the Texans' appeal for annexation, it took a hand in the struggle by recognizing Texas as an independent nation early in 1837. That deed outraged the Mexicans almost as much as the military provocation of the Texans themselves—and there were plenty of those.

Between 1837 and 1842, bands of Texans repeatedly invaded Mexican territory, taking advantage of the rebellions that wracked the country. In 1840, Texas made an alliance with rebels in the southern state of Yucatán, sending its small but aggressive navy to blockade Mexican ports. Far more serious, however, was the Texans' meddling in the revolts of northern federalists against the centralist government in Mexico City. By the fall of 1841, Texan-abetted bloodshed was so widespread in the north that General Mariano Arista, in charge of the region's defenses, implored all Mexicans there to join ranks against the real enemy. "In Texas," he declared, "you can find a field in which to display your warlike ardor without the pain and mortification of knowing that the blood you shed and the tears you occasion are from your brethren."

And now, suddenly, Santa Anna emerged once more to beckon Mexicans to his banner. His confused, trouble-torn nation, seeking a leader, forgave his past disgrace, and by October 1841, he was once again installed as president with dictatorial powers. Seeking to secure his position, Santa Anna fanned the flames of Mexican hatred for the Texans. The next spring, Mexican troops launched surprise attacks on San Antonio and the towns of Goliad and Refugio.

Emboldened by these successes, Santa Anna mounted a larger attack on San Antonio in August 1842. But this time, the Texans were ready. Although the Mexican force of nearly 1,000 men under General Adrian Woll managed to capture San Antonio, it soon became apparent that he could not hold it. On September 20, his army started home, harassed most of the way by nearly 500 Texans.

Without military triumphs to divert the public, Santa Anna's popularity faded amid rumors—substantially true—that he and cronies were guilty of embezzling up to 60 million dollars in public funds. The provincial federalists, cruelly suppressed ever since Santa Anna's return to power, rose in revolt again, and by the end of the year, all Mexico was in chaos.

The Mexican Congress, acting for the first time without its strings being pulled by some general, deposed Santa Anna and turned his authority over to a caretaker of its own choice. Santa Anna attempted to rally a force of loyal troops. But by now, mobs were raging through the capital howling "Death to Santa Anna, death to the robbers!" Santa Anna, too shrewd to die for a lost cause, surrendered and submitted to the indignity of imprisonment. Four months later, Congress passed an amnesty decree that permitted him to depart for exile in Havana. Yet Mexico would soon welcome him back—as its savior in time of war.

Mexico's imperious General Santa Anna was emphatically not a man to mourn his losses—either in battle or in his personal life. On August 23, 1844, his wife of 19 years, Doña Inez, died. The dictator ordered a funeral in the National Cathedral and a long period of public mourning. In a few days, however, the 50-year-old Santa Anna had chosen 15-year-old María Dolores Tosta *(left)* as his second wife. He promptly canceled the mourning and scheduled a gala wedding for October 3 in the very church where Doña Inez had lain. Mexico was scandalized. Santa Anna proceeded anyway, but years later, in drawing up his will, he attempted to retrieve a bit of propriety by insisting that the death and remarriage occurred six months apart.

Squat rows of adobe dwellings cluster around the tidy central plaza of La Mesilla, a typical 19th Century New Mexican town.

4 | A Society shaped by adversity

The province of New Mexico, undisturbed by the foreigners who repeatedly invaded Texas, made slow but steady progress in the decades just before and after the turn of the 19th Century. Yet the towns that sprang up in the period owed their general layout and their very existence to another form of adversity: marauding Apaches and Comanches.

So easily could these raiders pick off the isolated New Mexican homesteaders that in 1772 Governor Pedro Fermín de Mendinueta urged his colonists to emulate the peaceful pueblo Indians and form communities "in plazas so that a few men could defend themselves." A haughty Spanish grandee, Mendinueta lamented in an official report that "these churlish settlers live apart, as neither fathers nor sons wish to associate with each other." He never understood that the New Mexicans, like all pioneers, valued their freedom highly enough to take great risks.

All the same, increasing numbers of colonists built secure settlements along the Rio Grande, Pecos and Santa Cruz rivers. These classic New Mexican towns offered more than protection from savages. The towns became centers of trade and culture that made New Mexico the most stable and populous province of the Spanish West.

Manuel Chaves y Garcia de Noriega

"The bravest and most hardy subjects of New Spain"

By the modest standards of the village of Tomé, 25 miles south of Albuquerque, Don Ignacio Baca qualified as a wealthy man, a *rico,* in 1768. He was far from the richest of New Mexico's great hidalgos, some of whom dwelt in grand haciendas and owned as many as one million sheep. But he was a man of substance and much respected by the 50 or so Spanish families in the locale. Because of his wisdom and tact, he was Tomé's natural spokesman in important affairs, such as dealing with the Comanches.

In those days, despite the combustible nature of relations between Spaniard and Indian, the fearsome Comanches would sometimes, for purposes of trade, make peace with one village or another—while continuing to pillage other settlements. The Spaniards were happy to accept these occasional arrangements, even though they knew that the truce was unlikely to last long and would be broken at the Indians' pleasure. Some relief was better than none.

That year, Don Ignacio negotiated such a village treaty with the chief of a band of Comanches who came from somewhere to the northeast, probably the Sangre de Cristo range. It proved to be a most unusual truce, for it endured unbroken nine full years. It also proved to be personally advantageous for Don Ignacio; each year the chief arrived bearing gifts of horses or buffalo robes for the don and his family.

Both the longevity of the pact and the Indian leader's generosity were the consequence of a remarkable bargain between the two men. During the negotiations,

An eighth-generation New Mexican, Manuel Chaves bore witness to a time of drastic change. Born a Spanish subject, he alternately advised and opposed revolutionary Mexican governors. Later he swore allegiance to the U.S. and fought Indians as an officer in the New Mexico Volunteers.

the chief's 10-year-old son played in the village plaza with Don Ignacio's small daughter, María. The chief, much taken with the vivacious María, was seized with a notion and solemnly broached it. Now that peace was made, he told Don Ignacio, would it not be well to seal the compact by betrothing their children?

With equal outward gravity—and sly inner amusement—the Spaniard agreed. And so the years passed pleasantly, profitably and in peace. Tomé was an island of calm in a countryside often wracked by terror. But gradually, as the Comanche gifts mounted up, a sense of unease grew in Don Ignacio's mind. In the spring of 1777, María's 16th year, Don Ignacio suspected that the time was upon him and sent the girl to relatives in the nearby village of Valencia. Soon after, the Comanche leader and his 19-year-old son arrived, arrayed in their finest, to claim the bride.

Don Ignacio led them to Tomé's cemetery and sadly pointed to a fresh grave. María lay there, he said, an untimely victim of the dread smallpox. The chief accepted the falsehood in good faith and left with his son, in mourning.

But shortly thereafter they learned of the deception from local Indians in the upriver pueblo of Izleta. One summer day, the people of Tomé were assembled in church to hear a mass for Santo Tomás, their patron saint. The thunder of running horses startled them from their meditations, but before they could react, the door burst open and the church filled with Comanche warriors. The priest died on his altar; Don Ignacio died where he stood, as did 18 other men. María was carried off to be the bride of her kidnapper. Eventually she became reconciled to her savage husband, bore him numerous children and passed the remainder of a long life among the Comanches.

The story of Don Ignacio and of Tomé—"the village of the broken promise" the Indians called it—re-

119

flected, in microcosm, the plight of all of New Mexico in the late 18th Century. Despite diligent efforts to re-colonize the area after Diego de Vargas subdued the rebellious pueblo Indians in 1690, the land was not yet truly tamed. Perhaps even more than the Texans, the New Mexicans lived by the sword and the gun, the lance and the bow. In their harsh world, survival hung on a precarious balance of power between Spaniard and Indian—a balance that could tip tragically at any moment. Until that situation was resolved, the New Mexicans—although proud and independent—remained a haunted people, dissatisfied with the present and deeply uncertain of the future. As it turned out, they proved able to master their own fate far more successfully than the Texans, even if the ultimate results were the same.

The New Mexican province—or "kingdom" as Madrid preferred to call it—was an immense wilderness in 1777 when María Baca became a Comanche wife. Within its claimed boundaries lay all of what was to become the state of New Mexico, most of Colorado and Arizona, and slices of Utah, Wyoming, Kansas, Oklahoma and Texas. Much of this area was as inhospitable as it was remote, being either searing desert, jagged mountain or trackless, semiarid prairie. But in the south-central portion of the kingdom, along the Rio Grande, conditions were benign enough to readily support settlement. And it was here that the Spaniards had established their colonies.

At that, there were probably not more than 7,000 people of Spanish blood in the whole area in 1777. Aside from Santa Fe, the main centers were Santa Cruz de la Cañada, founded in 1695; Albuquerque, founded in 1706; and Taos, where Spaniards settled among the pueblo Indians around 1750. Santa Fe boasted a population of about 2,000; the others were mere villages with only a few hundred inhabitants. Despite the region's elevation—7,000 feet at Santa Fe—and the skimpy rainfall of a foot a year, this was good farming and ranching country. Its rivers were fed by snowmelt from the mountains, and the Spanish knew how to tap these watercourses to irrigate their crops, using techniques that they had learned centuries earlier from Spain's Moorish conquerors and that they now passed along to the New World Indians. In ad-

Holding an ox prod on his shoulder, a child at Tesuque Pueblo in the vicinity of Santa Fe waits for his *carreta* to be loaded. Such carts, a prime mode of transport, wobbled along on wooden wheels that were seldom perfectly round.

dition to growing the native corn, they had long since introduced European grains such as wheat and barley, along with European vegetables and such fruits as grapes and peaches.

The sere slopes of the mesas furnished surprisingly luxuriant grazing for livestock. The hillsides were covered with grama grass, a short, pale growth unpromising in appearance but rich in nutrients, even when burned dry by winter sun and wind. The grass supported the province's major industry: sheep. Whereas Texans and Californians favored beef cattle and horses, New Mexicans had concentrated on sheep ever since Don Juan de Oñate and the first Spanish colonizers brought 3,000 head to New Mexico in 1598. For one thing, sheep were far better suited than cattle to the mountainous terrain. And even though Indian raiders occasionally stole sheep — or slaughtered a flock to gall the Spaniards — the animals could not be stolen in large numbers because it was difficult to round them up and drive them away.

The New Mexican sheep were not highly bred animals. The stock had degenerated since first being imported from Spain, and the wool was of inferior quality, but the animals were healthy and reproduced abundantly. And so the hillsides everywhere seemed swathed in gray, the meandering flocks tended by an old man or a boy and a dog. Except for buffalo hides and later some copper, sheep comprised New Mexico's only export. In good years as many as 500,000 of the animals were herded south to market in Chihuahua, capital of the state of Coahuila.

It was an arduous 600-mile trek, and it served to emphasize the New Mexicans' isolation. There was virtually no communication with either the Texans or the Californians; the only trails ran south, back into Mexico. Along those trails, supply trains of ox-drawn two-wheeled *carretas* took two months to carry merchandise — sugar, coffee, hardware and textiles — up from Chihuahua. Other trains, bringing military equipment and ammunition from Mexico City, needed five months to complete the 1,800-mile journey, and they arrived three years apart.

As in Texas, this remoteness from Spanish power greatly increased the vulnerability of New Mexicans to the warlike tribes that surrounded and outnumbered them on every side. In 1777, the year of the Tomé tragedy, Governor Pedro Fermín de Mendinueta sent a desperate message to Mexico City pleading for help. The fearsome Apaches and Comanches, he cried, were "harrying the kingdom with incessant robberies, attacks and murders." During the previous five years, no fewer than 1,674 Spaniards had been killed by Indians.

Even in the most populated parts of the Rio Grande valley, communities were subject to devastating Indian raids. In 1773, two villages near Albuquerque—Carnué and Las Nutrias—had to be abandoned because of constant Apache harassment. During the summer of 1774, Albuquerque itself was raided by Comanches while most of the town's soldiers were off chasing Navajos. In the fighting, five settlers were killed and four more taken captive; the Comanches also drove off much of the town's horse herd and wantonly slaughtered 400 sheep. Only Santa Fe could count itself more or less secure from attack by marauding tribes.

In part the enmity of the Indians grew out of their continuing faith in the old gods and the obstinate refusal of the medicine men—whom the Spaniards bitterly called caciques demoniados (demonic chiefs)—to yield their sway over the ancient superstitions of the people. But, in good measure, the Spaniards had only themselves to blame for failing to convert more tribesmen than they did. All the New Mexican missions —numbering 37 at the peak in the mid-1700s—were Franciscan, and the Franciscans never learned to treat the Indians as anything more than serfs and servants. The choicest sections of mission lands were set aside for the subsistence of the friars, yet the friars did not till their own fields. Instead they required the vassal converts to do the work. Also, in some missions, the priests charged so exorbitantly in cash or kind for marriage, baptism or burial that the faithful—Indian converts and settlers alike—had to choose between the sacraments and perpetual bankruptcy. After a father had paid for his baby's baptism he often did not have enough left to clothe him.

By the 1770s the morale of the friars as well had fallen to low ebb. There were reasons for this decline of the crusading spirit: the sullen or frankly scornful rejection of the faith by most Indians, a chronic lack of funds despite the sacramental fees, and ever-hovering danger. In 1776, Fray Francisco Atanasio Domínguez was sent up from Mexico to inspect the state of the missions in the province. His report was written in anguish and despair. In some missions he discovered that the fathers dared not venture abroad to seek new converts because no military escort could be had—and it was worth a friar's tonsure to move without protection. At one outpost, he learned that the impoverished father had had to sell land belonging to the church to a local rancher in order to repair the church roof. In another, where a band of Navajos had promised to come in and accept baptism, "their inconstancy and fickleness compelled them to get on their high horse, retire to their old hiding places and abandon all that had been started."

Nearly everywhere, the missions had fallen into inexcusable neglect. The inspecting friar found baptismal and marriage record books with whole sections missing and learned that pages had been torn out to stuff broken windows, fashion sunshades and even to roll cigarettes. "In a single mission I found the books of Marriages and Burials without a single entry recorded in them for a period of five years. What grave carelessness! What injurious omission!"

Fray Domínguez also complained that the missionaries were neglecting their duty in the classroom. "There is no teaching of the Indians and consequently no care taken to have them attend catechism and learn it." And he sadly concluded: "Their ministers aspire only to possess many temporal goods and obtain them at the cost of the poor Indians' sweat and labor." The final blow fell when the distraught Fray Domínguez was compelled to acknowledge that some of the friars had been carrying on in a scandalous fashion "with women who are not only suspect but leading notoriously evil lives."

That same year, almost as though to do penance before God for the shortcomings of his fellows, Fray Domínguez, with another indomitable Franciscan, Fray Silvestre de Escalante, set out on a remarkable journey. Leaving Santa Fe in July, the two friars probed 2,000 miles through the wilds of Ute country, looping across the northern parts of present-day New Mexico and Arizona to Colorado and then northward into Utah. They hoped to blaze a trail from New Mexico through the mountains to Monterey in California, converting many Indians along the way. Their journey started out auspiciously, and the two missionaries traveled as far as Utah Lake by mid-September. "Here we found the most docile and affable nation of all that have been known in these regions," Domínguez recorded. "We proclaimed the Gospel to them with such happy results that they are awaiting Spaniards so that they might become Christians."

However, in early October Domínguez and Escalante encountered a vicious mountain snowstorm. Suffering from the bitter cold and dangerously short on provisions, the two men turned back toward Santa Fe. During the long homeward trek, they were forced to kill their horses for food, and when that was gone they had to subsist on grass seeds and prickly pear.

Domínguez and Escalante were the first to explore and chart extensive stretches of the interior country of the Southwest. But they did not find a route to California and could not convince their complacent New Mexican brothers to follow up their initial contacts with the Indians.

Domínguez's failure to expand Spanish influence into the American wilderness and his discouraging reports about the state of the local missions showed that Spain's grasp on New Mexico was both weak and deteriorating. Soon the situation became threatening enough to alarm officials not only in Mexico City, but in Madrid as well. When the Crown considered its New World empire, New Mexico stood at the center of a 1,500-mile arc of Spanish presence that stretched from the Mississippi River to the Gulf of California. No less than Texas in the east, the great, amorphous province stood as a buffer against the pressures of England and France. Its collapse would loose the savageries of the Comanches and, more particularly, the Apaches on the lower, richer, more productive states of Coahuila and Sonora.

In 1777, King Carlos III took action: he replaced Governor Mendinueta with a new governor who was explicitly charged with blunting the Indian menace in New Mexico. This man was Don Juan Bautista de Anza, the distinguished soldier-explorer who had won great royal favor the year before by blazing the first overland trail to California. Anza reached his new command in Santa Fe in 1778 and confronted New Mexico's imperative needs with understandable dismay. He had pitifully little to work with. The presidio of Santa Fe was garrisoned by only 80 regular officers and men;

the nearest other regulars were stationed at El Paso, 280 miles to the south.

For the work of fighting the elusive Indians, the regulars could scarcely have been more ineffectively armed. The New Mexican trooper's major weapon was the *escopeta,* a woefully inaccurate flintlock blunderbuss in no way modernized since its invention in the 16th Century. The gunpowder allowance per man was three pounds a year; if he used any more, he had to pay for it himself, an extravagance he was not likely to indulge on a salary of a quarter peso a day. Consequently no Spanish soldier wasted ammunition on target practice and, even in battle, the troops preferred to fight with lance and sword.

To reinforce the regulars, Anza had authority to call upon the civilian population, since every able-bodied male settler was, by law, a member of the militia. These citizen soldiers, however, were responsible for arming themselves and, because few had firearms, most expected to meet their Indian enemy on even terms — with bow and arrow.

The heart of Anza's Indian problem in that season was the Comanche. And the most dreaded of the Comanche leaders of the time was a chief called Green Horn, so named for his resplendent battle headdress of green-painted buffalo horns. Green Horn was notorious for cunning, for savage courage and for his implacable hatred of the Spanish, who had killed his father years before in one of the frontier's many skirmishes. His sanctuary between raids was known to lie somewhere in the Front Range of the Rockies, more than 200 miles to the north of Santa Fe in what later became the state of Colorado. Nobody had hitherto dared follow him into these fastnesses, but Anza was determined to track him down.

In early August 1779, the Governor stripped the presidio bare and put together a motley force of 575 men. There were his 80 regulars plus 200 militia — about all the able-bodied settlers available — and the rest friendly Indians, mostly Utes.

For two weeks, Anza pushed his ragtag force northward, keeping scouts far ahead and also on both flanks, marching at night to avoid being betrayed by any dust cloud, and lighting no fires despite the mountain cold, "so that it shall not happen to me so easily what has always come to pass, that is, to be discovered long be-

A master of war and diplomacy, Juan Bautista de Anza is portrayed here in a wistful mood that belies his cunning. As governor of New Mexico, Anza secured Spanish control by turning Indian against Indian.

fore reaching the country in which the enemy lives."

For once, the Spaniards were able to achieve surprise. One morning, Anza's outriders met a band of Comanches encamped near the Front Range. The Governor quickly drew up his forces for an attack.

"It was inevitable that they should discover us," wrote Anza afterward concerning the incident. "They had already caught their horses, but they did not sally forth as customarily to meet the troops. All being mounted, even to the women and children, they undertook precipitous flight, notwithstanding that the number of families equaled more than 120 tents. Disregarding this, we pursued them in best order possible. In three leagues we began to overtake the men, who faced us. The fight with them lasted about another three leagues, during which we succeeded in killing 18 of the most valiant and wounding many."

The rest of the warriors — about 800 men — escaped, but Anza captured 64 women and children and 500 horses. The prisoners told him that they had been on their way to rendezvous with Green Horn to the south of the Arkansas River. Their chief, they said, had been away for 16 days on a raid into New Mexico and should now be returning in triumph. "I determined to follow the trail of Green Horn to see if fortune would grant me an encounter," the Governor later wrote in his report.

Two days later, a Spanish scout sighted the returning Comanche warriors. In the fading light of afternoon, Anza drew up his troops in three columns and concealed them in a wooded area beside a narrow valley. As soon as the Spaniards saw dark Comanche forms descending into the valley, they burst from cover and charged from three directions. In the first melee, the Spaniards and their allies killed eight Comanches. But then the main body of warriors scattered and melted into the gathering darkness.

More determined than ever, Anza prepared to resume his pursuit the next morning. He did not have to go far. Just as his troops were getting underway, Green Horn emerged on the wooded mountainside directly in front of Anza's column. The Spaniards knew him: there was no mistaking that horned war bonnet. The chief, "his spirit proud and superior to all his followers, left them and came ahead, his horse curvetting spiritedly," the Governor wrote. "Accordingly I determined

to have his life. His pride and arrogance precipitated him to this end."

By a feint, Anza was able to cut Green Horn and his bodyguard off from the Comanches' main body. Trapped, the chief chose to make his stand in a narrow gully. He put up a gallant fight, as Anza later reported with soldierly formality: "There without other recourse, they sprang to the ground and, entrenched behind their horses, made in this manner a defense as brave as it was glorious. Notwithstanding the aforesaid, Green Horn perished, with his firstborn son, four of his most famous captains, a medicine man who preached that he was immortal, and ten more." With some amazement, Anza testified that Green Horn had been too proud "even to load his own musket, which was done three times for him by another."

The elimination of Green Horn did not by any means end the Indian problem. But it did measurably improve matters for the Spanish. For the time being at least, the Comanche were chastened and uncertain. New Mexico had a tolerable breathing spell, and Governor Anza, brevetted to colonel for killing Green Horn and his war leaders, could turn to other problems. Foremost among them was how to neutralize those other ferocious predators, the Apaches.

The Spaniards in the New World had never been noted for diplomacy. But patient negotiation and clever diplomatic maneuver were weapons Anza employed with Machiavellian skill against the Apache clans spread across southern New Mexico. His grand design was to make peace with the Comanches and Navajos, then unite them with the Utes against the Apaches, who were not only Spain's enemy but practically everyone else's as well. The Comanches and the Apaches had long contested for control of the Plains to the east; eventually, the Comanches drove the Apaches into New Mexico, where they preyed on all the less warlike peoples — meanwhile losing no chance to strike back at the Comanches. In 1756, the Apaches had killed 500 Comanches in a surprise attack in northern New Mexico. Some years later, the Comanches came upon a group of 300 Apache families — perhaps 1,200 people in all — and slaughtered every last one.

Creating an alliance to combat the Apaches was slow work and touchy. A central and almost insur-

Indians forge iron in a New Mexico smithy. To the dismay of the Franciscans who taught them such skills and expected payless work in mission shops, native artisans usually opted for the secular marketplace.

mountable difficulty flowed from the anarchic democracy of the Indians: warriors within a band felt under no obligation to obey a chief if they disagreed with him; and bands within a tribe usually went their own way in matters of war and peace. Still, Anza was not without resources. He could deny trade, for the Indians had grown dependent on such goods as guns, blankets and cooking utensils. He could threaten, a technique likely to be effective only to the extent that he could contrive to make the threat credible. He could offer outright bribes of horses and weapons, which the Crown was willing to supply in some quantity as payment for dependable peace and alliance. He could shower distinctions—medals and titles and fancy uniforms—on tractable leaders. And he could subsidize assassination of the intractable by their more cooperative fellows.

The Comanches began to make tentative peace feelers in July 1785. A deputation came to call on the Governor in Taos, wishing to talk about amnesty and trade. This was a development that Anza might have anticipated. France's cession of Louisiana to Spain in 1763 had effectively cut the Comanches off from their former French suppliers. But Anza temporized. He could not, he explained, be expected to make peace and trade with a fraction of the tribe while other bands still warred on him.

The Comanche envoys protested their sincerity and explained that the only Comanche band still attacking the Spanish was led by a holdout named White Bull. If it would facilitate peace, they said, they would be pleased to see to it that White Bull was murdered. Publicly Anza deplored this proposition as a "dark deed"; privately he hoped that they would not lose any time about it—and he subtly communicated his approval by telling the envoys that it would be wise to unite all the tribe under one eminent and reliable lead-

127

Mission San Xavier del Bac, a flamboyant mixture of Spanish, Moorish, Byzantine and Indian styles, looms out of the southern Arizona desert. Franciscan friars laid its cruciform foundation in the homeland of the Upper Pima Indians about a hundred years before this photograph was made in 1881.

er. As a candidate, the delegates suggested a famous chief with the name of Leather Cape, who controlled a band of about 600 Indians.

The negotiations dawdled along for seven months, during which Anza was pleased to learn that White Bull had expired of unnatural causes. Meanwhile messengers went back and forth, bearing gifts and assurances of good intent. At last in February, Leather Cape arrived in Santa Fe, bringing along 200 leaders of the Comanches to bear witness to the peace. With so many witnesses, the chief explained, none could later plead ignorance of the treaty. Leather Cape was received with high ceremony, and Anza presented him with a saber, a banner and a royal medal. The pact established Leather Cape as supreme chief of the Comanches with a governing council consisting of 11 subchiefs, 31 other tribal leaders and Governor Anza himself. For Spain's part, the Governor promised free trade, frequent fairs to facilitate these exchanges, and reasonable prices from Spanish traders. Leather Cape pledged perpetual amity with the Spaniards and perpetual war on the Apaches.

Anza then turned to the Utes, a fierce tribe of horsemen distantly related to the Comanches, and like them, seething with hatred for the Apaches. The Governor staged a marathon four-hour council that ended with Ute and Comanche chiefs embracing, exchanging gifts of cloth, pledges of fraternity and promises to kill Apaches together.

Next, the Governor focused his attention on the Navajos, the last major element in his coalition. Though raiders upon occasion, the Navajos were a semisettled people with cultivated fields and domesticated livestock; in any concerted attack by Apaches they stood to lose property they could not replace. Well aware of this, they were ready to palaver. The problem, once again, was to unite the tribe under responsible leadership. After some negotiation, the Navajos nominated one supreme chief and one auxiliary chief, upon whom Anza bestowed Spanish names and the insignia of rank.

Not above stooping to intimidation, the Governor had one of Leather Cape's leading war chiefs accompany him to the treaty-making. When the ceremonies were completed and pledges exchanged, Anza gave the floor to his guest. The Comanche arose, stepped to the center of the treaty circle and made the closing address of the occasion:

"You Navajos," he told them, "have made a solemn treaty of peace. Do not break it. Do not impose upon or betray our Spanish friends. For if you do, we Comanches will come and destroy you."

The *pax Anza* may not have been the perfect peace, but it endured for a generation and saw Spanish New Mexico into the 19th Century in tolerably good order. Although Apaches continued to strike viciously at outlying targets, they increasingly were on the defensive.

Leather Cape and his Comanches applied themselves with particular zeal to the task of neutralizing the enemy. In the spring of 1786, Comanches and Apaches clashed near the Pecos River; seven Apaches were killed and four captured without the loss of a single Comanche warrior. Later that year, Leather Cape sent a party of warriors to join Anza and his Spaniards in a successful campaign against the foe along the Rio Grande. In yet another series of skirmishes, Leather Cape was twice wounded in the course of inflicting bloody defeats on his enemies. Anza was duly grateful: with great solemnity he rewarded the chief with a colorful suit, a complete Spanish officer's uniform festooned with embroidery and a large medal bearing King Carlos III's likeness.

From the 1780s on, the Comanches, Utes and Navajos bartered with the Spaniards at Pecos east of Santa Fe and at the annual fair at Taos, which grew into a major regional occasion. Each August, wrote a Spanish chronicler, the Indians arrived in Taos with "pieces of chamois, many buffalo skins, and, out of plunder they obtained elsewhere, horses, muskets, munitions, knives, meat." The Spanish came with blankets, beads and other trade goods, plus any surplus from their farms and pastures. So successful was the fair that the Spanish population of Taos jumped from a few hundred in 1780 to 1,350 by the end of the century.

An even more popular event, this one devoted mainly to exchanges with their own brethren, drew New Mexican traders southward to Mexico proper. Every November, a caravan of hundreds of people and scores of wagons would start out along the northern reaches of the Rio Grande. As the train moved south, it steadily acquired additional traders — many of whom brought their whole families along with them — and by the time the caravan reached El Paso, close to 2,000 people would have joined up. Cargoes included woolen blankets, dried meat, tanned buffalo and deer hides, strips of red and green chili. Some of these goods were locally produced; some had come from the Indians at Taos a few months before.

The destination of the procession was the January fair in Chihuahua, where for two weeks the New Mexicans renewed ties with their countrymen and bargained, gambled and celebrated to exhaustion. When the New Mexicans were finally ready to start the 600-mile journey home, they loaded their wagons with coffee and chocolate from South America, silk hats and gloves from China, jewelry from the Philippines, boots and saddles from Mexico City and stationery, utensils, arms and ammunition from Europe. These luxuries and necessities cost dearly. Yet some of the bigger sheep ranchers not only came away with goods, but with bags of gold or silver coins, for trade at the Chihuahua fair was in cash as well as in kind.

As life settled into a calm pattern of trade and agriculture, growing numbers of settlers ventured north from Mexico. The Arizona desert and the high mountain regions remained dangerous and empty, but the Rio Grande and other river valleys blossomed with new communities. Between 1780 and the census of 1799, the Spanish population of Spain's New Mexican kingdom almost doubled to 18,826. The friars got back to working in the vineyards of the faith, though without outstanding success: the same census listed the Christian Indian population at 9,732, barely 600 more than it had been in 1760.

Some of the pueblo-dwelling Hopis, who had been devastated by Navajo raids and by several years of calamitous draught, came in to the Rio Grande valley and accepted the faith in lieu of starvation. But the Navajos, though at peace with the Spaniards, wanted no part of Christianity. Reluctantly they agreed, as one Indian said, to "give some of their children to have water thrown upon them"; however, as for the adults, they "were grown up and could not become Christians because they had been raised like the deer."

By 1800, Santa Fe boasted 3,795 citizens of Spanish blood. It was a thriving capital despite the drab appearance of its squat, whitewashed buildings. The universal building material was adobe, sun-dried brick laid up in walls three feet thick and roofed over with more adobe that was supported by horizontal timber poles. The Governor's palace and the church were the largest and most imposing buildings in town — and the only ones with glazed windows — but even these edifices had only a single story. Except around the plaza, Santa Fe presented a haphazard appearance, with no clearly defined streets or regular pattern of houses. The Spanish cherished their privacy and preferred ample space between neighbors. Thus, to a wayfaring American, Santa Fe resembled nothing so much as "a disorderly brickyard of kilns scattered here and there among cornfields beside a bright, cascading little river."

The society within these walls was rigidly structured. There were the very many poor, the very few rich — and between these two social layers a mere handful of metal craftsmen, leatherworkers, and carpenters equipped with the crudest tools. Aside from the Franciscan friars, New Mexico had no professional class. No lawyers practiced in the province; in criminal matters the alcalde, or chief magistrate, served as both judge and jury, consigning culprits to the *calabozo* as the justice of the matter struck him. Now and again, a doctor would show up and stay awhile before moving on; but there were no trained physicians residing in the province on a permanent basis.

Public schools were unknown and private teachers few. A wealthy man who desired an education for his heir might send him to Mexico City or even to Madrid. He could, of course, turn the boy over to the Franciscans for instruction, but the Franciscans were often lightly endowed with knowledge: A New Mexico friar once asked an outsider in all seriousness whether George Washington and Napoleon were not one and the same person. Girls, even the daughters of the well-to-do, were educated only in the household arts. Practical illiteracy was the rule.

The poor were poor indeed, living almost entirely on the produce of their irrigated gardens and the milk and flesh of sheep and goats. The dimensions of a poor man's adobe home, called a *jacale*, were determined by the length of roof poles he could cut from the scrubby trees near at hand. A *rico* enjoyed more roomy surroundings because he could afford to send woodcutters to fetch longer poles from timber in the mountains. ◉

The santos: folk art for the faithful

During the late 18th and early 19th centuries, a unique form of folk art flourished in New Mexico. Self-taught artisans — a few of them clergymen, but most of them ordinary laborers — spent their free time creating thousands of holy images, or *santos,* like the ones shown here and on the following pages.

The men who made these statues and paintings of saints or of the Holy Family were known as *santeros,* and they traveled on foot or burro to homes and churches throughout the province, often crafting their religious figures on the spot in accordance with their customers' preferences. Reciprocally they might receive food, clothes, animals, tools or perhaps a small amount of money for payment.

The *santeros* gathered inspiration from religious texts and prints, but when these were lacking they did not hesitate to draw upon their own fanciful notions of beatific demeanor. Their materials, too, were improvised. For example, to create statues, called *bultos,* they first

whittled the figure from the soft root of the cottonwood tree; next, the carvings were coated with a plaster made from gypsum and animal glue; then the artisans, using hog's-bristle brushes, painted their works with eye-catching pigments, many of them locally concocted. Plants and roots supplied the yellows and greens; the browns came from iron ores; the grays and blacks were made with charcoal.

The result was a charmingly unsophisticated beauty reminiscent of the Spanish Romanesque art of the Middle Ages. And like that art, the *santos* played an important role in the daily lives of the New Mexicans. To obtain good crops, a speedy recovery from illness, a safe childbirth or protection of livestock, the people plied the *santos* with candles and beseeched them with prayers. Should heaven fail to respond, however, the pious petitioners were not beyond retaliating by turning the image to the wall, locking it away or even by breaking off a limb in their anger.

A three-foot carving of Jesus dying on the Cross dominates the images of his grieving mother and his disciple John. In their humble statuary, the *santeros* often scaled the figures according to their importance.

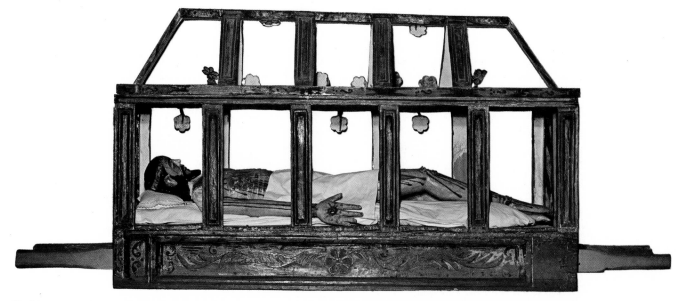

For his mission of Santa Cruz, Fray Andrés Garcia made a life-sized statue of Christ's reposing body, with carrying handles for processions.

Emanating heavenly rays, Our Lady of Guadalupe is framed by an arch. The Virgin was patroness of all Mexican provinces under this title, which refers to her wondrous appearance in a Mexican village.

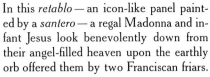

In this *retablo* — an icon-like panel painted by a *santero* — a regal Madonna and infant Jesus look benevolently down from their angel-filled heaven upon the earthly orb offered them by two Franciscan friars.

Called Our Lady of St. John of the Lakes, this statue of a prayerful Virgin is a replica of an image residing in the Mexican village of San Juan de los Lagos, to which numerous miraculous favors were attributed.

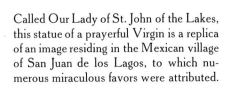

133

Cartouches on an amber-toned *retablo* portraying Our Lady of Guadalupe tell of her revelations to a Mexican Indian, Juan Diego, in 1531, when she supposedly made her only appearance in the New World.

Saint Isidore, the patron of farmers, tills the soil with miniature oxen. A missing hand and plow handle show time's toll, but a later devotee has made amends by providing the *bulto* with satin seed bags.

Bearing a sword to fight Satan and a scale to weigh souls for transport to heaven or consignment to hell, Saint Michael the Archangel is depicted wearing a 17th Century Spanish doublet and pantaloons.

Although drenched with blood, the head of Christ has the serene look often found on *santos*. The foot-high image is the remains of a crucifix that once hung in a church in what is now northern New Mexico.

This *bulto* of the Virgin Mary was constructed in an unusual way. The flat fan-shaped skirt—emblazoned with a crescent moon to symbolize purity—consists of a stick frame covered with cloth and plaster.

The *jacale,* with whitewashed inner walls and a packed-earth floor that was sometimes covered with a coarse wool rug, offered few of the basic amenities other than shelter. Beds, tables or chairs were frequently lacking. Dining was done picnic-style, with a plate held on the knees and generally no tableware except perhaps a spoon (many people found even that utensil superfluous, since a flake of tortilla would serve well enough to scoop up a dish of frijoles and chili, beans and red pepper with mutton).

By contrast, the hacienda of a *rico,* though made of the same unburnt adobe brick, was often downright opulent. One showplace hacienda south of Albuquerque boasted a dozen rooms, all opening onto a central patio; the interior walls were papered with calico and the windows decorated with crimson worsted curtains; the mansion was furnished with massive tables topped with white marble, many gilt-framed mirrors and Brussels carpets on the floors. The grounds of this estate sprawled over both sides of the Rio Grande and embraced extensive cottonwood groves and pasture lands. A guest at the slightly less lavish home of a Taos merchant of the same period described "a handsomely furnished room with a fireplace in one corner and walls hung with portraits of holy characters and crosses. At supper I sat at table and ate potatoes for the first time in several months. A mattress was unrolled from the wall where in daytime it served as a seat, and I turned in between sheets. Yes, sheets!"

Rich or poor, the New Mexicans enjoyed many fiestas, generally coupled with elaborate religious processions in celebration of some saint or holy occasion. And it seemed to an American visitor that no night passed without a fandango: "From the gravest priest to the buffoon—from the richest nabob to the beggar—from the governor to the ranchero—from the soberest matron to the flippant belle—from the grandest *señora* to the kitchen *cocinera*—all partake of this exhilarating amusement. To judge from the quantity of tuned instruments which salute the ear almost every night of the week one would suppose that a perpetual carnival prevailed everywhere." Not even convicts were excluded from the dancing, as was noted with homegrown honesty by a local chronicler. The prisoners, he observed, had "as much fun as anybody because at night they escape and go to dances." The jailers wanted to go to the dances themselves, so they let the prisoners join the fun on a promise to return after the dance was over.

Most of those in prison were, in any case, guilty only of the crime of poverty. One of the few laws that New Mexico got around to enforcing with any regularity was a statute providing imprisonment for debt. A man who fell into arrears had a narrow choice: he could go to jail or he could work out the debt as an employee of his creditor. With wages running between two and five dollars a month, his chances of getting clear often were slight. The system went a long way toward explaining how the *ricos* got rich and why the poor stayed peons all their lives.

When the New Mexicans were not spending their free hours dancing, they were gambling. Their favorite game was monte, a Mexican invention in which a player bets on his luck in matching cards against a dealer. Throughout the 1830s, the favorite gambling den in Santa Fe was run by a highborn woman named Doña Tules Gertrudes Barceló, who was reputedly the sharpest monte dealer in the territory; she was also the Governor's mistress. Another gambling game was called *chuza* and somewhat resembled roulette. Of an evening, a wealthy rancher might win or lose hundreds of sheep playing monte or *chuza* at Doña Tules Gertrudes Barceló's establishment.

The universal petty vice was the *cigarrito.* Everybody smoked, even the children. While Mexico remained under the Spanish Crown, the sale of tobacco was a king's monopoly; consequently the New Mexicans did not try to raise the weed privately for fear of confiscation. As a substitute, those who could not afford royally priced tobacco smoked *punche,* a pale, less noxious plant. The *cigarrito* was rolled in cornhusk, and a *vaquero* could roll and light his smoke with one hand while riding at full gallop—or so an awed foreigner related.

The standard dress for women was a short, full, brightly colored skirt topped off with a loose, low-cut blouse and a *rebozo,* or head scarf. This attire struck some outsiders as shocking and prompted one American visitor to comment that these clothes were worn "in profound ignorance of the fine art of lacing." Highborn ladies, however, were beginning to try out European fashions, and the formerly critical stranger,

Unkempt and weather-worn, U.S. Army
Lieutenant Zebulon Pike *(foreground)* and
his men are led into Santa Fe under guard.
Frederic Remington re-created the scene
nearly a century after Pike was seized for
trespassing on Spanish territory in 1807.

having observed several women who had been done up in corsets and bustles, felt obliged to confess that the simpler, more revealing dress was at least "a very graceful sort of undress."

But the birds of truly brilliant plumage in New Mexico were the men. A *caballero,* or gentleman on a horse, was such a sight to behold that Josiah Gregg, an early visitor from Missouri, felt compelled to describe the outfit from top to bottom: "The riding costume generally consists of a *sombrero*—a peculiarly shaped low-crowned hat with a wide brim—surmounted with a band of tinsel cord nearly an inch in diameter; a *chaqueta* or jacket of cloth gaudily embroidered with braid and fancy barrel buttons; a curiously shaped article called *calzoneras* intended for pantaloons, with the outer part of the leg open from hip to ankle—with the borders set with tinkling filigree buttons and the whole fantastically trimmed with tinsel lace. The nether garment is supported by a rich sash which is drawn very tightly around the body and contributes materially to render the whole appearance of the *caballero* extremely picturesque. Then there are the *botas* which somewhat resemble the leggings worn by the bandits of Italy and are made of embossed leather, embroidered with fancy silk and tinsel thread and bound around the knee with curiously tasseled garters. The *sarape saltillero,* or fancy blanket, completes the picture. This peculiarly useful garment is commonly carried dangling carelessly across the pommel of the saddle, except in bad weather when it is drawn over the shoulders, or the rider puts his head through a slit in the middle, his whole person is thus effectually protected."

The *caballero's* horse furniture was as gaudy as the rider and almost as heavy. Altogether the embossed

137

saddle with its silver ornaments, a bridle that was sometimes made of solid silver, spurs with five-inch rowels, goatskin chaps for riding through brush, and saddlebags called *coquinillos* would often weigh a hundred pounds or more. Fancy as all the equipage could be, it was also supremely utilitarian for men who spent much of their lives aboard a horse.

At the turn of the 19th Century, this somnolent society of gentlemen on horseback, sheepherders afoot and handsome women in seductive blouses stood on the brink of momentous changes. The signal of the new era's start was Napoleon's sale of Louisiana to Thomas Jefferson in 1803. Suddenly New Mexico's neighbors were no longer the representatives of distant European powers but pushy Americans pressing westward in pursuit of their destiny.

There was nothing especially alarming about these new neighbors at first. In 1804, William Morrison—a merchant in Kaskaskia, Illinois—dispatched one of his agents, Baptiste Lalande, on a trip up the Platte River

to trade with Indians, further instructing him to push on to Santa Fe to test the prospects of trading with the New Mexicans. Lalande found both himself and Morrison's merchandise so popular in Santa Fe that he decided to stay and settle; he also neglected to remit the proceeds to Morrison.

Two years afterward, when United States Army Lieutenant Zebulon Pike set out from the Missouri River town of Belle Fontaine with 75 men to explore the Arkansas and Red rivers, Morrison gave him his bill to collect in the event that he should meet up with the absconder. Early in 1807, after sighting the noble mountain that now bears his name and spending a dreadful winter in the Rockies, Pike pushed southward until he came upon a sizable river. He halted his expedition and built a fort on a tributary that joined it from the west. Pike later claimed that he thought the larger stream was the Red, and that the fort was needed for protection until he could gather up all his men, some of whom had suffered frostbite and were straggling. Whatever he had in mind, he sent the expedition

138

LOSSING. Sc.

physician, Dr. John Robinson, off alone to find Santa Fe and collect from Lalande.

Actually the larger stream was the Rio Grande and the smaller the Rio Conejos. Whether he knew it or not, Pike was flying the Stars and Stripes over a fortification on Spanish soil. A month later, any possible doubt he may have had was removed when a force of 100 New Mexican dragoons and militia, alerted by scouts, arrived and took him into custody. The dragoons approached with caution, for there were frightening rumors that Pike was merely the advance guard of a very large invasion force. They were mightily relieved to learn that the lieutenant and his ragged, woebegone crew were the only interlopers within hundreds of miles of them.

Pike and his men were escorted under guard to Santa Fe where they were courteously received by Governor Joaquín del Real Alencaster. However, Pike, according to the 19th Century historian Hubert Howe Bancroft, was "suspicious, independent and disagreeable to the point of insolence." When the Gov-

ernor asked to inspect the lieutenant's papers, Pike surreptitiously parceled out the most important of them among his men before turning over his strongbox; after the Governor had checked the strongbox and given it back that night, Pike gathered up the documents and returned them to the container. The Governor was probably aware of the subterfuge, since he demanded the box again the next morning.

The Governor then informed Pike that he would have to be taken to Chihuahua to be interviewed by General Nemesio Salcedo, the commandant-general of all Spanish forces in northern Mexico. Soon after leaving Santa Fe under guard, Pike was rejoined by Dr. Robinson, and together they made the 600-mile trek to Chihuahua. Whatever else the lieutenant learned en route, he discovered that the Spaniards, when they were so inclined, could be superbly hospitable to a prisoner. In Albuquerque, he was splendidly feted by a priest, and in El Paso the prettiest girls of the countryside were rounded up to entertain him at a *baile,* or ball. General Salcedo received him with the same gen-

139

In Doña Tules' crowded New Mexico gaming house, the famed lady gambler (underneath the window at left in the picture) deals for a select circle of Santa Fe patrons. After watching her at work in 1839, a foreign visitor wrote: "The cards fell from her fingers as steadily as though she were handling only a knitting needle."

tility in Chihuahua — but took away his papers for good — and sent him home under escort.

At one point while he was in New Mexico, Pike came across Lalande; he concluded the man was a spy, but apparently he failed to collect any money for Morrison's bill.

Pike did manage to hide from the Spaniards one journal of his expedition by rolling up its pages and placing them in gun barrels. He finished his manuscript back in the States and published it in 1810. However curt and surly he might have been to the New Mexicans, he had come away hugely impressed by both the land and its people. In his journal he reported: "Being cut off from the more inhabited parts of the kingdom, together with their continual wars with some of the savage nations who surround them, render them the bravest and the most hardy subjects of New Spain." He told of their hospitality, and painted shining pictures of the land: "The water of the Rio Grande fertilized the plains and fields which border its banks on both sides, and we saw men, women and children of all ages and sexes at the joyful labor which was to crown with rich abundance their future harvest and insure them plenty for the ensuing year." He continued: "Their remote situation also causes them to exhibit in a superior degree the heaven-like qualities of hospitality and kindness in which they appear to endeavor to fulfill the injunction of the scripture, which enjoins us to feed the hungry, clothe the naked, and give comfort to the oppressed in spirit."

Pike's book enjoyed wide popularity, and his tales of those isolated people and their beautiful country ignited the venturesome spirit of many an American wanderer. Soon the whole frontier throbbed with tales of the forbidden Spanish province.

But, however well they had treated Pike, the Spaniards felt no compulsion to be so kind to all future intruders. In 1810, when news of the Hidalgo revolt against Spanish rule filtered into the United States from Texas, American traders jumped to the conclusion that it had succeeded. They began to think that the Crown's old prohibition against trade with foreigners no longer obtained. Not knowing that Father Hidalgo had failed, an American named Robert McKnight and a party of 10 other merchants reached Santa Fe in 1812. Their goods were immediately confiscated, and they were conveyed to Mexico City; there they moldered in prison until the second successful revolt under General Agustín de Iturbide finally separated Mexico from Spain in 1821.

Word of the Iturbide revolt did not reach Santa Fe for months, and it was received with no great excitement. But after a while, the real significance of the news sank in: the King could not longer forbid trade with foreigners.

That year, a group of New Mexicans hunting buffalo on the plains to the east encountered a party of traders led by one William Becknell, from Franklin, Missouri. The New Mexicans advised the Americans that the gates to Santa Fe were open at last. And so Becknell and his crew took their goods, intended for Indians, across the Sangre de Cristo range by way of Raton Pass, then on to the city. There, to their intense pleasure, they disposed of the whole stock at a huge profit; one man headed home with $900 from an investment of $60. Arriving back in Franklin, the traders were met by a curious crowd. One of them lifted a rawhide sack, drew his knife and slashed it open. A shower of gold and silver coins spilled out onto the street around him, and with that the opportunities of the Santa Fe Trail were announced to the restless men of the American West.

The next spring saw a tide of American adventurers begin to flow over the plains and mountains to ply the lucrative Santa Fe trade. Becknell himself outfitted another expedition of 30 men, but he led this caravan toward New Mexico by a new route. Instead of heading toward the Rockies when he arrived at the Great Bend of the Arkansas River, he went south, across a land of rock and sand near the headwaters of the Cimarron River. As the traders trudged through the desert region, their water ran out. They killed their dogs and mules and drank the blood of the animals. They were close to death when at last they sighted a buffalo, its stomach distended with water. The men shot the animal, slashed open its stomach and drank the contents. One of the party later declared that nothing ever had given him such exquisite pleasure as his first draught of that liquid.

Becknell's party soon found the stream where the buffalo had gone to drink. They pushed on to Santa Fe, where they turned a $100,000 profit, and their

shortcut, known as the Cimarron Cutoff, ultimately became the favored trail to New Mexico.

For New Mexicans as well as for Americans, the trading route kindled an excitement and a prosperity that had been unknown previously. When the wagons approached Santa Fe, reported one witness, "even the animals seemed to participate in the humor of their riders, who grew more and more merry and obstreperous as they descended toward the city. I doubt whether the first sight of the walls of Jerusalem was beheld by the Crusaders with much more tumultuous and soul-enrapturing joy. Native cries of 'Los Americanos! Los Carros! La entrada de la Caravana!' were to be heard in every direction, and crowds of women and boys flocked around to see the newcomers. The wagoners were by no means free from excitement on this occasion. Each one must tie a brand new cracker to the lash of his whip, for on driving them through the streets every one strives to outshine his comrades in the dexterity with which he flourishes his favorite badge of authority."

Arriving in the main square, the teamsters immediately pulled out their wares and started trading in the streets. New Mexicans replaced their old clothes with colorful American calicoes; they exchanged their rugs, furs, blankets, and gold and silver coins for American tables, chairs and chests, new foods and spices, medicines, wines, tobacco, tableware, oil lamps, inks and paints. In 1824, the 25 wagons that left Missouri carried $35,000 worth of merchandise that was sold for $190,000 in gold, silver or the equivalent in barter. Within a few years, hundreds of wagons made the 800-mile journey from Independence, Missouri, and the annual volume of business rose to almost one million dollars.

Though the New Mexicans were backward in many things, they proved as progressive as anybody when it came to recognizing the prospect of a profit. Before long, the Santa Fe Trail became a two-way street, with Spanish-owned pack trains traveling north into the United States to compete with the merchants of St. Louis and Independence. One of the choicest items the New Mexicans had to sell was the mule. Faster than the ox, tougher and more sure-footed than the horse, the Santa Fe mule journeyed to the United States by so many thousands that eventually it passed

through a crisis of nationality and became the very symbol, even the personality, of the state of Missouri.

In the early and middle 1830s, the director of customs at Santa Fe was a former governor of the province named Manuel Armijo. The Missourians were at first greatly taken aback when he advised them that the duty on imported goods was 100 per cent, but they were relieved when they learned that Armijo was a reasonable fellow and would compromise. The director's idea of a square deal was to split the duty into three equal shares: one for the government, one for the merchant and one for Armijo. Later, when he became governor again, Armijo simplified the collection of customs duties by charging a flat $500 for each wagonload of goods. "How much of these duties found their way into the public treasury," said one trader, "I will not even venture to guess."

Armijo's second term as governor came about in 1837 through a peculiar chain of circumstances — most of which he apparently engineered himself. As a rule, New Mexico's governors, with the notable exception of Anza, were appointed from prominent local families because, in the introverted society of the province, outsiders were looked upon with suspicion. This had been the case two years before, in 1835, when Mexico City sent in a regular army officer, Colonel Albino Pérez, to rule the province. As if that were not irritant enough, the stranger Pérez was called upon to administer the first direct tax in the history of the republic. The tax was both resented and not very clearly understood; one rumor held that a man was to be taxed for cohabiting with his wife.

Suddenly, in August 1837, all of New Mexico rose up in wrath. The rebellion began among small farmers and pueblo Indians, but some thought it had been instigated by malcontent *ricos* — among them Armijo, who had been dismissed as chief of customs and was smoldering with fury.

Pérez attempted to quell the revolt with a few troops from the Santa Fe presidio, but was defeated by the enraged farmers and Indians. Trying to get away, the terrified Governor was run down by a mob in the outskirts of Santa Fe and was decapitated. The same mob dragged the secretary of state, Jesus María Alarid, from his house and lanced him to death. Then, turning to a former governor, Don Santiago Abreu, they cut

off his hands and tongue and pried out his eyes before they killed him.

Although he took no active part in the revolt, Armijo now rushed to the capital from his hacienda near Albuquerque, fully expecting to be named governor by the revolutionary junta. Instead they appointed José González, an honest but illiterate buffalo hunter. Armijo returned to Albuquerque and began plotting a counterrevolt. By September, having put together a sizable force, he marched on Santa Fe to "suffocate the rebellion," as he put it. Meanwhile, the revolutionaries had returned to their homes for the autumn harvest, leaving Governor González in helpless isolation. Wisely, he fled, and Armijo occupied the capital without any real resistance.

The brazen Armijo thereupon appointed himself governor and sent a dispatch rider rushing to Mexico City with an account of his glorious counterrevolution so colorfully mendacious that the central government was bamboozled into confirming him in office. Mexico City, moreover, sent him a force of 200 dragoons to help maintain "civic peace, harmony and good order."

When the troops arrived, Armijo marched them north to Taos, put down the remnants of rebellion and seized the fugitive González. Then, just to make sure there would be no argument about who was governor, he had his predecessor murdered.

As governor, Manuel Armijo cut an imposing figure. He was a large, florid man, running to paunch, and he affected a brilliant blue uniform with gold epaulets and a white ostrich plume in his helmet. He traveled about in a grotesquely carved and gilded gubernatorial coach that his subjects called "the wheeled tarantula." The spider analogy could have applied almost as well to the Governor himself: he was unprincipled, greedy and brutal, a sinner of omnivorous appetites. If Juan Bautista de Anza was the best and most effective Spanish governor New Mexico ever had, Manuel Armijo was certainly the worst.

Armijo's only discernible virtue was his frank acknowledgment of his accomplishments as a rascal. He liked to boast that he got his start in the world as a sheepherder who never hesitated to steal from his employer. He enjoyed recalling that he had stolen the same ewe 14 times and each time had sold it back to the original owner.

One of his palace favorites for a while was a nephew, Manuel Chaves. But with Governor Armijo, blood was thinner than water. It ran especially thin when it came to the matter of a racehorse named Malcreado that was owned by the 21-year-old Chaves. Malcreado was a big bay Arab. Manuel loved the animal, pampered it and made much money betting on it. But the Governor was jealous of his nephew's great horse, for that was his nature.

And so the Governor proposed a race, saying that he too owned swift horses in his stable. Chaves demurred. He knew perfectly well that Malcreado could outrun anything in New Mexico, and he also knew that his uncle could not abide being beaten. But his uncle insisted. Manuel had no choice except to agree. He bet his all on Malcreado, and set a day for the race. He also took to keeping Malcreado in a locked stall and appointed his young half brother, Román Baca, to sleep with the horse.

On the day of the race, Román awoke with an unaccountable headache, but the pain wore off in the excitement of getting ready to ride Malcreado to victory.

A main street in Santa Fe, photographed in the 19th Century, leads to the parish church. One American visitor in the 1830s found the churches "poverty-stricken and shabby-looking" compared with those of Mexico, and a European-born cleric said they recalled "the stable of Bethlehem."

The race, in the meantime, was the subject of great excitement among the citizens of Santa Fe, and the Governor, smilingly confident, covered all the Malcreado money offered—and there was a lot of it, for Malcreado's fame was great.

When the gun went off, Malcreado, with young Román Baca in the saddle, sped away like the wind. It was no race until—50 yards from the finish line—Malcreado fell dead. Still smiling, the Governor collected. Manuel Chaves was both heartbroken and broke.

A few days later, Manuel had a distinguished visitor; he was Dr. Philippe Auguste Masure, a French physician who had arrived in Santa Fe in 1831. The good doctor was obviously troubled and had a burden he wished to get off his mind. The Governor, he confessed, had hired him to poison Malcreado, promising him $1,000 if he did the deed and threatening to run him out of town if he did not.

Bullied into it, the doctor said, he had gone to Malcreado's stall the night before the race, anesthetized Román with a soaked handkerchief poked through the window on a stick, then climbed through the window and dosed the horse with a slow-acting poison. Now, he said, the Governor had reneged on his promise: he had given him only $300 and threatened to have him killed if he blabbed.

Stunned but not really surprised, Manuel swore to avenge his horse. He armed himself with bow and arrow—a weapon that he could wield as skillfully as any Apache—and took station that night in the black shadows near the palace. He thought to ambush his uncle on his way to his mistress, the gambler Doña Tules Gertrudes Barceló. But for once the Governor unaccountably stayed at home, and Manuel never got another chance. Somehow the Governor learned that Manuel planned to kill him. True to his nature, he planned to have Manuel killed instead. Forewarned, Manuel left town with a party of American traders whose destination was St. Louis. He found Dr. Masure in the same company.

Manuel Chaves' exile in St. Louis lasted two years, and during that time he learned English. By 1841, Governor Armijo found himself in sore need of somebody trustworthy who knew that tongue. Manuel, although suspicious of his uncle's good faith, accepted a "pardon" brought to St. Louis by another uncle. The Governor needed him, he was told. In Santa Fe, Manuel learned what Armijo wanted.

The Americans were coming, and the Governor required help in dealing with them—as did the whole of the Spanish-speaking New World. Thirty years before, when he was addressing the Spanish legislature, New Mexico's delegate Don Pedro Pino had warned his colleagues against the intentions of the United States. Its citizenry, he claimed, "knowing that by possessing New Mexico they would be masters from the North Sea to the South Sea, have tried with lucrative commerce and promises of protective laws to unite this territory to Louisiana."

In 1841, the threat of takeover was becoming a reality, although the immediate source of concern was not the United States but the young republic of Texas. The New Mexicans were well aware that, as early as its first congress in 1836, Texas had claimed the Rio Grande as its western border. Should that boundary be established in fact, Santa Fe and Taos would be swallowed up. Now, for more than a year, Mirabeau Lamar, Texas' second president, had been addressing to the New Mexicans a seductive invitation to "full participation in all our blessings. The great river of the north which you inhabit is the natural and convenient boundary of our territory and we shall take great pleasure in hailing you as fellow citizens, members of our young republic, and co-aspirants with us for all the glory of establishing a new and happy full nation."

In the spring of 1841, word reached Santa Fe that Texas was raising an army to implement this barefaced incitement to rebellion. President Lamar clearly believed that his effusive invitation would prove irresistible to the misgoverned peons of the Rio Grande valley; no Spanish or Mexican administration ever had paid heed to Don Pedro's other warning that "the means of establishing peace in New Spain lies in giving every one an interest in the property of the territory." However, the New Mexicans—peons included—considered the Texans to be godless freebooters bent upon pillage and arson and murder, the ravishment of women and the desecration of the Church. Despite injustices in their own land, they preferred to remain Spanish, untainted by heathen Texas blood.

Governor Armijo began the task of raising an army, and in September of 1841, he sent out scouts to the eastern frontier. As a fighting force, it was not much more formidable than the one that Governor Anza had been able to raise against the Comanches nearly three quarters of a century before. There were a few more regulars in the presidio garrison, but most of Armijo's 2,000 men were peasant militiamen armed for the most part with bows and arrows, swords and spears.

The Texas expeditionary force coming from the east was no overpowering legion of conquest either. The force, under command of General Hugh McLeod, consisted of about 300 Texas dragoons and several civilian commissioners who carried proclamations of friendship and Texas citizenship. There were also a few guests, including the founder and editor of the New Orleans *Picayune*, George Wilkins Kendall. The expedition was planned and put into execution with almost inconceivable incompetence. Although the distance from Austin to Santa Fe was about 700 miles, the Texans actually traveled a circuitous 1,300 miles. To make matters worse, they started out at a time when the Plains were almost waterless. And, as if incompetence were not enough, they had hard luck on the way. Kiowa and Comanche war parties harassed them and ran off their horses. A fire in camp destroyed tents and ammunition. Men sickened, starved, grew wild with thirst; some discarded their weapons as too heavy a burden.

It is possible that Governor Armijo knew into what sorry straits the Texans had fallen, for his scouts had word of them while they were still bogged down on the Staked Plains of west Texas. The situation ended abysmally for the Texans in September. Near the border, McLeod divided his force, sending ahead a party under a civilian commissioner by the name of William Cook. The commissioner was instructed to inform the New Mexicans that the Texans came to them in peace and to ask them to furnish supplies for their distressed men. Advised of this advance party, Armijo, dressed in his blue uniform and wearing his plumed headpiece, rode out of Santa Fe leading 1,500 men. Before leaving, he imposed a strict quarantine on all American traders then residing in the city.

Thirty miles out, the Governor met a detail bringing in five prisoners. One of them was Captain William T. Lewis, an artillery officer who, on being questioned, claimed to be a civilian trader. Seizing Lewis by the collar of his uniform jacket, Armijo pointed to a button and bawled, "Texas! I can read Texas."

With Lewis thoroughly intimidated, Armijo made him a tool to obtain the surrender of others. He assigned him to the custody of his nephew and secretary, Manuel Chaves, and employed both of them to persuade other parties of McLeod's exhausted men to give up their arms. Among the Texans who did so were Cook and his group, discovered wandering about in the desert. In return for surrender, Armijo promised to provide the Texans with supplies and to escort them safely back to the border.

It quickly became apparent, however, that Armijo had not the slightest intention of keeping his part of the bargain. As soon as he had rounded up the bulk of the force—more than 300 officers and men—he sent them off by foot to Mexico City, 2,000 miles away. He placed the prisoners under the command of a sadistic officer named Captain Damasio Salezar, saying, "If any pretends to be sick or claims he cannot march, shoot him and bring me his ears."

Editor Kendall, after witnessing the first occasion on which Salezar carried out his macabre orders, wrote: "Once more the bloodthirsty savage, pointing to the main body of prisoners, ordered the cripple to hurry forward and overtake them—*he could not!* 'Forward!' said Salezar, now wrought up to a pitch of frenzy, 'Forward, or I'll shoot you on the spot!' 'Then shoot!' replied McAllister, throwing off his blanket and exposing his manly breast, 'And the quicker the better.' Salezar took him at his word, and a single ball sent as brave a man as ever trod the earth to eternity! His ears were then cut off and his body thrown by the roadside as food for wolves."

Upon his return from his mission, Captain Salezar presented the Governor with five sets of Texan ears. Armijo nailed these souvenirs to the wall of his office in the Santa Fe *palacio*.

Five years later, advised of a more substantial threat in the approach of General Stephen Watts Kearny and 1,700 troops of the United States Army, Governor Armijo disbanded the militia and fled south to Chihuahua. When General Kearny entered the Governor's office, without the firing of a shot, he found a small property that Armijo had forgotten to take along. Nailed up on the wall were five pairs of Texan ears.

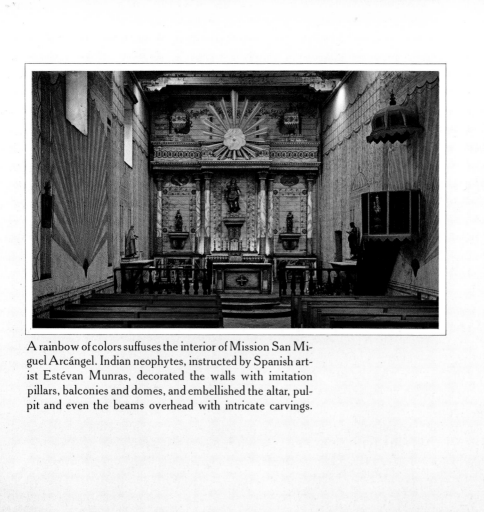

A rainbow of colors suffuses the interior of Mission San Miguel Arcángel. Indian neophytes, instructed by Spanish artist Estévan Munras, decorated the walls with imitation pillars, balconies and domes, and embellished the altar, pulpit and even the beams overhead with intricate carvings.

Constructed of sturdy adobe, San Miguel in the 1870s exhibits very few signs of having been abandoned for more than 20 years. Later, it was reactivated and restored.

5 | Prosperity and piety along the Pacific

Nowhere along the frontiers of New Spain did the mission system succeed in such grand style as in Alta, or Upper, California. Between 1769 and 1823, the visionary Franciscan Junípero Serra, his equally able successor Fermín Francisco de Lasuén, and three subsequent padres built a chain of 21 missions stretching from San Diego 650 miles north to the great bay named for the patron saint of the Franciscans.

Linked by *El Camino Real,* or The Royal Road, these self-supporting centers of Spanish civilization were about a day's journey apart, and most were within easy access of the sea.

Six decades after the first mission was founded, the padres could report almost 17,000 converts. The Indians tended the fields and orchards, looked after the flocks and herds, and labored at improving the mission buildings. The neophytes also had a talent for music, and their choirs and orchestras often performed at weddings and fiestas.

In the mid-1830s, however, the Mexican government secularized mission lands and began breaking them up for ranchos. The Franciscans' dream of smoothly assimilating the Indians into Spanish culture was undone, but it had clearly pointed the way to a cultured society of plenty on the Pacific Coast.

In its capped buttresses and high, narrow windows, Mission
San Gabriel Arcángel reflects the strong Moorish influence
that was so much a part of Spain's heritage. Established in
1771, it was the fourth in the string of Alta California
missions and quickly became one of the most successful.

San Gabriel boasts a spectacular trove of holy images. According to tradition, when San Gabriel's founding fathers encountered hostile Indians, one of the friars pacified them by holding up a painting of the Virgin *(left of the altar)*.

The small chapel used for baptisms and weddings at San Francisco de Asís is dominated by an elaborately carved altarpiece brought from Mexico. The striped ceiling beams are of redwood, and so are the columns above the two side altars, despite their painted disguise as Italian marble.

One of the early links in the mission chain, San Francisco de Asís was established in 1776 and later gave its name to the great American city that grew up to surround it. In the cemetery at the side of the church were buried 5,500 Indians, most of them victims of the white man's diseases.

Santa Inés is celebrated for unique pink-and-green wall dec-
orations that simulate marble, and also for the exquisite statue of its patroness, Saint Agnes, over the altar. Built in
1804, it was badly damaged in 1824 when mission Indians
staged a one-day revolt, but was restored the next year.

As seen in the 1870s, Santa Inés' weathered bell tower has been stripped of plaster, exposing its adobe brick construction. The mission, in a valley north of Santa Bárbara, was the last built between San Diego and San Francisco, and like most of the others, faced east to greet the sunrise.

155

San Luis Rey de Francia, sited in a fertile valley north of San Diego, was the largest of all the Franciscan settlements in California, with buildings that covered more than six acres. Said one European visitor in 1827: "In the still uncertain light of dawn, this edifice has the aspect of a palace."

Sinuous Indian paintings cover the pillars and ceilings of San Luis Rey, known early on as the "King of Missions." Its cruciform layout, with an octagonal dome above the transept, was unique among California missions. The modern banners decking the altar area proclaim Easter tidings.

The Californios: "We live here like princes"

The history of California might arguably have been very different if young Ignacio Vicente Ferrer Vallejo had obediently hewed to the path laid out for him. At his birth in Jalisco, Mexico, in 1748, Ignacio's parents had dedicated him to the Church, and as a youth he duly entered upon studies for the priesthood. But Ignacio had no bent either for sanctity or scholarship. "At the last moment," according to one account—presumably, the very instant he was to be ordained—Ignacio bolted through the sacristy door to freedom, and with the help of friends fled to the western Mexican city of Compostela. There he remained in hiding until he got the chance to enlist as a soldier for service in Alta California.

In September of 1774, Ignacio Vallejo arrived in San Diego. The first chapter of one of California's most colorful family chronicles was about to be written—a chronicle that would reflect not only the vicissitudes and triumphs of one family but the evolving fortunes of California itself, from Spanish colony to Mexican province to its ultimate destiny as part of the United States of America.

Ignacio found himself in a struggling colony that was barely past its infancy. Gaspar de Portolá and Father Junípero Serra had led the first Spaniards into California only five years earlier, and the overland trail from Mexico had just been blazed. Everything was still in short supply, including Spanish women. The 28-year-old Ignacio, displaying exceptional foresight, took steps to remedy this situation by betrothing himself to María Antonia Lugo on the day of her birth in 1776 to a Spanish couple in San Luis Obispo. A solemn

covenant of engagement was drawn up, subject to María's future consent.

Ignacio, as it happened, was a catch far superior to the average frontier soldier. Not only was he a full-blooded Spaniard, but he also came from a distinguished family. One of the Vallejos had been a captain under Cortés, who rewarded him with the governorship of a province rich in silver mines. Another forebear, Admiral Alonso Vallejo, had commanded the ship that, in the year 1500, carried Columbus back to Spain in irons to face charges of maladministration. (The Admiral, feeling that Columbus still deserved respect, offered to have the chains removed, but Columbus would have none of it.) Don Pedro Vallejo, the Admiral's brother, had served as Viceroy of New Spain. Ignacio was Don Pedro's great-grandson—and very proud of it.

While he waited for María to grow up, Ignacio kept busy with his military career. It took him, after San Diego, to San Luis Obispo, to San Carlos (present-day Carmel), San José, Soledad, Monterey, Branciforte (Santa Cruz) and back again to Monterey, where he settled permanently. During his prolonged bachelorhood, it became abundantly clear that he had done the right thing—from the Church's viewpoint, at least—when he bolted through the sacristy door. A blistering letter written by an irate governor shows that when Ignacio was appointed *alcalde* (chief magistrate) of San José, to put an end to dissolute living there, he joined the offenders instead and set a scandalous example by his "too intimate acquaintance with the daughter of one Gonzales."

Ignacio was frequently in trouble with his superiors, for he was haughty and insubordinate as well as something of a rake. Despite his impressive ancestry, he never advanced beyond the rank of sergeant. On the other hand, he won commendation for his bravery in In-

Master of an 80-square-mile rancho south of the pueblo of Los Angeles, Don José Andrés Sepúlveda was a true son of California, racing horses, making wagers and entertaining guests, all on a lavish scale.

dian campaigns, and for his services as a civil engineer. Extensive irrigation projects at several missions were laid out under his direction, and the same governor who had deplored Ignacio's peccadillos gave him credit for bringing about San José's eventual prosperity.

Gradually the pioneering labors of men like Ignacio Vallejo began to transform California into a bountiful as well as beautiful land. Because they were so few, the transformation took time — especially after the overland route from Sonora was severed by the bloody Yuma rebellion of 1781. Once again, supplies had to be brought by ship from San Blas on the Mexican mainland, and their arrival remained unpredictable. Still, by 1781 the new Californians — "Californios," as they came to be called — were no longer in danger of starvation. And there were plenty of Indians to take over the hard work once they had been taught how. The Californios' isolation might deny them some niceties available in less remote parts of the world; but on the whole, theirs was beginning to be a relatively good life.

It was not good enough, however, to suit the wife of the redoubtable Pedro Fages. Fages, another of the rambunctious characters in which California history abounds, had taken part in the first Spanish expedition to the California wilderness and — as soldier, explorer, and bear hunter — had been one of the young colony's mainstays. As a reward, he had been appointed governor in 1782. Hastening back north to take up his new gubernatorial duties, he had left his wife, Doña Eulalia, and their little son, Pedrito, behind in Mexico. Doña Eulalia, a Catalan like her husband, was a high-spirited woman with a streak of stubborn independence. She seemed to be in no hurry to change her abode. Fages wrote letters pleading with her to join him, and even had friends intercede on his behalf to assure Doña Eulalia that California was not totally barbarous.

Finally the lady consented. Fages made the arduous journey to meet her ship at Loreto, in Baja California, where a joyful reunion took place in the spring of 1783. Then they began a triumphal progress back to Monterey, the capital, finally arriving in January 1784. As the first truly aristocratic lady to reach California, Doña Eulalia was welcomed ostentatiously at every point along their route and was viewed with approbation and awe by soldiers, friars and Indians alike. When she had been installed in the governor's prim-

itive palace, Fages wrote enthusiastically to his mother-in-law in Mexico that "the Señora Gobernadora is getting on famously, and Pedrito is like an angel; so rest assured, for we live here like princes."

The Governor's report was not entirely accurate. Doña Eulalia was, in fact, distressed by the rude frontier conditions in which she was forced to live, and appalled at the sight of so many naked Indians. She began to distribute clothing with a free hand, not only from her own wardrobe but from her husband's as well. Fages had to caution her that if she kept this up, both the Governor and his lady would be going about as naked as the Indians.

Thereafter, Doña Eulalia continued her charitable ways along more sensible lines, winning praise for her kindnesses to the poor and sick. She also bore her husband a daughter; but alas, by the end of the first year, she announced that she had had enough of California and wished to leave. Fages had no intention of giving up his post, and there followed a family row that fascinated all within earshot.

And there were many within earshot. Neither the Governor nor the *gobernadora* spoke softly, and soon, as they warmed to the argument, the very walls trembled with roars and shrieks of rage. Finally, the overwrought Doña Eulalia resorted to her ultimate weapon: she barred the Governor from her bed. In the days — and nights — that followed, she observed with alarm that Fages was not reduced to contrite submission, as she had hoped. In fact, the Governor did not seem to be unduly upset by this denial of privileges. Her suspicions fell on a young Indian maidservant named Indizuela, a girl whom Fages had brought back with him from the last campaign against the Yumas on the Colorado. On the morning of February 3, 1785, she followed her husband when he appeared to be headed toward Indizuela's quarters. With the abusive vocabulary any true Catalan can wield like a cat-o'-nine-tails, she loudly accused him of adultery — so loudly that the news was soon all over Monterey. Among other things, she threatened divorce.

Fages went to the friars of the San Carlos mission for their advice. The priests spoke with the irate lady, but she declared emphatically that she would rather be in hell than live with her husband again. They submitted the case to their bishop for adjudication, meanwhile ordering Doña Eulalia to remain in her quarters.

When Fages had to leave Monterey on official business, he asked the friars to confine his wife in the mission. Doña Eulalia refused to budge from her room. Finally Fages kicked the door down, and threatened to tie her and carry her off to San Carlos by force if necessary. Most grudgingly and reluctantly, she went. However, once there, she raised such a ruckus that the friars too resorted to threats, promising her chains and flogging if she did not moderate her behavior. But separation and time eased tempers on both sides, and after Fages returned to the capital the pair was reconciled. Fages subsequently wrote a friend: "It is now about five or six months since Eulalia suddenly called me one morning, and with a thousand excuses and tears, humbly begged my pardon for all the past. She spontaneously confessed that it had all been a mere illusion and falsity. Thanks to God that we are now living in union and harmony."

Doña Eulalia fired only one more shot. She wrote to royal authorities asking that her husband be transferred elsewhere because the Monterey climate did not agree with him. Catching wind of this, Fages hastily did some writing of his own, ordering a strategically placed friend to intercept her letter before it could be sent along to Spain. After that, so far as anyone knows, they lived together in peace, until Fages resigned the governorship and in 1791 departed the scene for Mexico, where Doña Eulalia had preceded him.

Among those watching with lively interest as the *escándalo Fages* developed was Ignacio Vallejo. The affair pointed a moral for him: wasn't a man better off with a wife who had never known any place but California? Ignacio's long wait for such a helpmate ended in 1790, when Maria gave her consent and they were married. The groom was 42, the bride 14. Like most Californios, they soon began producing a numerous family. And in Mariano Guadalupe Vallejo, the eighth of their 13 children, they were to provide California with one of its most illustrious native sons.

Once upon a time, the world had firmly believed that California was an island. During the childhood years of the first Vallejo offspring, it seemed to be just that—in spirit if not in fact. Isolated and inaccessible, California lay dreaming like some Sleeping Beauty, in innocent and almost total ignorance of what went on in the rest of the world. News consisted either of intramural gossip or tedious official documents brought by supply ships from Mexico. The isolation was reinforced by a Spanish proscription against trade with foreigners, and also against admission of foreign visitors, let alone settlers, without express advance permission.

But Spain's legal wall around California had one great chink: the innate hospitality—whetted by chronic curiosity—of the Californios. Thus, in 1786, when the first non-Spanish ship ever to call at a California port put in at Monterey for supplies and water, its captain was cordially received. He was the French navigator-scientist Jean François de Galaup, Comte de la Pérouse, and he had been searching for the Northwest Passage—the mythical shortcut to the Orient that explorers had been yearning to find since the days of Columbus. La Pérouse did manage to discover the strait between Japan and Russia that bears his name, but not long afterward he perished in a shipwreck.

Six years later, in 1792, the English ship *Discovery,* commanded by George Vancouver—who had also been searching in vain for the Northwest Passage and had effectively proved that there was no such thing—came into San Francisco Bay, followed a few days later by a sister ship, the *Chatham.* The acting commander of the port, Hermenegildo Sal, made them welcome and provided stores of food, wood and water.

Vancouver then sailed down the coast to Monterey, where another of his ships, the *Daedalus,* was already anchored. Throughout their 50-day stay there, the Englishmen were entertained with balls, banquets, fandangos and lavish picnics called *meriendas.* When the visitors sailed away, their ships were well-stocked with supplies that had cost them nothing. Among other things, the *Daedalus* carried a cargo of live cattle that were the first ever delivered to Australia and that started the cattle business there.

Vancouver returned to California twice more, in 1793 and 1794. In his journal, he expansively referred to the entire Pacific Coast as "New Albion," after the literary name often given Britain. He also wrote that California's meager defenses looked as if they were "totally incapable of making any resistance against a foreign invasion" and that the Spaniards in the colony "have thrown irresistible temptations in the

Miners kneel before a priest blessing the Enriquita quick-silver (mercury) mine at New Almadén, California, while members of the gentry prepare to set off fireworks in celebration. Quicksilver was the only metal discovered in California prior to annexation by the United States.

way of strangers to trespass over their boundary."

It was curious, in view of Spain's fear of foreign encroachment, that the English had been permitted to land at all. It indicated that the reins of Spain's Empire were very slack, a situation that the great European colonizing nations might have exploited aggressively had they not soon become wholly absorbed in the Napoleonic wars. An even more curious event occurred a bit later—this one involving the Russians, whom Spanish authorities considered to be at least as great a menace to California as the British.

Through the 17th and 18th centuries Russian fur traders had steadily pushed eastward across the Siberian wilderness. In the 1740s they reached the Aleutian Islands, where an abundance of sea otters provided them with the most luxurious pelts in the world. When the supply was almost exhausted, they pressed farther east, looking for more. By 1784, there was a Russian settlement on Kodiak Island and later a more important one at Sitka, in southeastern Alaska.

After the founding of Sitka in 1799, the Russians in America experienced at least as many hardships as had the first Spaniards in California. In 1805, the Czar sent out a Russian nobleman, Nikolai Petrovich Rezanov, to inspect the Alaskan colony and to try to improve the lot of its struggling colonists. He found them dying of scurvy and starvation. Luckily, an American ship, the *Juno,* put in at Sitka. Rezanov bought not only the entire cargo of Yankee merchandise but the vessel as well. He then set sail for California to look for food to relieve the Sitka settlers.

On April 5, 1806, Rezanov steered the *Juno* through the narrow passage that later was known as the Golden Gate, mooring his ship well inside San Francisco Bay. He sent ashore his surgeon-naturalist companion, Dr. George Heinrich von Langsdorff, who held a preliminary conversation with a mission priest —in Latin, since there was no one who could understand both Russian and Spanish.

By following the letter of Spanish regulations, the Californios could have refused to cooperate. But as usual, their curiosity and generous nature carried the day. The Russians were allowed to land and revive themselves, Rezanov himself being entertained in the home of the port commander, José Darío Argüello. The visitors were impressed with the happy, well-fed lives the Californios led—the food, the wine, the gaiety and indolence, the abundant time for hunting and gambling and, above everything, the beauty and lively nature of the womenfolk.

In this Rezanov was highly susceptible, and he was particularly taken with the post commander's 16-year-old daughter, Concepción Argüello, acknowledged by all to be the prettiest young woman in California. Rezanov courted the girl assiduously, charming her with tales of court life in Saint Petersburg. Concepción —nicknamed Concha—was overcome and accepted Rezanov's proposal of marriage. The family agreed, and the mission priests promised to petition the Pope for permission for the girl to marry outside her faith. Rezanov got his shipload of flour, peas, beans and dried meat—and tried to wrest from California's governor, José Joaquin Arrillaga, a promise of future trade between the two isolated colonies. Arrillaga finally agreed to forward the request to his superiors.

Rezanov planned to deliver the supplies to Sitka and return to Russia, then travel on to Spain, to Mexico, and finally to California, where the wedding would take place. But he never completed his journey. During the long trek across Siberia, he became ill with fever and exhaustion, suffered a fall from his horse and died. Concepción heard nothing from or about her fiancé. She ignored her many suitors and finally became a sister of the Dominican order, devoting her life to charity and teaching. She died in a convent in 1857 at the age of 66.

The Rezanov-Argüello affair was to become one of the most famous in the romantic annals of California. Apparently, Concepción did not learn what had hap-

---

THE FRANCISCANS' PROGRESS REPORT FOR 1803

A meticulous 1803 accounting by Father Estévan Tapis, president of the Franciscan missionaries, summarizes the state of the 18 missions thus far established in California. The left-hand column lists the missions in geographic order from San Diego to San Francisco, with the date of their founding as well as the distance from the preceding mission. Across the page are entries for cumulative baptisms, marriages and deaths; current neophyte population; numbers of cattle, sheep, goats, pigs, mares, other horses, mules; and output of wheat, barley, corn, beans, *garbanzos,* peas, lentils, oats (the two figures indicate amounts planted and harvested). The report had to be done yearly and in triplicate with copies to Franciscan headquarters in Mexico City, the order's California archives and the Spanish governor.

Estado de las Misiones de la Nueva California sacado de los Informes de sus Misioneros en fin de Diciembre del año 1803.

Nombres de las Misiones, sus Edades, Alturas de Polo, y sus Distancias	Bautismos	Casamientos	Difuntos	Existentes	Ganado Mayor	Idem de Lana	Idem de Pelo	Idem de Cerda	Yeguas y Crias	Caballos Mansos	Bestias Mulares
Sn Diego, 16 de Julio de 69, 32 gr 42 m. Dista de ... de la antigua Calif. 23 leguas.	3085	730	1321	1567	5000	5000	000	15	730	100	45
Sn Luis Rey de Francia, 13 de Junio de 98, 33 gr 3 m. Dista de la antec. 13 y m. leguas.	670	135	132	615	2200	5400	000	000	190	66	23
Sn Juan Capistrano, 1 de Nov. de 76, 33 gr 26 m. Dista de la antec. 12 y m. leguas.	2245	516	1118	1027	9124	15345	000	000	600	190	58
Sn Gabriel, 8 de Sept. de 71, 34 gr 10 m. Dista de la antecedente 16 leguas.	3605	815	2251	1123	9500	12000	200	300	1000	130	75
Sn Fernando, 8 de Sept. de 97, 34 gr 16 m. Dista de la antec. 9 leguas.	1111	233	230	820	1000	2200	000	130	150	110	60
Sn Buenaventura, 31 de Marzo de 82, 34 gr 36 m. Dista de la anteced. 22 leguas.	1665	353	781	1075	15340	5400	20	200	1730	270	126
Sta Barbara, 4 de Diciembre de 86, 34 gr 42 m. Dista de la antec. 6 leguas.	3102	694	1133	1792	2260	11221	000	000	439	201	67
Purisima Concep., 8 de Diciembre de 87, 35 gr. Dista de la antecedente 20 leguas.	2033	473	610	1436	3230	5400	000	14	240	66	37
Sn Luis Obpo, 1 de Septiembre de 72, 35 gr 36 m. Dista de la antecedente 12 leguas.	2003	542	1033	919	5400	6000	000	100	800	200	70
Sn Miguel, 25 de Julio de 97, 35 gr 44 m. Dista de la antec. 13 leguas.	1077	243	225	908	409	3223	000	52	257	85	29
Sn Antonio de Padua, 14 de Julio de 71, 36 gr 30 m. Dista de la anteced. 13 leguas.	2914	695	1609	1156	2912	6151	000	30	504	150	44
Soledad, 9 de Octubre de 91, 36 gr 36 m. Dista de la antecedente 11 leguas.	944	245	442	627	1150	5000	000	30	550	120	40
Sn Carlos, 3 de Junio de 70, 36 gr 44 m. Dista de la antecedente 15 leguas.	2452	653	1559	591	1600	6000	000	000	750	170	36
Sn Juan Bautista, 24 de Junio de 97, 36 gr 56 m. Dista de la antec. 12 leguas.	1278	256	287	1017	1036	4660	000	22	500	40	8
Sta Cruz, 28 de Agosto de 91, 37 gr. Dista de la antec. por la costa, fuera del camino de Sta Clara, 13 leguas.	1062	317	625	437	1457	3512	000	117	2002	67	48
Sta Clara, 18 de En. de 77, 37 gr 20 m. Dista de la antec. atravesando la sierra, 11 leguas.	4544	1060	3119	1271	5000	7000	000	000	2000	200	30
Sn Jose, 11 de Jun. de 97, 37 gr 30 m. Dista de la antec. al Norte del camino de Sn Franco, 7 leguas.	1073	292	354	729	900	4600	000	000	257	70	8
N.P.S. Francisco, 9 de Oct. de 76, 37 gr 56 m. Dista de la antec. 7 leguas, y de Sta Clara, 15.	2878	864	1695	1059	9240	10250	000	000	600	200	30
Totales	37976	9174	18584	18185	77574	117362	220	1010	13306	2455	467

Son 210 leguas desde Sn Diego hasta Sn Franco por la derecera, de la que se desvian las Misiones de Sta Cruz y Sn Jose en sus anotadas Distancias.

Total de Siembras .... 2784 f. 8 alm.

Total de Cosechas ..... 48003 f. 5 alm.

Fr. Estevan Tapis

Self-contained settlements from a brilliant master plan

If Spanish civil officials had only been half so well organized as the Franciscan mission builders, California might still be a jewel in Spain's crown. At their peak, the Franciscans numbered only 38 padres, but they worked from a brilliantly thought-out master plan.

They assumed that it would take at least 10 years from the founding of a mission to change pagan Indians into proper Christian workers. As start-up money, every new mission received a contribution from a special fund for the purchase of bells, vestments, seeds, tools and other necessities. Established missions were expected to help out with grain, cuttings, breeding stock, fowl, wine and anything else that could be spared. If all went well, the mission developed by stages into a thriving complex like the one below.

This particular success story, Santa Bárbara, got its start on December 4, 1786, when Father Fermín de Lasuén blessed the site and, with the help of two companion padres, erected a temporary chapel and some rude dwellings of logs and boughs. As soon as the makeshift buildings were up, the Franciscans began proselyting the local Chumash Indians, smoothing the process with gifts of glass beads, clothing, blankets and food. Once an Indian agreed to convert to Catholicism, he was not allowed to leave the mission grounds without permission; a small detachment of soldiers, armed with muskets, enforced the edict.

The padres soon had their charges tilling fields and replacing temporary structures with permanent ones. Over the years, the residents repeatedly expanded and upgraded the compound into a self-sufficient little world of living quarters, workshops and storage areas. Rising above all this was the mission church, which was not completed in its final form until 1833, nearly 50 years after the mission's founding. On first seeing it, a 19th Century French visitor to California was awed by the Franciscans' ability to create such an imposing structure "in a wilderness land so far from European refinements."

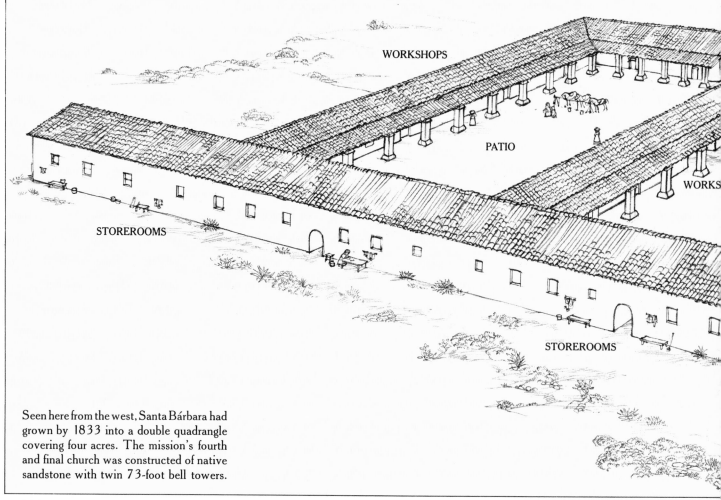

WORKSHOPS

PATIO

WORKS

STOREROOMS

STOREROOMS

Seen here from the west, Santa Bárbara had grown by 1833 into a double quadrangle covering four acres. The mission's fourth and final church was constructed of native sandstone with twin 73-foot bell towers.

Viewed from the east, as the mission appeared in 1787, Santa Bárbara's first thatched church was flanked by a kitchen, storerooms, and stockaded quarters for the priests, servants and single Indian women.

A vantage from the south in 1800 shows tile-roofed adobe mission buildings arranged in a quadrangle. Most neophytes still occupied their traditional domelike dwellings of grass woven around a skeleton of poles.

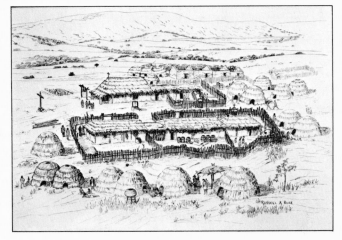

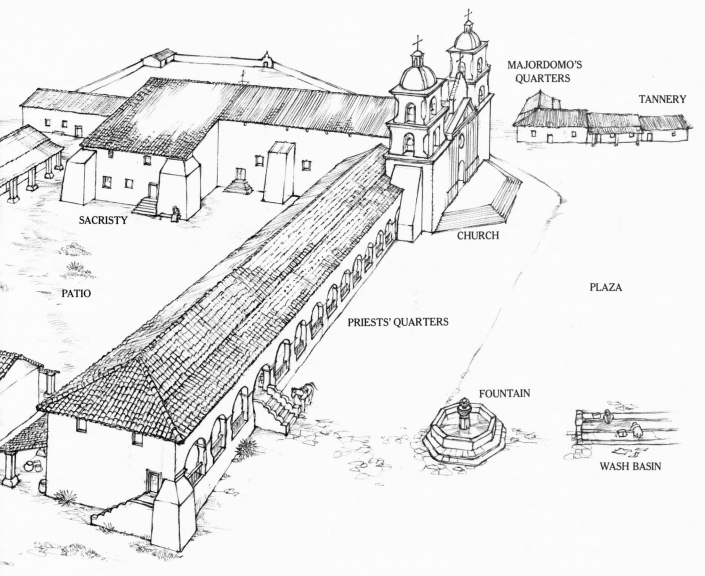

MAJORDOMO'S
QUARTERS

TANNERY

SACRISTY

CHURCH

PATIO

PLAZA

PRIESTS' QUARTERS

FOUNTAIN

WASH BASIN

pened to her lover until 1842, when Sir George Simpson of the Hudson's Bay Company visited Monterey. A poem by Bret Harte tells how, during a banquet for the English visitor, someone mentioned Rezanov.

Quickly then cried Sir George Simpson:
"Speak no ill of him, I pray!
He is dead. He died, poor fellow, forty years
  ago this day.
Left a sweetheart, too, they tell me. Married, I
  suppose, of course!
Lives she yet?" A deathlike silence fell on
  banquet, guests, and hall,
And a trembling figure rising fixed the
  awestruck gaze of all.
Two black eyes in darkened orbits gleamed
  beneath the nun's white hood;
Black serge hid the wasted figure, bowed and
  stricken where it stood.
"Lives she yet?" Sir George repeated. All were
  hushed as Concha drew
Closer yet her nun's attire. "Señor, pardon, she
  died, too!"

Not long after Rezanov's visit to California, Don Ignacio Vallejo's wife, the former María Antonia Lugo, gave birth in Monterey to their eighth child and fourth son, Mariano Guadalupe. The date was July 7, 1808. Monterey and California were still Spanish, and still so isolated that not only could Concepción Argüello go for years without news of her lover, but the colony could remain ignorant of revolutionary rumblings in Spain's Empire.

What little political sentiment existed in California was largely royalist. Mexico's struggle for independence from Spain excited no particular interest when it began in 1810; it was too remote. The only contact that Monterey — and the Vallejos — had with the war was the raid of a French adventurer, Hippolyte de Bouchard, and his two-ship "fleet" of the so-called Republic of Buenos Aires, a new splinter from the shattered Empire of Spain.

Bouchard and his men claimed to be waging a patriot's war against the King of Spain and his property, but they behaved like plundering privateers. When the two ships showed up at Monterey on November 20, 1818, Ignacio and his eldest son, José, stayed to fight

Two tableaus, done by an Indian in a naïve but vivid style, dramatize Pilate's judgment of Christ and the journey to Calvary. Along with 12 other

the invaders, while the younger children and their mother fled inland with most other residents of the town. The local forces were overwhelmed and Monterey sacked and burned, along with a few nearby ranchos. (The Californios had one moment of glory when *vaqueros* put three of the pirates out of commission by skillfully lassoing them.) When the raiders finally moved on, Monterey had to be rebuilt, and not until the following April were all its inhabitants once more at home and able to resume a normal life.

California at this period was idyllically pastoral, a paradise of beauty and abundance. The seeds and cuttings brought in by the missionary priests had multiplied into a cornucopian plenty. More important, cattle flourished with almost no attention. Although there were sheep and pigs (the Californios seldom ate pork, but raised swine for the fat used in making soap), California was primarily cattle country. The livestock roamed the open range and were rounded up by the hard-riding *vaqueros* twice a year — in spring for branding of calves, and again from July to October for slaughter.

The slaughter, or *matanza,* was solely for home needs in the early years of the province. Cattle sup-

plied beef to be eaten fresh or dried for future use; hides for shoes, lariats and outerwear; cooking fat; and tallow for candles and soapmaking. Only a few hundred pounds of the carcass could be used. The remainder was left where it had been killed, to be picked clean by coyotes, vultures and bears. In areas where wood was scarce, the bones and skulls would sometimes be gathered up later and made into corral fences, with the horned skulls at the top. Even so, most ranchos were littered with bones.

Anyone could become a rancher. Range land was readily available, and seed cows and a bull or two could be borrowed from a mission or an established rancher, with the debt to be repaid as soon as the new herd was thriving. Travelers needing meat were expected to help themselves, leaving the hide on the remote chance the owner might find it and want it. Later, after annexation by the United States, many Californios were astonished that such free use of livestock was regarded as theft under the new country's law.

Horses brought in by the Spaniards had run wild and multiplied, and they were as plentiful as the cattle. The best specimens were culled from the wild herds

Stations of the Cross, they were executed at Mission San Fernando about 1800 and may have been the first neophyte paintings in California.

and broken to saddle, for California life was to a great extent conducted on horseback. The Californios—men, women and children—were seldom without their favorite steeds and rarely went anywhere afoot. A long trip involved several overnight stops at ranchos along the way. At each halt, the rider would be given a fresh mount for the following day, and on the return trip, the horses would be returned to their owners.

Despite the often rough-and-ready conditions typical of any frontier, a certain amount of Spanish *punctilio* survived. Rigid obedience and deference to one's elders were expected of young people; a youth did not begin shaving until given permission by his father, usually at about the age of 21. Instead of being addressed as *ciudadano*, or citizen—the approved practice in Mexico after it became a republic—prominent Californios continued to be called Don or Doña, indicating distinction, achievement or important antecedents.

Social activity was limited by distances and the difficulty of travel—but it was intensified as well. Once arrived at the scene of a wedding or holiday celebration, the traveler was expected to stay for a while, and the celebrations usually went on for several days and nights. Food and drink were offered in staggering quantities: wine and fruit from the nearest mission, olives from San Diego, pastries and wheat bread from another mission, slabs of beef roasted on iron spits over beds of live-oak coals. (Milk, butter and cheese were rare, however, because it was so difficult to milk the wild cows, and sweets were limited because of the chronic shortage of sugar.) Indian musicians, trained to play the guitar and violin by mission fathers, usually provided the music for dancing the *jarabe, jota, son, contradanza* and waltz.

William Heath Davis, an American, described one such exuberant occasion in his memoirs. "In November, 1838," recalled Davis, "I was a guest at the wedding party given at the marriage of Don José Martinez to the daughter of Don Ignacio Peralta, which lasted about a week, dancing being kept up all the night with a company of at least one hundred men and women from the adjoining ranchos, about three hours after daylight being given to sleep, after which picnics in the woods were held during the forenoon, and the afternoon was devoted to bullfighting. This program was continued for a week, when I had become so exhausted

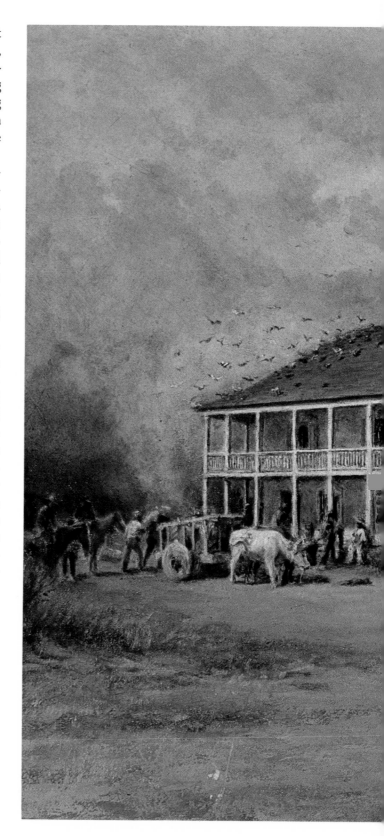

The mansion of adobe that American emigrant Alpheus Thompson built in 1835 for his Spanish bride, Francisca Carrillo, was the envy of Santa Bárbara. By the end of Mexican rule, many rich Californians had discarded the low rancho dwellings of earlier days for roomy two-story homes.

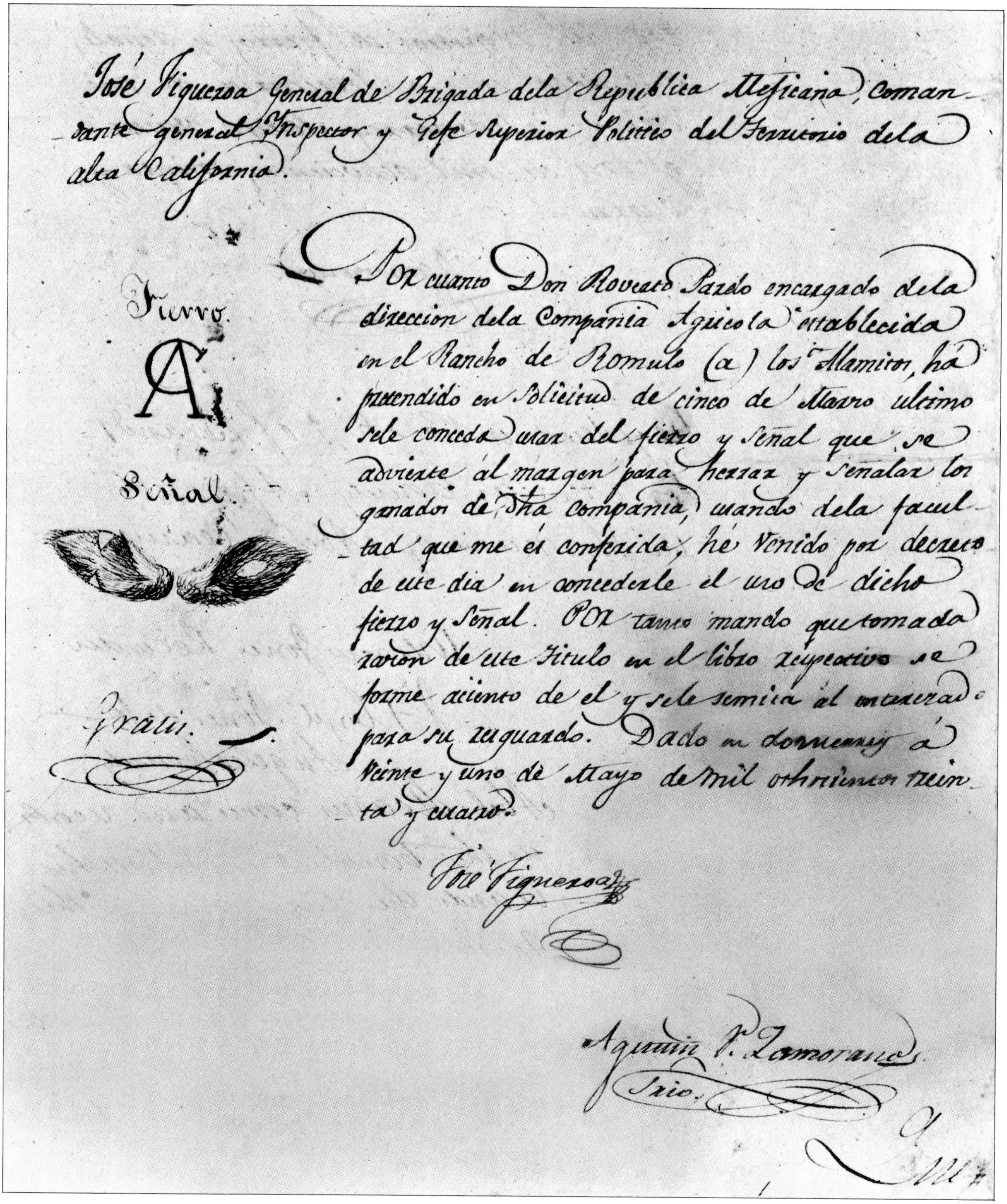

José Figueroa General de Brigada dela Republica Mexicana, coman-
dante general Inspector y Gefe superior politico del territorio dela
alta California.

Fierro.

A

Señal.

Gratis.

Por cuanto Don Rosendo Pardo encargado dela
direccion dela Compañia Agricola establecida
en el Rancho de Romulo (a) los Alamitos, ha
pretendido en solicitud de cinco de Marzo ultimo
sele conceda usar del fierro y señal que se
advierte al margen para herrar y señalar los
ganados de dha compañia, usando dela facul-
tad que me es conferida, he venido por decreto
de este dia en concederle el uso de dicho
fierro y señal. Por tanto mando que tomada
razon de este Titulo en el libro respectivo se
forme asiento de el y sele sirva al interesado
para su resguardo. Dado en Monterey á
veinte y uno de Mayo de Mil ochocientos trein-
ta y cuatro.

José Figueroa

Agustin V. Zamorano
Srio.

for want of regular sleep that I was glad to escape.

"During this festivity, Don José Martinez, who was a wonderful horseman, performed some feats which astonished me. For instance, while riding at the greatest speed he leaned over his saddle to one side as he swept along and picked up from the ground a small coin, which had been put there to try his skill, and then went on without slackening his speed."

Thanks to the Californios' urge to show off their riding skill, bullfighting was "far different from the brutal exhibitions of Spain and Mexico," according to one eyewitness. The object of the exercise was not to kill the bull but to tire him into panting immobility. Meanwhile, as the horseman repeatedly waved his red cloak, then dodged out of the way of the charging bull, his dexterity and panache would evoke cries of admiration and a mad fluttering of handkerchiefs from the pretty señoritas watching on the sidelines.

Not that the Californios shrank from a bloody spectacle: they relished a cockfight, and another of their favorite diversions was to chain a wild bull and a grizzly bear together and goad them into fighting to the death. Hunting, too, was a passion, especially since the Californios could shoot game from astride their beloved horses. By the same token, fishing held little appeal because it had to be done afoot. An American visitor in the mid-1840s joked: "If they could go to sea on their horses and fish from their saddles, they would often be seen dashing through the surf; but to sit quietly in a boat is entirely too tame a business."

One thing notably lacking in this Spanish Garden of Eden was book learning; as everywhere on the frontier, even literacy was rare. Mariano Guadalupe Vallejo was more fortunate than most; at seven he began attending a class taught by a bad-tempered old soldier. The young scholars were made to memorize religious

tracts, to copy out customs-house documents in a careful hand, and to endure the sting of a lash when they stepped out of line.

A more palatable kind of enlightenment appeared with the advent of the last Spanish governor, Pablo Vicente de Sola, who served from 1815 to 1822. Sola first tried, unsuccessfully, to establish a good school for Monterey. Failing that, he interested himself in the community's brighter boys, among them Mariano, Juan Bautista Alvarado and José Castro, all about the same age and all to become famous in California. He gave them books to read, including *Don Quixote,* lent them newspapers and journals from abroad and encouraged them to broaden their horizons.

Still another opportunity for an intelligent, ambitious lad developed when the first mercantile establishment in California opened in Monterey in 1822. One of its principals was William Edward Petty Hartnell, a well-educated and cultured Englishman who was fluent in Spanish and eager to share his learning. Under his direction, Mariano and the other young men of the area learned English, French and Latin, and they made free use of the books in Hartnell's personal library. In return, they did odd jobs around the store, and Mariano became a kind of junior clerk with a chance to acquire some arithmetic and bookkeeping skills.

Mariano Vallejo's training was put to good use when he served as secretary to Luis Argüello, brother of the unhappy Concepción and California's first governor under Mexican rule. Mexico had achieved its independence from Spain in February 1821, but news of the event reached California only the following year and at first was greeted with disbelief. Argüello finally took office in November 1822. One of young Vallejo's first duties as his secretary was to draw up articles transferring California's allegiance to Mexico.

With independence from Spain, the old Crown regulations against foreigners were relaxed. Foreign-flag vessels brought trading goods from China, from England and from the United States. California's tremendous surplus of cattle products was quickly recognized as a profitable export, readily exchangeable for foreign merchandise. The heretofore-casual slaughter of cattle was put on a more systematic basis. At a *matanza,* the Indians would carefully cut away the fat from the freshly killed beef carcass, separating the fat just under the

THE SPECIAL MARKS OF RANCHO LOS ALAMITOS

To protect his ownership of free-roaming livestock, a California ranchero designed unique brands and submitted them to the provincial Governor for approval. In the illustrated branding permit at left, Governor José Figueroa grants a *fierro* (rump brand) and a *señal* (ear-notching pattern) to Don Roberto Pardo at Rancho los Alamitos in southern California. A third mark called a *venta* — not shown — was emblazoned on the animal's shoulder when it changed hands.

A hearty fare based on corn, meat and spices

"The dawn is breaking. Let us all sing 'Ave Maria.'" With that call to song and prayer, the owner of a California estate would invite his household to partake of a simple yet nourishing breakfast: ground-corn porridge served with milk and accompanied by a cup of hot chocolate or coffee. Both the corn and the choc- olate were native to the New World, as were such additional staples of the California cuisine as beans, pumpkins, chilies and tomatoes. But the Californians also enriched their daily diet by transplanting the common European grains and a wide variety of fruit trees — and this range of makings helped to ensure meals that were entirely wor- thy of the sunny paradise on the west coast of North America.

The cooks, usually Indian women, were charged with preparing three full meals and two snacks (mid-morning and mid-afternoon) each day; some of the recipes they followed appear in modernized form opposite. Except for breakfast, every meal featured the Cal-

Making flour for tortillas, the cook at a California rancho grinds parboiled corn kernels between a heavy stone roller and a slab.

ifornians' staff of life, the tortilla — a flat pancake made of corn flour. At noon and in the evening, the main dishes were likely to be hearty beef stews (though game abounded, the Californians disliked it). The meat was placed in copper kettles, seasoned with chilies and wild herbs, then simmered for hours over an open hearth. So spicy were such dishes that a diner might pay his compliments with the exclamation: "Ah, this broth is capable of raising the dead!"

Nixtamal (Parboiled Corn)

1 gallon water	2 quarts (8 cups)
1/3 cup unslaked lime	whole dry corn (maize)

Mix the water and lime in a galvanized kettle and stir the combination with a wooden spoon. Add the corn kernels and stir until the mixture no longer effervesces. Bring to a boil, then lower the heat to a simmer. Stirring frequently, cook for one hour, then drain the corn and wash the kernels in cold water until all traces of lime taste are removed. Rub the kernels between your hands until they are free of their hulls. The result is a mixture that is very much like hominy, which can now be ground into masa, or moist corn dough. Place one cup of *nixtamal* in a blender or food processor, and reduce it to a medium-fine flour. Then add just enough water to keep the mixture moist. Cover with a damp cloth until used. This recipe makes about two dozen tortillas.

Tortillas de Maiz (Corn Tortillas)

Break off a small piece of masa and form it into a two-inch ball. Place this ball on a cloth-covered board. Press and pat round and round from the center to the circumference with your fingertips, until the cake is thin and six inches in diameter. Bake both sides on a hot, ungreased griddle until slightly brown and blistered.

Puchero (A Stew)

1 sun-dried beef or veal knuckle bone	3 dried tomatoes
1/2 teaspoon pepper	2 green chili peppers
2 teaspoons salt	1 pound green string beans tied in bunches
2 pounds cut-up veal	
2 pounds cut-up beef	1 bundle turnip leaves
3 ears corn	3 small green pumpkins or summer squash
3 sweet potatoes	
1 cup *garbanzos* (chick-peas)	
2 whole onions	1 hard apple
	1 hard pear

Cover the knuckle bone and meat with cold water. Add the pepper and salt. Bring to a boil and skim scum from the water. Place all the vegetables and fruit over the meat in the order listed, the corn at the very bottom, the pear at the top. Simmer for three hours. Do not stir. To serve, place the vegetables and fruit on one platter, meat on a second platter and broth in a tureen. Serves 12.

Sopa de Carne Seca y Arroz (Jerky-and-Rice Soup)

1 pound dried beef	1 green chili pepper
1 tablespoon fat	1 onion
1/2 cup rice	1/2 teaspoon salt
1 ripe tomato	Pepper

Roast the beef at 400° for one hour to soften the dried meat. Then pound it on a wooden block until it shreds. Heat the fat in a kettle and fry the rice, tomato, chili and onion. Season. Add meat, cover with one quart boiling water and simmer 15 minutes or until rice is cooked. Serves six.

Enchiladas

1 cup black olives, pitted	6 tablespoons fat
	1/2 clove garlic
1 tablespoon olive oil	1 tablespoon vinegar
1 teaspoon salt	12 corn tortillas
12 red chili peppers	1/2 pound white cheese, grated
3 tablespoons toasted bread crumbs	
	1 large onion, minced

Mix the onion with olive oil and salt. Wipe the chilies; stem them; then slit and remove seed veins and seeds, and boil until pulp separates from hulls, producing a purée. Continue simmering. Brown crumbs in 2 tablespoons of fat in a skillet; stir in mashed garlic and vinegar. Add to chili purée and simmer 20 minutes. In another skillet, heat 4 tablespoons of fat, and lightly fry tortillas one at a time. Immerse each in chili sauce, place on a warm platter and fill with cheese, onion and olives. Fold in thirds. When all tortillas are filled, cover with the remaining chili sauce, cheese, onion and olives. Place in an oven to keep warm. Serves six.

Champurrado (A Thick Chocolate)

6 teaspoons grated chocolate	1/2 cup masa
	2 eggs, well beaten
6 teaspoons sugar	2 teaspoons vanilla
1 cup hot water	Dash of cinnamon
5 cups milk, scalded	

In a double boiler, combine the chocolate and sugar. Add the hot water slowly, stirring until a smooth paste is formed. Add the milk, a little at a time, then the masa, which has been thinned with a little of the hot liquid. Before serving, fold in the eggs, vanilla and cinnamon. Serves four to six.

hide, called *manteca* (lard), from the interior fat, called *sebo* (tallow). Both were then tried out in iron pots bartered from whaling ships. The higher grade *manteca* was generally saved for domestic use, the Californios preferring it to the lard obtained from swine. The *sebo* was almost all for export. After rendering, it was poured into *botas*, or bags sewed from fresh cattle hides. In trade, the tallow brought six cents per pound, and from 75 to 100 pounds was obtained from each carcass. Hides brought from one dollar to $2.50 apiece; American sailors called them "California banknotes."

It was a malodorous business. Even the swarms of vultures, coyotes and other scavengers could not keep up with the unwanted meat, and the killing grounds could be smelled for miles around. At the ports, the warehouses used for storing skins that were waiting to be shipped retained their stench for many years after they had fallen into disuse.

Incoming ships would arrange their merchandise on deck, and the Californios would come aboard to choose what they wanted in exchange for their hides and tallow. The array generally covered the full gamut of human needs and desires: silks, satins, woolens, jewelry, liquors, hardware, pins and needles, crockery, tinware, cutlery, spices, sugar, tea, coffee. Richard Henry Dana, a young American seaman who arrived aboard the *Alert* in 1835, observed uncharitably in his book *Two Years before the Mast:* "The Californians are an idle, thriftless people, and can make nothing for themselves. The country abounds in grapes, yet they buy bad wine made in Boston; and buy shoes (as like as not, made of their own hides which have been carried twice round Cape Horn) at three and four dollars. Things sell at an advance of nearly three hundred percent upon the Boston prices."

Dana frequently rowed the California customers out to the ship and back to shore again, and the New England Puritan in him could be extremely disapproving: "The fondness for dress among the women is excessive and is often the ruin of them," wrote Dana. "A present of a fine mantle, or of a necklace or pair of earrings, gains the favor of the greater part of them. Nothing is more common than to see a woman living in a house of only two rooms, and the ground for a floor, dressed in spangled satin shoes, silk gown, high comb, and gilt, if not gold, earrings and necklace. They

used to spend whole days aboard our vessel, examining the fine clothes and ornaments."

Such righteousness was the exception, however, and a great many Yankee mariners found the girls of California irresistible. Henry Delano Fitch, an American skipper from New Bedford, eloped with a beautiful daughter of the wealthy Carrillo family of San Diego, the family into which Mariano Guadalupe Vallejo would himself marry within a few years *(page 183)*. Before long, every comely señorita was boasting that she would wed a blue-eyed man. Encarnación Vallejo, one of Mariano's sisters, was wooed and won by Captain John Roger Cooper, who arrived in California in 1823 as master of the Boston schooner *Rover,* carrying a cargo of goods from China. Following the custom among these seaborne romantic invaders, Cooper adopted the Catholic faith, was rebaptized Juan Bautista, and became a Mexican citizen.

Meanwhile, the Yankees had begun arriving overland—a feat that astonished the Californios. On November 27, 1826, Jedediah Smith and a party of fellow fur trappers from the Rockies showed up at the San Gabriel mission. Searching for beaver pelts, Smith and his men had wandered through what he called "Starvation Country"—southern Utah, northwestern Arizona and the Mojave Desert of southern California. His hosts concealed their uneasy surprise beneath the usual generous hospitality. One of Smith's trail-worn companions, Harrison Rogers, was dazzled by their reception in what seemed to be the Promised Land.

The Californios, wrote Rogers in his diary, "all appear to be gentlemen of the first class both in manners and habits. There was a wedding and Mr. S. and myself invited. Mr. S. and I endeavored to apologize, being very dirty and not in a position to shift our clothing, but no excuse would be taken, we must be present. They treat us as gentlemen in every sense, although our apparel is so indifferent. I make a very grotesque appearance when seated at table amongst the dandys with their ruffles, silks, and broad cloths."

Smith's presence in California was illegal, of course, for he carried no passport. Because the beaver-trapping trade was all but unknown to the Californios, he was described in official records as "a fisherman." When Smith asked for spare horses and permission to travel wherever he pleased, the California governor, José

Echeandía, conceived a deep mistrust of his intentions and placed him under house arrest in San Diego. He was finally released on condition that he and his men leave California at once by the way they had come.

Instead, he spent the winter hunting and trapping in the San Joaquin Valley. In the spring, he blazed a new route home, traveling across the Sierra Nevada and the Great Salt Lake basin. After a brief restorative pause, he headed west again in 1827 along his Mojave Desert route. At his reappearance, the angered and alarmed Californios clapped him in jail. On this occasion, as previously, the persuasiveness of American ship captains brought about his release—contingent upon his promise to leave immediately and forever. Again Smith broke his word, camping in the Sacramento valley before leaving California for Oregon.

Three years later, Smith was murdered by Comanches on the Cimarron River in New Mexico. He was only 32 but had already carved a deep gash in history. In a letter written to explorer William Clark and later reprinted in a St. Louis newspaper, he had described California as a land once "veiled in obscurity, and unknown to the citizens of the U. States." Now California had been forever breached. Smith's own observations on the Sacramento valley suggest how potent was the lure: "The soil is good and the climate pleasant. A country rather calculated to expand than restrain the energies of man. A country where the Creator has scattered a more than ordinary Share of his bounties." The Americans soon to pour into California over the trails he had opened would discover that it was all true.

Like his father and elder brother before him, Mariano Guadalupe Vallejo had decided to become a soldier. In 1823, at the age of 15, he petitioned to be enrolled as a cadet in the presidial company at Monterey. Mariano thus launched himself on adult life and responsibilities at almost the same time California was entering its Mexican period. The years ahead would be marked by extreme political confusion.

Many factors contributed to the disarray. At the base of it was a strong disposition of the Californios toward home rule and a distaste for the governors, administrative apparatus and legal restrictions imposed by faraway Mexico. Local resentment of centralist tendencies on the part of the Mexican government was as strong in California as it was in Texas and elsewhere in the Southwest. In addition, there were regional rivalries for political supremacy within California, between San Diego and Los Angeles in the south and Monterey and San Francisco in the north. On top of this were the personal ambitions of many California leaders—the sort of ambitions that are the inevitable by-product of a governmental vacuum or near vacuum.

As a result, during much of the period from the establishment of Iturbide's independent Mexican "empire" in 1821 to the Treaty of Guadalupe Hidalgo in 1848, California existed in a virtual state of civil war. Rival factions showed a commendable tendency not to spill one another's blood, however, and warred mainly with speeches and pronunciamentos. The succession of governors, some locally chosen, some sent from Mexico, was dizzying. The provincial capital switched from north to south to north and back south again.

The Indians, too, were restless. In 1829, soon after the 20-year-old Vallejo was made ensign of the San Francisco presidio, he was ordered to take the field at the head of an "army" of 107 men to put down a rebellion led by a native named Estanislao.

Estanislao had been born and educated at the San José mission, where he showed so much promise of leadership that Father Narciso Durán, the missions' president, appointed him alcalde. But during the course of visits to neighboring native villages, Estanislao had conceived the burning desire to lead a revolt against the white man. In late 1827, he deserted his mission and joined a marauding band of ex-neophytes and pagan Indians that hid out in the San Joaquin Valley. By the next year Estanislao had gathered together some 40,000 Mariposa Indians and set them to raiding and terrorizing the countryside.

Vallejo, not yet 21 in 1829, was hardly an experienced Indian-fighter, but he had just led a campaign in the Tulares, a marshy section of the San Joaquin Valley, where his 35-man troop had killed 48 Indians without suffering a single casualty. For the mission against Estanislao, he bolstered his 107-man force with a piece of heavy artillery.

Crossing the San Joaquin River on rafts, Vallejo's men approached the site where the Indians were entrenched: a dense woods at the edge of the Lasqui-

Making the rounds on horseback, the ranchero host of a grandly scaled fiesta near Santa Bárbara doffs his sombrero to a group of picnicking señoras and señoritas. The guests at such fiestas enjoyed a succession of entertainments — like the rodeo in the background — that sometimes lasted a week.

simes (later the Stanislaus) River. They were greeted with a murderous hail of arrows. Realizing that the forest was impenetrable, Vallejo ordered it set afire, meanwhile positioning his soldiers and the artillery piece on the riverbank opposite. The flames forced some of Estanislao's warriors to the river's edge, within range of the Californios' guns; exactly how many were killed could not be determined since the Indians carried off their dead and wounded under cover of darkness.

Later, Vallejo pressed the attack into the burned-out woods — where he discovered abandoned trenches and defensive barricades planned with great cunning — and on through chapparal thickets to a second stronghold. On the evening of the third day, when part of Estanislao's forces seemed to be cornered in a new stretch of woodland, word raced through Vallejo's camp that the Indians were escaping by swimming downriver. After a vigorous pursuit, the Californios found they had been duped: they were chasing bundles of grass, tied together to resemble swimmers floating downstream in the twilight. Meanwhile, the Indians had escaped in the opposite direction.

By the fourth day, Vallejo's forces had exhausted their ammunition and provisions and were obliged to withdraw. But they had effectively dispersed the raiders, capturing 300 Indians and 18 horses, and no doubt inflicting heavy casualties. On their own side, they had suffered 13 casualties but no deaths. Despite the withdrawal, the revolt was broken.

In the autumn of that year, trouble erupted from another quarter. Vallejo was serving as commandant of the Monterey presidio in November when the post's garrison revolted under the leadership of a former convict, Joaquin Solis. Owing to the dilatoriness of the Mexican government, the soldiers had long gone without pay. Vallejo and the other officers were thrown into the presidial dungeon for three days by the mutineers, and Vallejo was released only on condition that he leave Monterey immediately aboard a ship sailing for San Diego.

His enforced visit to that city had a most happy result: he met and fell in love with the beautiful Francisca Benicia Carrillo, "a spinster of fifteen years of age of honorable family," as she was described in subsequent correspondence. As an army officer, Vallejo was required to secure the permission of the Ministry of War in Mexico City before marrying. A messenger was sent off on burro-back to carry Vallejo's petition. By the time the authorities had duly considered the request and granted their consent, 18 months had elapsed and Señorita Carrillo had become almost 17 — considered a somewhat advanced age for marriage in Mexican California. It was, nevertheless, both a happy and productive union. There were 16 children, although several died in childhood. Vallejo gave some of his sons literary names: Andrónico (for Shakespeare's *Titus Andronicus*), Plutarco (for Plutarch), Platón (for Plato). Later, there was also to be a Napoleon. Most of the children were born in the Vallejos' home at Sonoma, on California's northern frontier.

What had brought Vallejo to the north was a long-overdue concern with the Russians, whose interest in California had been only temporarily halted by the death of Rezanov, the fiancé of Concepción Argüello. In 1812, the Russians, hoping to find both sea otters and a source of food for their outpost at Sitka, had moved south from Alaska to California coastal land they had purchased from Indians for three blankets, three pairs of trousers, two axes, three hoes and an assortment of beads. They established Fort Ross about 100 miles north of the Golden Gate, and founded a second settlement at Bodega Bay, 25 miles closer.

This peaceful invasion had caused great concern in Spain and, later, in Mexico. While powerless to evict the Russians, the Mexican government had decided that California should be settled and colonized as far north as the 42nd parallel (the present boundary between California and Oregon). Toward that ambitious end, two missions had been founded. One of them, San Francisco Solano, established 40 miles north of San Francisco Bay in 1823, was to be the last of the Franciscan missions in California. Little else had been done about securing the northern wilderness.

When José Figueroa, the greatest of California's Mexican governors, assumed office in 1833, the Russian problem was high on his agenda. Figueroa dispatched Vallejo, whom he had quickly grown to like and trust, on an inspection tour of the area. Vallejo was to visit Fort Ross and select a site for nearby Mexican colonies that might serve as buffers against any further Russian encroachment. The 24-year-old ensign was graciously received by the Russians and took a careful look at what they possessed. He noted the shipyard, the grist mills, the tannery, the carpentry and blacksmith shops, the armory, and the gun emplacements in the wooden fortress. He recorded that they had 800 cattle, 700 horses, 2,000 sheep, 400 fruit trees, 700 vines and a total population of about 300. Only 70 of the inhabitants were Russians; the remainder were either California Indians or Aleut hunters brought down from Alaska.

Vallejo also reported back to Figueroa that the Russians apparently planned to expand their holdings inland. The upshot of this was that Figueroa appointed Vallejo as Military Commander and Director of Colonization of the Northern Frontier. He had already named the young soldier as administrator to supervise the secularization of the San Francisco Solano mission; by an 1833 order of the Mexican Congress, all the missions in the California chain were to be divested of Franciscan control immediately.

It had always been the practice in New Spain to secularize missions automatically after a period of 10 years; that meant replacing the friars with ordinary parish priests and turning over mission lands and property to the Indians—for whom, by law, they had been held in trust until such time as the Indians were Hispanicized and could manage successfully on their own. But in California, many decades had gone by without secularization, and the Indians as a whole seemed to be more dependent, not less, on the missionaries. Meanwhile, the missionaries' virtual monopoly of Indian labor, their control of the vast bulk of the good land, and their resistance to new land grants and new settlers had built up acute economic pressures—and an often bitter resentment among the laity.

Governor Figueroa, recognizing that immediate secularization could produce chaos, developed a plan to spread the process over three years. Ten of the missions were secularized in 1834, six more in 1835 and the last five in 1836.

San Francisco Solano, whose secularization Vallejo was to direct, was among the first group of 10 removed from Franciscan authority on August 9, 1834. Meanwhile, beginning in 1833, Vallejo had instituted a series of colonizing efforts at settlements called Petaluma, Santa Rosa and Santa Ana y Farias. Although the first two were to become established California

towns, none was very successful at the outset. Missionary priests, trying to stake out as much territory as possible before the decree went into effect, had established prior claims to land that would have been ideal for colonization. And various Indian tribes persistently harassed the new settlers, stealing livestock and burning fields. Vallejo persevered, however, and on property that had belonged to the Solano mission he built a town named Sonoma, the Spanish version of an Indian name meaning Valley of the Moon.

As the Solano mission declined in importance, many neophytes who had had mission land assigned to them moved away, abandoning both their land and cattle. Through a succession of official grants much of this land and stock fell into Vallejo's hands. He came to own most of the fertile land in the Sonoma Valley as well as an immense tract stretching from the Carquinez Strait to Petaluma. These holdings—approximately 248,682 acres—made him one of California's largest landowners. Eventually he ran 50,000 head of cattle on this huge acreage (he was the single largest cattle owner in the province), along with 24,000 sheep and as many as 8,000 horses—1,000 of which were broken to saddle use. At times, he had a hundred men at once plowing his fields, and at a Vallejo *matanza* as many as 8,000 cattle might be killed.

Critics who resented his lordly sway and his haughty, dictatorial style called him "the autocrat of Sonoma." Since the Mexican government was derelict in sending troops to protect the area, Vallejo maintained what amounted to a private 40-man army, uniformed, armed and supplied largely at his own expense. The big adobe house on the plaza at Sonoma, which he built in 1835 as his home, incorporated a watchtower and was, in effect, a fortress. That same year, Vallejo moved his wife and young son Andrónico to Sonoma from San Francisco.

From the outset, there were Indian troubles on this frontier. The Suisun tribe, under the leadership of Sem-Yet-Ho (Mighty Arm), at first opposed the settlers, but Vallejo treated him in friendly, diplomatic fashion. In the end, the Suisun chief, baptized and renamed Solano, became Vallejo's staunch ally in the struggle to end the depredations of less friendly tribes. Solano, six feet seven inches tall, learned to speak Spanish fluently and adopted many of the white man's ways. ◉

Yanqui bridegrooms for Mexican daughters

"My most highly esteemed sir:
For some time I have wished to speak with you regarding a matter so delicate that . . . words have failed me. . . . Perhaps the attentions I have shown to your very charming daughter Doña Anita, have been observed, as also, no doubt, my desire always to attend the many gatherings graced by her presence. Her attractions have persuaded me that without her I cannot live or be happy in this world. Consequently, I am begging for her hand."

This formal proposal of marriage, written three days after Christmas in 1834, was addressed to José Antonio de la Guerra y Noriega, who was among the most prominent and prosperous citizens of Santa Bárbara. The requisite elegant prose, rendered in flawless Castilian, came from the pen of a certain José María Alfredo Robinson, a highly successful shipping agent in the California port—and an ex-Yankee who hailed from Boston.

Robinson was one of dozens of Americans who had journeyed west to California to make his fortune—in his case in the hide and tallow trade—and he had subsequently fallen under the spell of the salubrious climate and the leisurely way of life. Like many others of his transplanted countrymen, he had become converted to the Catholic faith and had Hispanicized his name (although he remained widely known as Alfred). Pledging his troth to a local señorita was the next logical step—and it was one that many of the expatriates followed.

It was no accident that he and his fellows usually found their overtures welcomed by leading California families. For the rich ranching clans of the isolated colony, the acquisition of a shrewd Yankee trader as a son-in-law was a good way to obtain needed business expertise. It also helped establish contact with the wider world—especially with the Californian's increasingly important neighbor, the United States. The Americans in California, in turn, gained prestige from their influential kinsfolk as well as protection from hostile acts—deportation or worse—that suspicious Mexican governors sometimes directed against foreign residents.

As accustomed as the venturesome suitors were to Hispanic life and manners, even those from blue-nosed New England found the courting customs of their new land overly restrained. Trader William Heath Davis, for example, lamented that, during a two-year courtship, he and his Californian bride-to-be were allowed almost no chance to speak with each other in private.

"This was an unwritten law of Spanish families from time immemorial," he commented. "When the rule was invaded the young lady would expect a reprimand from her mother or father; hence it was a rare occurrence." Even after the wedding ceremony took place, Davis reported, "The bride and bridegroom were not given any seclusion until the third night." This delay was not the result of prudery, but rather because of a nuptial fiesta that continued around the clock until the celebrants were forced to call a halt to the revelry out of sheer weariness.

Taken some 15 years after their wedding in 1836, these photographs show an aging Alfred Robinson and his still youthful-looking wife, Anita de la Guerra. In keeping with custom, she was 14 when they married; he was 29. Their elaborate nuptials were immortalized by Richard Henry Dana in *Two Years before the Mast.* Dana wrote: "The great amusement of the evening was the breaking of eggs filled with cologne upon the heads of the company."

In artist Charles Nahl's portrayal of California's most dramatic elopement, Josefa Carrillo is spirited off to Henry Fitch's ship.

California was shocked in 1829 when Josefa, the oldest daughter of wealthy San Diegan Joaquin Carrillo, ran off with Henry Fitch, a Massachusetts-born sea captain. The elopement was not the act of headstrong youngsters. Fitch had correctly courted Josefa for three years, and the couple was at the altar when an edict banning the union came from Governor José María Echeandía, whom Josefa, it was reported, had spurned. The lovers fled to Chile, where they were wed.

All ended happily. Josefa and Henry made peace with the authorities the next year by, among other things, giving a bell to the church in Los Angeles.

Looking like the stern New England skipper he once had been, Henry Fitch led the life of a wealthy rancher and trader when this portrait was painted around 1840.

In the late 1870s, Josefa Carrillo de Fitch *(far right)* sits for a portrait together with her daughter, son-in-law and a thoroughly Americanized brood of grandchildren.

When he sat for this daguerreotype with his youngest daughter Margarita in 1855, Juan Bandini was a flinty-looking old patrician, but his performance of the fandango was still the high point of his famed fiestas.

In a photograph taken prior to his wedding to Ysidora Bandini, Tennessee-born Cave Johnson Couts displays the soldierly bearing of an officer trained at West Point.

Although their marriage was arranged, Arcadia Bandini and Abel Stearns (below) enjoyed a happy life together, and their home became the social center of Los Angeles.

Like many of his peers, San Diego grandee Juan Bandini was outspokenly pro-American and proved it by marrying off four of his five lovely daughters to Yankees. In 1841, he gave the hand of Arcadia to his friend Abel Stearns, a merchant and landowner. Since Stearns was on his way to becoming California's richest man, the fiesta-loving Bandini assured himself the funds to pursue his profligate life style as well as a congenial son-in-law.

Pragmatism may have also played a role in the betrothals of his daughter Dolores to innkeeper Charles Johnson and of Margarita to Dr. James Winston. But it was all romance in the marriage of Ysidora to Lieutenant Cave Johnson Couts. This lively, coquettish girl was admiring a column of cavalrymen from the roof of her home and fell into the arms of her handsome husband-to-be when the railing gave way.

While Vallejo worked at taming the north, Governor Figueroa reestablished some degree of tranquillity elsewhere by offering amnesty to all Californios who had, for one reason or another, been in a state of revolt before his arrival. But Figueroa was in poor health, and his administration lasted only from 1833 to 1835. Following his death, California relapsed into political turmoil, and the same rebellious spirit that had brought about war in Texas began stirring. The man who exploited it was Juan Bautista Alvarado, Vallejo's friend from childhood—and also his nephew, although Alvarado was only one year younger. In November 1836, Alvarado headed a small rebel band that fired one cannon shot—all they had—at the residence of Governor Nicolás Gutierrez in Monterey and forced his capitulation. Alvarado ruled as revolutionary governor from December 1836 to July 1837. Meanwhile, sectional jealousy had prompted San Diego and Los Angeles to mount a counterrevolution. The situation was resolved when Alvarado, evidently in a move to retain power, swore an oath of allegiance to Mexico that effectively kept him in office. He continued to function as California's legally recognized governor until 1842.

Alvarado had tried to involve his uncle, Mariano Guadalupe Vallejo, in the revolution, but received no open support from him. Vallejo apparently had some doubts about the outcome and declined to take part, on the grounds that his troops were too badly needed on the northern frontier. With the success of Alvarado's coup, however, Vallejo at the age of 28 became the supreme military commander of California and one of the most powerful figures in the province.

At the Vallejos' residence on the plaza at Sonoma, a steady parade of visitors made their appearance, all generously entertained regardless of their rank or importance. Maintaining the Vallejo family and attending to the needs of their guests required an army of Indian servants. One visitor asked Señora Vallejo how many there were. "Each one of my children," replied the lady of the house, "has a servant who has no other duty than to care for him or her. I have two servants for myself. Four or five grind the corn for the tortillas, for here we entertain so many guests that three grinders are not enough. Six or seven serve in the kitchen. Five or six are constantly busy washing the clothes of the

children and servants. And nearly a dozen are required to attend to the sewing and spinning. As a rule, the Indians are not inclined to learn more than one duty. She who is taught cooking will not hear of washing clothes; and a good washerwoman considers herself insulted if she is compelled to sew or spin. All our servants are very clever. They have no fixed pay; we give them all they need. If sick, we care for them; when their children are born, we act as godparents, and we give their children instruction. In a word, we treat our servants rather as friends than as servants."

At San Francisco Bay on December 27, 1835, Richard Henry Dana, the young Yankee seaman serving aboard the *Alert,* took note in his journal of a visit to the ship that day by Don Mariano Guadalupe Vallejo in his capacity of presidio commandant. Vallejo, wrote Dana, was "the most popular among the Americans and English of any man in California. He spoke English very well, and was suspected of being favorably inclined to foreigners." More proof of this suspicious inclination—if such it was—came the following summer, when Jacob Leese, one of the more recent foreign arrivals, gave an ambitious entertainment.

Leese, a native of Ohio, was a shrewd and enterprising trader who had reached California in 1833. In 1836, he built the first large frame building in Yerba Buena—as the little adobe village outside the San Francisco presidio walls still called itself—and celebrated its completion with a gay Fourth of July festival. Both Mexican and American flags were raised. American vessels that happened to be in the bay fired salutes, and Leese's combination store and dwelling, decorated with flowers and bunting, was thronged with Americans, their Mexican neighbors and the growing number of married couples of mixed nationalities. During a banquet, Vallejo delivered a much-applauded oration in praise of George Washington. Dancing went on all night, and it was impossible not to notice how much Leese admired Rosalia Vallejo, the Don's beautiful and spirited sister. The next day all the celebrants moved on to Rincón Point for a *merienda;* and the dancing lasted until the dawn of July 6.

The observance of the neighboring nation's Independence Day was repeated the following year—by which time Rosalia had become Señora Leese—and every

year after until 1841, when the Leeses moved to a house on the plaza at Sonoma. The Mexicans, who loved a social occasion no matter what its international implications, continued to participate enthusiastically.

If one kind of foreign infiltration was growing, another was ebbing. The Russians, whose presence was the reason for Vallejo's being on the northern frontier, had decided by 1839 that their coastal settlements at Fort Ross and Bodega Bay were not worth the trouble. The sea otters had become virtually extinct, and there seemed no hope of obtaining from Mexico fertile interior lands that might produce more food than the rocky coastland. Finally, in 1841, the Russians sold their properties to the Swiss-born John Augustus Sutter, another recent newcomer to California, who had already secured a huge tract of farming and grazing land in the Sacramento valley, on which he built a fortress and trading post. Sutter called his domain "Nueva Helvetia," New Switzerland, and ran it like a European principality. His acquisition of the Russian prop-

erties did not please the autocrat of nearby Sonoma.

But Sutter, at least, was a legal immigrant who had taken out Mexican citizenship. Genuinely alarming was the influx of parties of illegal immigrants that began in November 1841, when the first overland wagon train crossed the Sierra Nevada. The following month, Vallejo addressed a series of dispatches to the government in Mexico City, spelling out what he regarded as the perilous state of affairs in California.

The underlying problem, wrote Vallejo, was California's "lack of population." Without population, California could not defend itself; and without adequate defenses it was dangerously vulnerable. "Daily," he continued, "throughout the whole extent of the Department, with the exception of this frontier, where I maintain a military force of 40 men at my own expense, there are Indian raids which ravish the fields with impunity, and destroy the only effective wealth of the country, the cattle and horses." These and other ills had to be endured, he pointed out, "because we can-

187

not prevent them, since we have no troops. All that we have suffered and shall endure comes from one single cause: lack of troops."

As an example of the worsening situation, Vallejo cited the recent irruption of immigrants across the Sierra. He mentioned that he had been in San José when the first party — "thirty-three foreigners from Missouri" — arrived. "I had them appear before me to demand their passports, and I was told that they had none. They did not deem them necessary, since they did not use them in their country. It is said that a larger [party] is on the way.

"The total population of California does not exceed 6,000 souls," he reminded distant Mexico City, "and of these two-thirds must be counted as women and children, leaving scarcely 2,000 men. We cannot count on the 15,000 Indians in the towns and missions because they inspire more fear than confidence. Thus this lamentable situation in a Country worthy of a better fate." He concluded: "Excuse this burst of feeling in a soldier who laments not having arms, when he sees the treasure being stolen."

Vallejo appended specific suggestions: California should have a strong governor with supreme civil and military authority; an army of at least 200 men, with corresponding officers, "all secure in their salaries"; reform of customs collection and elimination of unnecessary civil servants; establishment of a post office; rebuilding of the San Francisco presidio; and immigration of large numbers of Mexicans, mostly artisans and farmers. He also urged a reduction in the vast amounts of goods imported into California, arguing: "If there were no English boots, nor American blankets, we might be able to sell Californian shoes and robes."

A new governor for California, Manuel Micheltorena, had already been appointed. Additional troops were soon sent, and Vallejo was promoted to a lieutenant-colonelcy in the regular Army. Otherwise little was done. And 1841 in retrospect had the look of a watershed year. From that time on, growing numbers of Americans pursuing their self-proclaimed "Manifest Destiny" made their way westward through the snowy passes of the Sierra into California. Juan Bautista Alvarado was to comment later: "Would that the foreigners that came to settle in Alta California after 1841 had been of the same quality as those who pre-

ceded them!" The newcomers were less disposed to blend harmoniously into the Mexican California scene than to dominate it. When United States Navy Commodore Thomas ap Catesby Jones seized Monterey and raised the American flag in October 1842, under the false impression that the United States and Mexico were at war, his mistake was soon made right with profuse apologies. But Jones's action gave the Californios much to ponder.

On March 16, 1846, Vallejo was summoned from Sonoma to take part in a meeting at Monterey to debate the future of California. The province was still recovering from the shock of John Charles Frémont's provocative action earlier in the month.

The brash young Frémont, a captain in the United States Army Topographical Corps and leader of what was said to be a mapping expedition, had arrived at John Sutter's fort on the Sacramento River the previous December. He had crossed the Sierra Nevada to get additional supplies from Sutter, whom he had met on an earlier trip, and had used the occasion to visit Monterey, where he met with U.S. Consul Thomas O. Larkin. Frémont insisted to Mexican officials that his mission was purely scientific and exploratory, but the arms and equipment of his men aroused Mexican suspicions. When he moved south instead of north, the suspicions were intensified.

General José Castro, the Mexican commander at Monterey (and Vallejo's friend since boyhood), sent word that Frémont and his men must get out of California. Instead, Frémont built a rude fortification on Gabilan Peak, 25 miles northeast of Monterey. There, he planted a sapling in the ground and raised the American flag in defiance of Mexican authority. After three days, however, two things happened: a Mexican force, including cavalry and artillery, gathered in the valley below; and the flagstaff toppled to the ground. Frémont interpreted the latter as an omen and, under cover of darkness, withdrew north toward Oregon.

Though Frémont had backed down, Vallejo and other members of the junta assembled at Monterey realized that a change was inevitable. It appeared doubtful that Mexico would be able to maintain its hold on California much longer. Some of the men present thought a British protectorate might be the solution;

Britain's government was eminently stable, and her mighty Navy could guard California's long coastline. Others favored France. There had been close—although sometimes stormy—relations between the French and Spanish for centuries, since they were both Latin peoples and shared the same religious faith.

Mariano Guadalupe Vallejo's voice, however, was raised in favor of American annexation. More than four years had passed since Vallejo, concerned with his responsibility as commander general of the province, had warned the government in Mexico City to take decisive action if it wished to save California. Mexico had given ample proof that it was incapable of such action. Now Vallejo, who no longer held the top military post, felt free to advocate what seemed to him the soundest and most realistic course open.

A young United States Navy lieutenant, Joseph Warren Revere, grandson of the man who had made the midnight ride, was in Monterey at the time and reconstructed what happened at the meeting in his 1849 book, *A Tour of Duty in California.* According to his version, which he later checked with Vallejo himself, Vallejo said: "To rely any longer upon Mexico to govern and defend us would be idle and absurd. We possess a noble country in every way calculated, from position and resources, to become great and powerful. I would not have her a mere dependency upon a foreign monarchy, naturally alien, or at least indifferent to our interests and our welfare. What possible sympathy could exist between us and a nation separated from us by two oceans? How could we endure to come under the dominion of a monarchy? We are republicans—badly governed and badly situated as we are—still we are all, in sentiment, republicans. So far as we are governed at all, we profess to be self-governed.

"I come prepared to propose instant and effective action to extricate our country from her present forlorn condition. We must persevere in throwing off the galling yoke of Mexico, to rid ourselves of what may remain of Mexican domination. We have indeed taken the first step, by electing our own governor." (Vallejo referred to the recent overthrow of Micheltorena, the Mexican governor, and his replacement by Pío Pico, a Californio.) "But another remains to be taken," Vallejo continued. "It is annexation to the United States. In contemplating this consummation of our destiny, I feel nothing but pleasure, and I ask you to share it.

"Discard old prejudices, disregard old customs, and prepare for the glorious change which awaits our country. Why should we shrink from incorporating ourselves with the happiest and freest nation in the world, destined soon to be the most wealthy and powerful? Why should we go abroad for protection when this great nation is our adjoining neighbor? When we join our fortunes to hers, we shall not become subjects, but fellow-citizens, possessing all the rights of the people of the United States, and choosing our own federal and local rulers. We shall have a stable government and just laws. California will grow strong and flourish, and her people will be prosperous, happy and free."

It was ironic, then, that the best friend the Americans had among the Mexican Californians should be one of the first victims of American hostility. Frémont, who was encouraging any spirit of rebellion among the Californios, returned south and camped in the Sacramento valley. To his camp came many American Californians, some respectable settlers, others reckless adventurers, all determined to join any pro-American enterprise Frémont had in mind.

Finally on June 14, 1846, a party of 33 Americans attacked the northern outpost of Sonoma. Although Frémont remained aloof, they were clearly acting on his orders. Vallejo and the few civilian inhabitants of Sonoma were arrested, their arms were confiscated and a makeshift flag of independence (the so-called "Bear Flag," incorporating a rude representation of a grizzly) replaced the Mexican flag. Vallejo spent the next six weeks imprisoned at Sutter's Fort.

By the time he was released, in early August, the Mexican-American War was raging. Monterey had fallen to the Americans, and the Stars and Stripes were fluttering over Vallejo's old adobe headquarters at Sonoma. His emotions at beholding it were not recorded, but several of his first actions were remembered. He burned his Mexican uniforms and shaved off his heavy beard—and for the rest of his life went clean shaven. If he was bitter, he did not show it. Only much later, and only in private, would Vallejo allow himself a pointed observation on what the coming of the Americans had done to California and to him. "Quien llama el toro aguanta la cornada," he said: "He who calls the bull must endure the horn wound."

An illustrious marriage that started a dynasty

When he married Francisca Benicia Carrillo in 1832, Mariano Vallejo, a young army officer and legislator, already seemed destined for greatness in California. One wedding guest, Governor José Echeandía, offered a fitting toast: "May their progeny be numerous and worthy of them and an adornment to our beloved California."

How prophetic the words of the Governor were could be seen some 50 years later. Of 16 Vallejo offspring, nine of the 10 who had survived childhood were busily raising families of their own. Two of Vallejo's sons had embarked upon successful careers in music and art; a third was a noted surgeon, having graduated first in his class from Columbia University's medical school.

By then Mariano Vallejo and his wife had long since retired to Lachryma Montis (Tear of the Mountain), a mansion they had built in 1851 near Sonoma. This New England-style home suited its master. Though Latin to the core, Vallejo as a young man foresaw that California's future lay with the U.S., not Mexico. He never voiced regret at annexation, even though, over the years, title disputes and squatters reduced his once-vast ranches to barely 280 acres. Like many other Californios, Vallejo endeavored to serve his new country, helping to draw up a state constitution in 1849 and later becoming a state senator. Not long before his death in 1890 at age 82, the patriarch could look back with satisfaction: "I had my day. It was a proud one."

Three young women of the Vallejo household about 1870 show off their long, long hair (front view, left to right): Lily Wiley Vallejo, wife of Mariano's son Platón; Vallejo's daughter Luisa; and Emily Melvin, governess of several Vallejo grandchildren.

Mariano Vallejo sits with daughters Maria *(upper left)* and Luisa *(lower right)* and three granddaughters.

In a mid-century portrait, Mariano Vallejo's brother Salvador—later a Union Army major—sits between state senator Pablo de la Guerra (*left*) and Andrés Pico, brother of Mexican California's last governor.

Mariano *(center)* and his consultants discuss his *History of California*. From left to right they are: General Henry Cerruti, who contributed his own papers to the work; former California treasurer Don José Abrego; Rosana Leese, Mariano's niece and researcher; and scholar Don Vicente Gomez. Though never published, Vallejo's work earned fame as a source for historians.

The proud bearing and high character of Mariano Vallejo are reflected in this succession of portraits, made over the years as he changed from a handsome young Californio into a white-haired elder taking his ease outside his Sonoma mansion. Among the contributions Vallejo made to California were fine wines—whites, red and champagnes—from his vineyards; his wine-making example helped launch a major industry, which flourishes today, around Sonoma and the neighboring Napa Valley.

In a dawn engagement on the outskirts of their capital, Mexican troops—some in sandals—attempt to stanch the American onslaught.

6 | "A war of race, religion and customs"

Twenty years before war erupted with the United States in 1846, the Mexican press began to view the colossus to the north with dread. The newspaper *El Sol* decried the "fanatical intolerance" of Americans for nonwhites, while *El Mosquito Mexicano* called the U.S. a parasite that "devours Mexico's entrails." The Texas revolution in 1836 seemed to prove the point. A few years later, diplomat Manuel Eduardo de Gorostiza warned that unless Mexico recouped Texas, nationality and cultural identity would be jeopardized in a larger "war of race, of religion, of language, and of customs."

Even a pessimist could not have been ready for the one-sidedness of the war when it came to pass. For 17 months, Mexico did not achieve clear victory in a major battle, and in the penultimate clash at El Molino del Rey on September 8, 1847, almost 2,000 Mexicans died in an attempt to save the capital. So bitter was this defeat that the anonymous Mexican artist who painted this scene could not bear to reflect reality. The Americans appear as tiny, smoke-obscured figures huddled in the background—while the Mexican cannons boom and troops charge from all directions in what seems a prelude to a momentous triumph.

The desperate struggle against the insatiable Americans

General Mariano Arista, commander-in-chief of Mexico's Army of the North, suffered no doubts as to his proper course of action when he gave the order that, on April 24, 1846, triggered the war with the United States. Provocation abounded. Six weeks earlier, several thousand American soldiers from Texas had crossed the Nueces River, invading the province of Tamaulipas. These troops had marched 150 miles south to the Rio Grande, which the U.S. claimed—entirely without justification, in Mexico's view—was the border between the two nations. There, they had begun building a fort just across the river from the Mexican garrison in Matamoros.

Repeatedly, the Americans had been warned to return home. They had refused. Therefore, a state of war already existed, and it was indisputably necessary for Arista to bring the trespassers to battle.

Arista had 5,000 troops at Matamoros, with more on the way. In preparation for a major offensive, he ordered General Anastasio Torrejón across the Rio Grande to cut roads and engage American units passing to and from the new fort.

On the morning of the 24th, Torrejón marched his 1,600-man brigade 14 miles upstream from Matamoros, well beyond American eyes. Then his cavalrymen swam their horses across the warm, muddy river, while his infantry and sappers crossed in small boats. The brigade reassembled on the river's left bank, and probed slowly upstream, keeping a sharp lookout for American patrols. All through the afternoon, Torrejón reconnoitered westward, his riders twisting easily in their saddles to avoid spiny cactus, the foot soldiers plodding behind, kicking up clods of soft red dirt. Finding no Americans, Torrejón camped for the night at a ranch 27 miles above the American fort.

Toward dawn on April 25, Torrejón's sentries spotted a U.S. cavalry patrol coming upriver toward them. The Americans—four officers and 61 troopers—may have sensed the Mexican presence, for they reined to a tense halt about three miles from the ranch house. Then they started up again—and rode straight into a perfect ambush.

Torrejón's men, concealed in the thick chaparral ringing the ranch, let the patrol pass, then opened fire as it was crossing an open field. The Americans desperately tried to fight their way clear, but the Mexicans hurled them back with a murderous musket volley, blasting several troopers out of the saddle. An American captain was carried off by his wounded horse and knocked unconscious when the pain-maddened animal plunged into a ravine. The U.S. troopers rallied behind a second captain and galloped toward the river, only to bog down in marshy ground. At this point, with 11 of their number dead and no chance of escape, they were compelled to surrender.

Torrejón himself escorted the prisoners to Matamoros, where the exultant Arista congratulated him for "the triumph achieved by the brigade which your Excellency so worthily commands." Later Arista said, "I had the pleasure of being the first to start the war."

As news of the clash spread south, Mexicans everywhere let out a lusty cheer. The national mood was precisely gauged in another statement by Arista: "Forced into war, we enter a struggle that cannot be avoided without failing in what is most sacred to man." Too long had the United States flouted Mexico's honor, its pride, its courage. In Mexican eyes, these arrogant, ruthless Yanquis had to be stopped before they seized or destroyed everything that Mexicans held dear:

Mexican guerrillas spy on American troops at a strategic river ford after the capture of Monterrey in September 1846. A U.S. dragoon sketched elements of the scene during the war and did this painting years later.

their land, their Catholic religion, their Spanish language and way of life, their very identity as Mexicans.

Mexico's case against the United States was summarized with uncommon forbearance in 1848 by historian Ramon Alcaraz and 14 associates, who knitted together hundreds of eyewitness reports and official documents to present their nation's first comprehensive account of the war. In tone and substance, their history inevitably differed from American accounts, yet its reportage of the fighting was no less enlightening; and in the sense that attitudes engender deeds, its analysis of the causes was no less true.

The chroniclers blamed the conflict on the "insatiable ambition of the United States" and asserted that the Americans "desired from the beginning to extend their dominion in such a manner as to become the absolute owners of almost all of this continent." The territorial avarice of the U.S. was obvious, said the team of historians. "The North American Republic has already absorbed territories pertaining to Great Britain, France, Spain and Mexico. It has employed every means to accomplish this — purchase as well as usurpation, skill as well as force, and nothing has restrained it when treating of territorial acquisition. Louisiana, the Floridas, Oregon and Texas have fallen successively into its power."

The loss of Texas was the biggest bone in Mexico's throat. The nearly 28,000 American settlers whom Mexico admitted to Texas between 1823 and 1835 had sworn oaths of loyalty as Mexican citizens and had acknowledged Mexico's ultimate ownership of the lands granted them for use. By Mexican lights, therefore, the Texas revolution of 1836 had no force of law, and the province remained a part, albeit a rebellious part, of Mexico.

The United States, meanwhile, had lost no opportunity to aggrieve its neighbor, or so the Mexicans believed. Hardly had the Texans won the battle of San Jacinto than Washington recognized the so-called "Republic of Texas." And through the years of vicious border fighting in the early 1840s, the U.S. press and public had sided with the Texans. Many of the sympathizers called for outright annexation, and in 1845 a bill was introduced in the U.S. Congress to admit Texas as a state. Mexico angrily protested, but to no avail. The bill passed in March; Texas would officially become the 28th American state on December 29, 1845. Mexico's minister in Washington, Juan N. Almonte, called the legislation "an act of aggression, the most unjust which can be found in the annals of modern history." White with fury, he demanded his passport, thereby breaking diplomatic relations.

The only thing that prevented Mexico from declaring war in March of 1845 was an all too familiar occurrence — there had been yet another revolution a few months before. The general who had taken over the reins of government was Jose Joaquín de Herrera, a well-intentioned moderate who arrived at the highly unpopular conclusion that negotiations were preferable to war. Herrera's foreign minister, Manuel de la Peña y Peña, sounded just like an appeaser when he declared that "war with the United States is an abyss without bottom which will devour an indefinite series of generations and treasure."

As it turned out, no formal talks were ever initiated because the American terms were so totally unacceptable. One item presented in preliminary conversations revived an old quarrel: back in 1837, the United States had lodged a six-million-dollar claim for damages suffered by its citizens during the various Mexican uprisings; Mexico, bankrupt because of these very revolutions, had defaulted on the payments — and a large segment of the American press had repeatedly urged the U.S. Army to act as bill collector. American belligerence about this claim had long annoyed Mexico, and now the United States stirred deep ire by offering to assume Mexico's reparations to American citizens if Mexico agreed to recognize the Rio Grande instead of the Nueces River as its border with Texas. Further, the United States proposed to buy California for $25 million, and would pay five million dollars more if New Mexico was thrown into the bargain. To Mexicans, this was the supreme insult — and final proof that Americans intended to rule the entire continent.

At last, the reluctant Herrera ordered Major General Mariano Paredes y Arrillaga to mobilize the Mexican army. Paredes, an archconservative, issued the call to arms — and then immediately turned the troops against Herrera, marching into Mexico City and installing himself as president on January 2, 1846. However, while Paredes was reassuringly warlike toward the United States, he had incurred grave public dis-

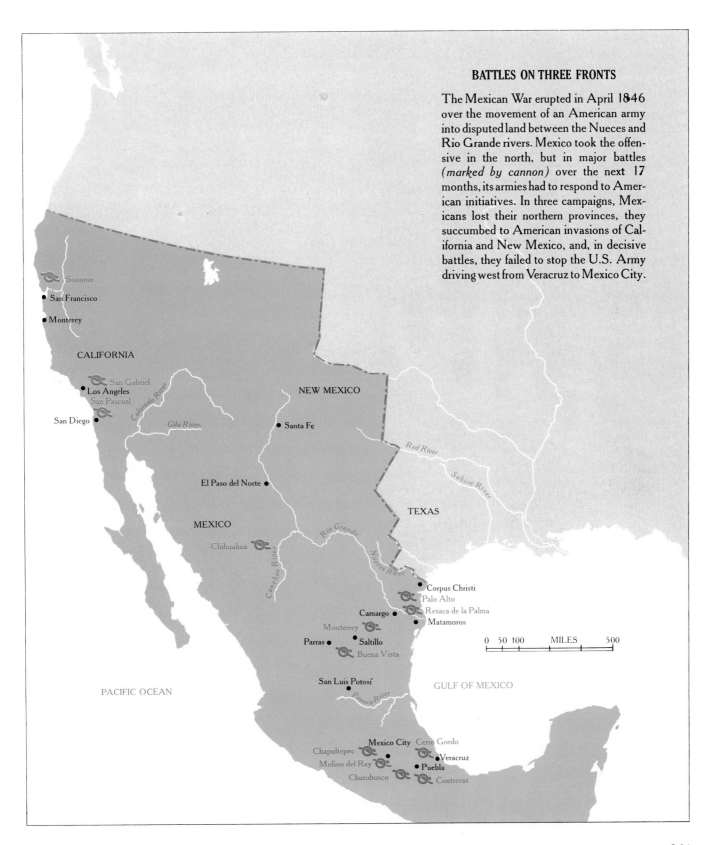

BATTLES ON THREE FRONTS

The Mexican War erupted in April 1846 over the movement of an American army into disputed land between the Nueces and Rio Grande rivers. Mexico took the offensive in the north, but in major battles *(marked by cannon)* over the next 17 months, its armies had to respond to American initiatives. In three campaigns, Mexicans lost their northern provinces, they succumbed to American invasions of California and New Mexico, and, in decisive battles, they failed to stop the U.S. Army driving west from Veracruz to Mexico City.

Sonoma

San Francisco

Monterey

CALIFORNIA

San Gabriel

Los Angeles

San Pascual

San Diego

Colorado River

Gila River.

NEW MEXICO

Santa Fe

Red River

Sabine River

El Paso del Norte

TEXAS

MEXICO

Rio Grande

Chihuahua

Conchos River

Nueces River

Corpus Christi

Palo Alto

Resaca de la Palma

Camargo

Matamoros

Monterrey

Parras

Saltillo

Buena Vista

San Luis Potosí

GULF OF MEXICO

0 50 100   MILES   500

PACIFIC OCEAN

Panuco River

Mexico City

Cerro Gordo

Chapultepec

Veracruz

Molino del Rey

Puebla

Churubusco

Contreras

Defending Monterrey, Mexican soldiers, civilians and even clergy mill bloodily with U.S. infantry in this contemporary lithograph by the French artist J. Michaud. The provincial capital, widely considered impregnable, fell to the invaders at a cost of 370 Mexican and 490 American casualties.

approval for harsh tactics employed in past revolts. As a result, his troops had to force citizens at musket point to fly flags to welcome their new president. "I come," he said coldly, "resolved to make my ideas triumph. I shall shoot anyone who gets in my way, whether he be an archbishop, a general, a magistrate or anyone else."

While Paredes was consolidating his power, the United States supplied the ultimate provocation for war: on March 8, 1846, an American army in Corpus Christi, Texas, crossed the Nueces River and began marching south through undefended country toward the Rio Grande. They reached the river on March 28, and were established there for nearly a month before Paredes' generals felt strong enough to mount an attack. And that first clash between General Torrejón's brigade and the American cavalry patrol seemed to promise a crushing lesson for the intruders.

In the beginning, most Mexicans shared their generals' optimism. Mexico had about 30,000 men under arms, four times more than the United States. A few observers were vaguely concerned about the quality of the army, but almost everyone believed that Mexico was too strong in its righteous wrath to be defeated. Geography, too, seemed to favor Mexico. Texas, presumably the main battlefield of the war, presented no terrain obstacles to impede a Mexican sweep eastward to New Orleans and even Mobile; then the United States would surely sue for peace. Should the Americans undertake an invasion of Mexico, however, their supply lines would be overextended, and they would have to traverse hundreds of miles of cruel desert before they reached the nation's rich central valley.

In military leadership, Mexico appeared to have an edge in vigor. The American commander-in-chief, Zachary Taylor, enjoyed a reputation as a successful tactician but was 61 years old and suffering from bilious attacks. His opponent across the Rio Grande, General Mariano Arista, was a youthful 43 and a highly respected veteran of Mexico's civil wars. Arista was light-haired — odd for a Mexican — and a handsome, elegant figure of a man. A Mexican acquaintance said that he was "of graceful address, always well dressed, with an expression, half sadness and half smile, which is not only interesting but invites confidence."

After his subordinate Torrejón captured the Amer-

Early in the war, leadership of Mexico's
forces alternated between Generals Mariano Arista *(left)* — a popular cavalryman
who had lived briefly in the U.S. — and
the whimsically cruel Pedro de Ampudia.

ican patrol, Arista itched to score an important victory, and he planned to seize the coastal town of Point Isabel, which the Americans were using to land supplies. Arista put this scheme into effect on April 30, taking about 3,000 troops from Matamoros and heading downstream to cross the Rio Grande under cover of darkness. Once on the other side, Arista's force would link up with Torrejón's 1,600-man brigade, which had remained on the left bank. The entire army of 4,600 men would then descend on Point Isabel before the Americans awoke to the fact that a general offensive was under way.

It was a sound strategy, but Arista immediately met the sort of evil fortune that would dog the Mexicans throughout the war. Most of the boats he had counted on to ferry his men across the river proved too leaky to use, so his 3,000 troops had to cross in two small scows — an operation that took 24 hours. During the delay, General Taylor acted, seemingly in anticipation of Arista's plan. Taking all but 500 of his 3,500 men, Taylor left his fort on the Rio Grande and head-

ed for Point Isabel, undoubtedly to collect supplies.

Realizing that Taylor had thwarted him, Arista changed his strategy promptly and cleverly. He sent most of his army 10 miles north to a place called Palo Alto, squarely athwart the road from Point Isabel. With the remaining troops, Arista prepared to bombard the American fort into submission. He knew that the sound of cannonading would carry to Point Isabel. He also knew it would bring the Americans back to relieve the besieged fort — and deliver them to the Mexican forces lying in wait at Palo Alto.

On May 3, Arista ordered the heavy batteries in Matamoros and four field cannon to open fire on the fort. For five days the cannonading continued, battering down the walls, killing a number of troops. Mexican soldiers were preparing to storm the bastion when word came that Taylor and his men had finally started back from Point Isabel. Arista broke off his attack and ordered most of the siege troops to join with the main army at Palo Alto. Nearly 4,000 Mexicans were waiting when the vanguard of Taylor's 3,000-man force hove into sight at noon on the 8th and stopped short.

Arista reviewed his army and delivered a short patriotic speech. "His remarks," according to the chronicle compiled by historian Ramon Alcaraz and his associates, "were received with enthusiasm. The banners floated to the winds, the soldiers stood to their arms, the horses pawed the ground, the bands performed inspiring and beautiful music, and shouts of *'Viva la Republica!'* filled the air."

Both generals deployed their troops for battle. At 2 p.m., Mexican observers reported that the enemy was advancing in columns along a mile-wide front. When they were within 1,000 yards, the Americans halted and formed a stationary line on open, level ground. Arista called for artillery fire. The Mexican field guns boomed impressively. But Arista watched with mounting dismay as the bulky copper cannonballs sailed slowly through the air and landed harmlessly in front of the enemy. Many of the Americans simply sidestepped the bouncing missiles.

Suddenly, American gun crews appeared with their light cannon, wheeled them swiftly into position and commenced firing. The highly mobile field pieces — "flying artillery," the Americans called them — fired with an absurd, barking report, but they sent vicious loads of grapeshot screaming across the field and cut swathes through the ranks of advancing infantry led by General Pedro de Ampudia, Arista's second-in-command. The Mexicans were witnessing the dawn of a new era in military technology. Henceforth, fewer and fewer battles would be won solely by weight of manpower; more and more victories would go to the side that kept the most metal flying toward the enemy.

The Mexicans fought, as they had at the Alamo a decade before, with old-fashioned raw courage. Arista sent Torrejón's brigade charging to turn the Americans' right flank. The cavalrymen rode hard, their lances cocked down, streamers fluttering from the tips. But the American cannon hurled their attack aside, tossing horses and men into tangled heaps.

Arista shifted his attack, hoping to crumple the American left. Yet here, too, American cannon moved into position with startling speed and sent storms of grape howling around the running infantrymen. The muzzle blasts set fire to the prairie grass, and a following wind blew choking clouds of smoke into the Mexicans' faces. Arista was forced to pull back 1,000 yards and suspend the attack.

By late in the afternoon, the Mexican troops were wilting under the incessant bombardment. "The artillery of the Americans, much superior to ours, made horrid ravages in the ranks of the Mexican army," the Alcaraz chroniclers reported. The men were crying in frustration, shouting for the chance to use the bayonet. At last, Arista moved among them and ordered his men to charge. But the light was fading, and in the smoky gloom one Mexican force crashed against another. Alcaraz later recounted: "Our troops being disconcerted, trampled on each other, and blundered within pistol shot of the American batteries, which broke them and destroyed them." Mercifully, it was now dark, and Arista was able to break off the fight without further damage to his troops.

At this point, neither side could claim a clear tactical advantage. Arista had hardly even touched the American army. However, Taylor and his troops had not broken through to relieve their beleaguered fort. Yet the Mexicans had suffered much heavier casualties, with at least 300 men killed and wounded, and the night was a hellish one for them.

The prairie fire flared up again. "Its sinister splendor," wrote the Mexican historians, "illuminated the camp, in which now were heard the heart-rending groans of our wounded. As most of these were from cannon-shot, they were horribly mutilated. Nothing could be done to alleviate their sufferings, for the surgeon who carried the medicine chests had disappeared."

At dawn on May 9, Arista withdrew to the south, looking for good defensive terrain. About five miles from Palo Alto, at a place called Resaca de la Palma, he deployed his army in and behind a long wooded draw, and in front of a thick forest of chaparral. He began to recover his nerve. It stood to reason that the dense foliage would slow any attack by the American infantry; more important, the American artillery would be almost impotent in these woods. By 10 a.m. his troops were in place, and Arista retired to his tent to prepare an analysis of the previous day's reverse at Palo Alto. He was certain the Americans would not dare attack him that day. But he was mistaken.

"The enemy advanced upon our troops at half-past four o'clock," the chroniclers reported. "The General-in-chief still persisted in his error, calling this attack a simple skirmish." Incredibly, Arista was so deluded that he delegated command to General Diaz de la Vega and returned to his tent.

The Americans' attack hit hardest at the Mexicans' left flank. There, the Mexican 4th. and 6th Light Infantry companies, gallantly commanded by Captains Barragán and Moreno, fought the enemy to a standstill. But then some American soldiers found a path through the woods and circled to the side and rear. "The two heroic companies," wrote Alcaraz and his chroniclers, "did battle with a great part of the North American army. Barragán fell mortally wounded. Moreno was taken prisoner. The soldiers, reduced to one-fourth their number, without officers, without hope, main-tained the unequal strife, but finally had to give way."

Now the Americans began enveloping the Mexican line. "The enemy's artillery decimated our ranks. Their dragoons rode up to our pieces, which they captured. The enemy surrounded our soldiers on every side, to cut off a retreat."

Arista finally emerged from his tent and tried to rally his men — to no avail. "The disorder which defeat had produced on the left of our line soon extended to the corps on the right. This last had not been under fire, but dispersed shamefully. The soldiers threaded their way through the briers of the woods. The most horrible confusion reigned on the field." The Mexicans were fleeing, throwing their weapons away. Arista raved and cursed, whipping the men around him with

In a savage melee at San Pasqual on December 6, 1846, tall-hatted Californios led by General Andrés Pico rout an American force under Genera

the flat of his saber. He mounted, organized a small cavalry troop for the charge and drove forward into the muzzles of the American guns, which blew his men back. Whole companies were running for the river, "not believing themselves safe while they were on the other side. The confusion and trampling on each other was astonishing. They began to dispute for priority in being ferried over the river in the only two boats. The lack of transports rendered the miserable fugitives desperate. Many drowned when they tried to swim."

The rout was complete. Arista reached Matamoros safely, but only to order the town abandoned. He already had left hundreds of wounded soldiers behind on the two battlefields; now he left 500 more in Matamoros. Some of the soldiers, according to the Mexican chroniclers, were so terrified of being captured by the Americans that they "crawled out of the hospital and followed, dragging their bodies along the ground, and leaving a track of blood."

Arista moved southwest toward Linares, about 180 miles away, with the remnants of his army staggering along behind him. José María Roa Bárcena, a young reporter from the south, wrote: "The retreat was disastrous. The infantry was abandoning pieces of artillery and wagons on their way; the cavalry was left almost completely without horses; some of the ammunition had to be rendered useless and buried, and the troops suffered for lack of food and water; the women assistants and officers in the vanguard came taking possession of everything they could find to eat and

Stephen Kearny, who was wounded twice in the fray. The victory was Mexican California's swan song: a month later, the province surrendered.

During the battle of Buena Vista, United States officers *(foreground)* direct defenses against a charge by troops under General Ampudia. Locked in a deadly dance, the armies took turns advancing and retreating until, too battered to continue, they broke off — with both sides claiming victory.

some resold the food to the troops at very high prices." A few men blew their brains out with their muskets.

When Arista's army reached Linares, it was totally shattered; of his original 5,000 men, fewer than 3,000 remained fit for duty. Mexico was stunned by the disaster, and pamphleteers rushed into print with ingenious explanations of what had gone wrong, often alleging treason on the part of certain Mexican generals. Yet as details of the catastrophe kept drifting in, the Mexican people began to glimpse the truth—that their army had grievous flaws.

Morale was abysmally low. This was a class army in which gentlemen officers considered soldiers peons; in consequence, soldiers hardly knew their officers and often resented them. Worse, the soldiers went for months without pay because of the nation's chronic insolvency. Even their white cotton uniforms were in short supply, and sometimes they fought in rags. Men were separated from their families for years, marched over some of the harshest terrain in the world and were expected to live off the land. They still carried old smoothbore muskets—a notoriously inaccurate weapon that was not meant to be aimed but to be fired en masse by soldiers working in unison. The Mexicans might have learned that their muskets were outmoded —and that the Americans' rifles were deadly accurate —during the Texas campaign. But they had not.

Indeed, the Texas revolution should have taught the Mexicans a good deal about Americans as fighting men. Though not trained as soldiers, most were expert with the rifle. They fought as individuals and placed their fire with devastating effect. And as they won battles, their morale naturally soared. Mexicans could fight as courageously as any soldiers on earth, but army for army, Mexico clearly was outclassed.

From Linares, the broken Army of the North was transferred to Monterrey, the principal city of northern Mexico, with a population of about 15,000. There, through the summer, the army was rebuilt to meet attack from the Americans. Meanwhile, some comforting news arrived: the U.S. forces were suffering an epidemic of yellow fever and dying like flies in Camargo, up the Rio Grande from Matamoros.

Command of the Mexican army now devolved to General Pedro de Ampudia, who had conspired to undo his former chief Arista. This Ampudia was a brute; years before, while suppressing a rebellion, he had executed 15 rebels and boiled their heads in oil so that he might display their skulls in iron cages. He fully expected to crush the Americans; he had more than 10,000 troops, and Monterrey seemed impregnable —rimmed by mountains, with the only large open area, to the east, guarded by three forts. To the west of town ran the road to Saltillo, Ampudia's supply line; it passed through a narrow gorge between two steep hills, Federación and Independencia, and Ampudia emplaced heavy artillery atop each.

Early in September, word came that the American army, now grown to some 6,600 men, was marching south from Camargo, led by their irregulars, the Texas Rangers. This corps of scouts was infamous for its ferocity in border clashes; at the mere mention of Texas Rangers, the townspeople of Monterrey turned panicky and—said Alcaraz's team of chroniclers—"abandoned their homes in fear and trembling."

The Americans arrived outside the ring of mountains on September 19, and the main force under General Taylor launched a frontal assault on the eastern side of the valley. Mexican defenders there fought gallantly and held firm. Two days later, however, it developed that the chief threat came from the unlikeliest quarter—the west. A secondary American force of 2,000 men had circled the mountains, cut the road to Saltillo and was attacking toward Mexican gun emplacements on Federación and Independencia hills.

Ampudia sent his cavalry to counterattack, but the charge of the lancers crumpled before the American cannon. In turn, the Mexican defenders of the vital hills threw back one American assault after another, inflicting awful casualties. The turning point came at dawn on September 22. Swiftly, silently, a 300-man American force stormed up the far side of the twin-peaked Federación hill and—according to Alcaraz —"reached the west peak, surprising the 70 men of the 4th Light who defended it, against the predictions and assurances of General Garcia Conde, who had insisted it was inaccessible." Incredibly, the Americans dragged cannon to the top and destroyed the Mexican batteries on the east peak, with their infantry swarming in behind the gunfire with bayonets. Then the Americans assaulted Independencia hill.

"The Americans," Alcaraz reported, "charged with

confidence, while ours, overpowered, fell back in disorder. The soldiers in their hurry, full of fright, descended and penetrated to the interior of Monterrey, spreading terror. This unlucky event infused a silent fear which comes before defeat."

On the 23rd, the Americans who had surmounted the two hills drove into Monterrey from the west while their main army broke through in strength in the east. They fought their way through the city streets, moving from house to house, engaging in small, deadly actions. The next day, their artillery was close enough to put Ampudia's central arsenal under fire. At nightfall on September 24, the threat of a major explosion there prompted General Ampudia to offer an armistice. General Taylor, his men thoroughly exhausted, his casualties mounting, accepted.

On September 25, Ampudia's men marched away, leaving the Americans a city "converted into a vast cemetery," as Alcaraz said. Broken once again, they headed for San Luis Potosí, 245 miles to the southeast, there to regroup. For all practical purposes, the fall of Monterrey brought the struggle for northern Mexico to a disastrous end.

While Mexico City was wringing its hands over this reverse, reports from the far north told of other debacles: both California and New Mexico had fallen to the Americans. The most dismaying part of this news was that both of the provinces had surrendered virtually without even a fight. Indeed, many Californians and New Mexicans seemed actually to welcome the Americans—at least at first.

In New Mexico, Governor Manuel Armijo had made a reluctant show of resistance by assembling a force of 4,000 citizens. But New Mexicans were far from Mexico City and not bound by close ties; their greatest trade was north along the Santa Fe Trail into the United States. Armijo himself had a lucrative partnership in an American trading firm and had little stomach for combat in any case. Thus, in spite of the imminent threat of American invasion, he ordered his force disbanded and sent home. He then left Santa Fe and headed into Mexico with one of his trading caravans—loaded with $50,000 worth of American manufactured goods, some New Mexicans said. Another story held that Governor Armijo's departure had been hastened along by 500 ounces of American gold. Whatever the truth, the New Mexicans were left without a strong leader, and they submitted quietly on August 19 when General Stephen Kearny led a column of 1,700 men into Santa Fe.

The Americans were so cocky after their trouble-free take-over that Kearny sent 1,000 of his troops on a long and fruitless invasion of the Mexican province of Chihuahua. Then, leaving a few hundred men to occupy all of New Mexico, he headed toward California with the tiny remainder of his army.

Soon after his departure, the full impact of what had happened suddenly struck the New Mexicans. Groups of citizens rose up to fight for their land and their Spanish heritage in the face of increasing arrogance on the part of the American occupiers. In the town of Mora, citizens killed eight Americans and announced, "We have declared war on the Americans and we shall take arms in defense of our abandoned country." In Taos, New Mexicans rebelled at the lawless behavior of the rowdy American troops, of whom one indignant townsman said, "A more drunken and depraved set I am sure can never be found."

The U.S. soldiers sobered up enough to quash the initial revolt. A month later, however, Taos rebelled again and six more Americans were killed, including the new American governor, the American sheriff and a Mexican who was sympathetic to the Americans. But one by one, the uprisings were put down, and the New Mexicans pragmatically reconciled themselves to their new government.

In California, most of the citizenry felt the same sense of isolation from Mexico City, and had enjoyed cordial relations with the Americans who had settled in the province or stopped in its ports to do business. Hence, few Californios stood to arms in June 1846, when a group of Americans and other foreign settlers proclaimed the province independent of Mexico. In fact, many Californios were fed up with their inefficient, often corrupt provincial government, and they actually favored the revolt.

All that changed, however, when the local rebels were joined by United States Army lieutenant John Frémont and his armed band of 60-odd Americans from the east. These newcomers, supposedly on a mission of exploration, soon began acting like advance

Assaulting Mexico City's Chapultepec Castle on September 13, 1847, American infantrymen advance on artillery units defending lowlands before the fortress. At left, a body of U.S. troops has broken through the breastworks and is racing up the mine-studded hillside to the bastion's walls.

agents for a United States takeover. Assuming command of the revolt, Frémont's men seized the village of Sonoma and San Francisco in early July — and promptly proved themselves to be bloodthirsty and utterly ruthless. A group of Frémont's men stopped an elderly Californio and his two young nephews on the road outside of Sonoma and demanded to know their business. Before the Californios had time to reply, the Americans shot and mortally wounded the two nephews. The old man cried out, "Is it possible that you kill these young men for no reason at all? It is better that you kill me who am old." The Americans obligingly shot the old man, and their leader later explained that they had "no room for prisoners." This leader was a frontiersman named Kit Carson.

The Californios' distrust of Frémont was confirmed when, on July 7, the local revolt was superseded by the start of an overt United States invasion. San Francisco, Monterey, Santa Bárbara and other coastal towns were occupied in quick succession by landing parties from United States naval vessels. Frémont's troop was quickly incorporated into this force. San Diego was captured on July 29 and Los Angeles on August 12 — both falling with scarcely a shot fired.

Belatedly, as in New Mexico, many Californios took up arms against the invaders. Southern California was the main battleground for the insurrection, and the Californios quickly won a series of encouraging triumphs. In September, they ousted the small American force from Los Angeles and won a brisk skirmish 25 miles to the east. Then in October, 150 Californios with one cannon repelled an attempt by 400 Americans to recapture Los Angeles.

South of Los Angeles, Californio soldiers had bottled up the invaders in San Diego. But at this crucial juncture, General Kearny finally arrived from New Mexico with what was officially designated the United States Army of the West. It was a ludicrous scarecrow of an army, consisting of 100 half-naked, travel-weary troops. But its union with larger American units already in action formed a force that outnumbered the Californios two to one. Under Kearny, the Americans launched a major assault at San Pasqual — a small Indian village about 35 miles northeast of San Diego — early on the chilly morning of December 6.

The Californios, led by General Andrés Pico, stood their ground as the Americans charged down from the top of a hill. The light cavalry bore the brunt of the attack and smashed it, killing 18 Americans and wounding 11 more while losing only one man killed. Later, a California officer explained that "since the site was a lowland, it had become very muddy; so much so that the heavy mules of the Americans could hardly maneuver, while our horses wheeled from side to side as if they were on solid ground."

The Americans fell back to regroup, and the Californios thought that a strong counterattack might force them to surrender. But for some reason, General Pico did not act immediately — and during the lull, an American soldier crept through the Californio lines and carried word of Kearny's plight to the American troops encircled in San Diego. By a herculean effort, they burst out and raced to relieve Kearny. When the two American forces linked up, the backbone of the resistance movement was broken.

In the next few weeks, the Californios gradually succumbed to the enemy's superior numbers and equipment. By early January of 1847, the Americans were again marching on Los Angeles — to an easy victory that terminated the bitter struggle within 10 days. Thereafter, the Californios submitted quietly to American rule, yet their epoch did not really end until 1849. Then, a mere 5,000 people, they were inundated by some 70,000 Americans in the first year of a great gold rush, which quickly converted their lost province into one of the United States.

Even before California's fate was sealed, Mexicans had heard more than enough bad news from all directions, and — taking their vengeance on the most accessible target — they overthrew General Paredes. But even as a shaky liberal president took over, many Mexicans found their thoughts turning to the only man who had ever shown himself capable of maintaining a semblance of order and waging a war: Antonio López de Santa Anna. In their desperation, Mexicans were willing to forget his blunders in Texas and his scandalous venality as president from 1841 to 1844.

Santa Anna, 52 at this point, was currently resting in exile in Havana, devoting most of his attention to cockfights and his comely 17-year-old wife (page 115). One diplomat's wife described the deposed Mexican leader as "a gentlemanly, good-looking, quietly-dressed, rather melancholy-looking person. He had a sallow complexion, fine dark eyes, soft and penetrating, and an interesting expression of face. Knowing nothing of his past history, one would have said a philosopher, living in dignified retirement — one who had suffered ingratitude and who, if he were ever persuaded to emerge from his retreat, would only do so, Cincinnatus-like, to benefit his country."

Presumably the lady knew something of Santa Anna's past history, and made her comment with tongue in cheek. For Santa Anna was in "retreat" only in the sense of a coiled cobra; his inner lust for power burned as fiercely as ever, and he needed little encouragement to seize any opportunity that offered itself. His problem was to find a way through the tight U.S. naval blockade of Mexico's Gulf Coast ports. It was a situation that called for a ruse, and the Mexicans devised a brilliant one.

Soon there appeared in Washington a gentleman who wangled a meeting with President Polk to suggest that, if only Santa Anna were allowed to return home and take the helm of his nation, he would formally cede California and New Mexico for $30 million — plus a half million dollars in expense money for himself. Polk was intrigued and sent an emissary to Cuba to talk to Santa Anna. Precisely what was said is not known, but shortly afterward the U.S. Navy received orders that Santa Anna was to be passed through the blockade without question.

On August 16, 1846, as "a most discordant band screamed national airs, and a crowd of boys squibbed and crackered on the wharf," recounted a witness, Santa Anna and his bride landed at Veracruz.

Traveling in easy stages, projecting an air of great calm and certitude, he arrived in Mexico City on September 14 and was virtually handed the government by the popular acclaim of the Mexican people. On September 28, he set out for San Luis Potosí, there to rebuild the army that the Americans had mauled at Monterrey. By December, he had raised more than 20,000 troops and supplied them with two million dollars donated by the Church.

Meanwhile, Santa Anna came into possession of some interesting dispatches, taken from an American courier who had been captured on his way to General Taylor in Monterrey. One letter, from General Winfield Scott, discussed American strategy in full detail. Since a broad desert separated Taylor from Mexico City, General Scott was going to land at Veracruz with an army that included some troops borrowed from Taylor. Scott would then drive inland to capture the capital and end the war.

This enemy plan, Santa Anna felt, gave him two very pleasant choices. He could leave immediately for Veracruz and there block General Scott's landing. Or he could go north to Monterrey, rout Taylor and still return in time to trap and destroy Scott on the mountainous road between Veracruz and Mexico City. Since the latter course was the more spectacular, Santa Anna naturally chose it.

On January 28, 1847, the Mexican army started the awful march across the desert to Monterrey. The Mexicans had 18,183 men, Santa Anna later reported, but many fell by the wayside. His report complained of the "bad quality of food," of water that was "brackish as well as scarce," of the troops' exposure to snowstorms and cold, which killed several men and led to many desertions.

His approach interrupted the Americans while they were maneuvering south of Monterrey. General Taylor's army had been reduced to 7,500 men. He fell back to a place on the Saltillo Road near the hacienda of Buena Vista and wedged his force into a gap in the mountains known as La Angostura — The Narrows. On learning of the American withdrawal, Santa Anna mistook it for flight and hurled his troops into a brutal forced march. The Mexican army traveled the last 50 miles in 24 hours. "The fatigue alone killed several soldiers, who remained stretched upon the road," Alcaraz wrote. On the morning of February 22, the Mexicans met the Americans, who were dug in "on two successive series of hills and gorges which formed a truly formidable position. Each hill was fortified with a battery, and ready to deal its murderous fire upon any attempting to take it."

Santa Anna grandly offered Taylor a chance to surrender. The American general refused, and the Mexican army struck his left side that afternoon. Early in the battle, Santa Anna noticed an undefended hill and ordered General Ampudia to take it and mount cannon there. About the same time, some Americans raced to seize the hill. The two forces collided bloodily at its base. Night fell with nothing settled.

At dawn the next day, the Mexican priests traveling with the army said a splendid mass to prepare the troops for battle. After the ceremony, Santa Anna sent his men smashing into the American left flank. Ridge by ridge, the Mexicans drove the Americans back with bayonets. But as the foe's left collapsed, the Mexicans ran into a fresh American regiment whose first volley broke the momentum of their charge. The Mexican line wavered, stopped and fell back.

At noon, Santa Anna's men charged again. But then, amid a violent rainstorm, the Americans counterattacked with bayonets and bowie knives. Locked together, half blinded with blood and rain, the two forces ripped at each other. Late that afternoon, the Americans put on a weak charge, and the Mexicans punched them back. Then, with the rain coming down in solid sheets, both sides stopped fighting, too tired and too hurt to go on.

Another attack by the Mexican army might well have finished the Americans. But on the morning of February 24, the Mexican army was in full retreat on orders from their commander. Santa Anna took some captured flags and called it a victory.

It was a dubious victory at best. According to a Mexican reporter, 800 wounded men were left on the battlefield: "They couldn't be transported to Aguanueva, the town the army was ordered to go to next, so most of the wounded were abandoned in the desert." Alcaraz added that these poor wretches, "steeped in their blood, shivering with cold, parched with thirst, without shelter, saw their companions disappear. In sight already were the jackals and the dogs who awaited their frightful banquet."

At Aguanueva there "was a slimy standing pond into which the soldiers plunged, dying with thirst. But scarcely had they tasted when they expired in frightful convulsions. Their blood, mixing with the scum upon the water, made the drinking intolerable. Yet there was no other water. Soon the sight of the dead bodies, the death rattle of the dying, the moaning of the wounded, and the cursing of all, added new griefs." By the time the army reached the town of San Luis Potosí 250 miles across the desert, it was no longer an army.

Two weeks after the battle of Buena Vista, the citizens of Veracruz saw Scott's men coming ashore in specially built surfboats. The city was a fortress, and it stood up to more than two weeks of bombardment by field artillery and naval ships lying at anchor in the bay. The people felt honored that the Americans would make war on civilians. "Patriotism was everything," wrote reporter José Bárcena. "Women made bandages out of bed sheets for the wounded. All the capable men enlisted in the national guard."

Finally, on March 27, the nightmare ended, and Veracruz belonged to these new invaders. The citizens watched in pain and foreboding a week later as the Americans started marching up the steep, winding National Road, which ran 300 miles between Veracruz and Mexico City.

Santa Anna, meanwhile, had reached Mexico City. Despair had been sweeping through the capital, but Santa Anna's commanding presence revived the hopes of the Mexicans. In an amazingly short time, he was able to restore order to the government, raise capital and start to build a new army that would eventually reach 30,000 men. "The nation has not yet lost its vitality," he proclaimed on March 31. "I swear to you I will answer for the triumph of Mexico. Veracruz calls for vengeance. Follow me and I will wash out the stain of her dishonor."

Santa Anna immediately set out at the head of 16,000 men to stop the Americans marching up the National Road. The place he had in mind was called Cerro Gordo. It was a narrow pass through which the road twisted and turned alongside a river.

To hold the National Road, Santa Anna lined up with troops and guns and mounted his main batteries atop two hills, Atalaya and Telégrafo. He held another body of troops in reserve behind the forward positions. His battle plan seemed quite sound, though his engineers politely suggested to him that the Americans would be able to outflank the two hills and strike them from the rear. Santa Anna looked over the rocky, wooden terrain and then sneered. Not even a rabbit could get through, he said.

Scott halted suspiciously at the entrance to the gorge on April 12. Several days passed, during which the Mexicans had indications that the Americans were seeking a way around the roadside gauntlet of guns. Sentries posted to the rear heard axes ringing in the dis-

Vicente Suárez, 13

Juan de la Barrera, 20

Fernando Montes de Oca, 17

THE BOY HEROES OF CHAPULTEPEC

When the fury of battle subsided at Chapultepec, these six young cadets of the Mexican Military Academy were dead, but their valor had earned them the lasting admiration of their countrymen. Refusing to retreat from their fortress-school, they had fought beside the regulars "like demons," as one U.S. correspondent said. Indeed, one cadet, Juan Escutia, reportedly snatched the academy flag from its staff, wrapped it around his body, and patriotically leaped to his death on the rocks below the castle.

Agustín Melgar, 18

Juan Escutia, 20

Francisco Marquez, 14

217

tance, and two of them reported the telltale sound to Santa Anna. The general laughed at the first sentry and threatened the second one with disciplinary action for spreading subversive rumors.

On April 17, Santa Anna discovered that Scott — no rabbit, but a mountain of a man, nearly six and a half feet tall — had somehow found a way to squeeze himself and 8,500 troops through the woods and ravines behind the lofty Mexican defenses. The Americans had cut a road through the woods down the full length of the Mexican line. Frantically the Mexican gun crews swung their cannon around and began firing at a long wave of American skirmishers. The guns, now loaded with American-style grape, did terrible damage, but it was too late to save Atalaya. Its defenders were driven off the peak, and the enemy turned the captured guns on the Mexican troops defending nearby Telégrafo hill.

On April 18, in a devastating reprise of the battle for Monterrey, the Americans atop Atalaya swept down its slope and up the west side of Telégrafo. Simultaneously, a second American force burst out of the woods below the hill and charged upslope from the north. The Mexicans fought desperately between and among the two assault forces; at one point in the fighting the heavy guns of both armies fell silent, unable to distinguish friend from foe.

The battle for Telégrafo raged on for three hours. "The 2nd Light and the 3rd and 4th of the line lost almost their entire force," Alcaraz wrote. "The enemy successively gained possession of the lower works of the position, and without losing an instant, rapidly ascended to assault the last crest of the hill. Some of our soldiers now began to leave their ranks, attempting to mingle with the wounded." Mexican officers ordered a bayonet charge, but the surviving troops were falling back; they and their commander, "sword in hand, were actually rolled together down the opposite declivity, borne along by the multitude which poured onward like a torrent from the height. On the summit of the hill now was seen, in the midst of a column of dense smoke, a multitude of Americans. Above the mass of blue formed by the Americans still floated our deserted flag. But the banner of the stars was soon raised by the enemy on the same staff."

Just then, another column of American soldiers emerged out of the woods and struck at the Mexican reserves, throwing them into complete and utter confusion. The Americans worked among them with bayonets, and as the United States troops on Telégrafo hill came pouring down in a new attack, the whole Mexican army broke and ran.

Of his 18,000 men, Santa Anna lost 3,000 captured and several thousand more killed or wounded. For the second time within two months, he had presided over the liquidation of an army. For the second time, too, Santa Anna made good his escape — although he left behind all his personal baggage, including a chest containing $20,000 in coin.

As catastrophes went, Cerro Gordo was far worse than Buena Vista; it left the enemy a clear route to Mexico City. Defeatist talk swept the capital. José Ramírez, a minor government official, wrote that Cerro Gordo was "a rout as complete as it was shameful," and said that most soldiers "surrendered their arms almost without defense." In another letter, he reported, "Officers declare that the Yankees are invincible, and the soldiers are telling terrible tales. Some say that the enemy soldiers are such huge, strong men that they can cut an opponent in two with a single sweep of their swords. It is also said that their muskets discharge shots which, once they leave the gun, divide into fifty pieces, each one fatal and well-aimed." A few days later, Ramírez added, "Our situation is truly desperate. Everything is lost."

Santa Anna, himself depressed, rode hard toward Mexico City with the remnants of his army strung out behind him. His pell-mell passage through the city of Puebla started a panicky civilian exodus. Ramírez, reporting the news from Puebla, wrote: "There's no means of transportation; you can't even find a donkey; the families travel by foot, they live in fear."

At this point, the Americans gave Mexico City a new lease on life. Scott's army made a detour to capture Santa Anna's home town of Jalapa. "The wounded in Jalapa," Ramírez wrote, "are suffering many deprivations and miseries; urged by necessity they leave the hospital and die in the fields which are covered with corpses in a state of corruption."

Then the Americans moved on to Puebla, where they tarried for a full 10 weeks, regrouping and bringing in reinforcements from Veracruz. When the American army finally resumed its march toward the capital on August 7, it numbered 14,000 men.

Santa Anna used the hiatus to prepare what he was certain would be a lethal reception for the Americans. Recovering his natural self-assurance, he raised still another army of close to 30,000 men; more volunteers than ever before fell out to take arms. A smashing victory here might yet win the war for Mexico; Scott's army would have no place to fall back on but Veracruz, and it could be picked apart during its 300-mile retreat to the Gulf.

Surely Scott would be inviting disaster when he attacked the well-nigh impregnable capital. The glittering sprawl of Mexico City was ringed with mountains and lay near the center of an obstacle-strewn valley about 32 miles wide and 46 miles long. Barring the National Road from the east was El Peñon, a fortified hill whose gun batteries commanded a long causeway running between Lake Texcoco and an impassable marsh. Lake Texcoco protected the city to the north, and guarding it to the south and east was an arc of fortresses interspersed with jagged beds of lava and more lakes and marshlands. A tactician could not choose a better place to defend, or a more horrendous one to attack.

On August 15, Mexican patrols reported that the American army had topped the last pass and paused while its engineers reconnoitered the valley below. Santa Anna took personal command of 7,000 troops manning El Peñon. In Mexico City, the 200,000 citizens braced themselves for the onslaught, waiting with a confidence born of desperate resolve.

To Santa Anna's great surprise, the Americans merely feinted toward El Peñon and swung off to the southwest. In a swift march of about 25 miles, they wheeled past two large lakes, waded through a huge marsh and seized the town of San Augustin, located nine miles due south of Mexico City, on a road that ran north between a lake and the massive lava fields known as the Pedregal. Santa Anna responded swiftly, shifting the biggest part of his troops to block the southern approach to Mexico City.

The American occupation of San Augustin threatened to cut off the Mexican troops defending Contreras, a village four miles farther west. So Santa Anna sent orders to the troops there to withdraw northward, past the western edge of the lava fields. Tragically,

however, the commanding general at Contreras was a flamboyant fool named Gabriel Valencia, who hated Santa Anna and refused to obey a command that denied him a chance for glory. Instead of retreating, Valencia chose to advance—and actually won some skirmishes. But at dawn on August 20, Valencia woke up to discover that the greater part of the American army was attacking his troops from the rear. Incredibly, the enemy had found a ravine leading through the impassable lava fields and had made the crossing in the dead of night, with no light to guide them but the shellbursts of their artillery.

Behind Contreras, Mexicans and Americans crashed together in a frenzy that lasted less than 20 minutes. When the battle was over, Valencia's army had been broken and routed, leaving a gaping hole—and an open road—through the Mexican right flank. Realizing the danger, Santa Anna ordered his troops to fall back to the village of Churubusco, situated on a small river five miles from Mexico City. The Mexicans emplaced themselves around a bridge crossing the river and fortified a strong stone convent on the edge of town.

General Pedro María Anaya, in command of a large force of militiamen defending the road to Mexico City, understood that Churubusco must be held by Mexico as long as possible at whatever cost. In the convent, General Manuel Rincón readied his 1,400-odd troops for a last-ditch stand. General Francisco Pérez, commanding a small force at the bridge, prepared his soldiers for almost certain death. These three generals would make Churubusco Mexico's most brilliantly fought battle of the war.

On August 20, an overwhelming mass of about 8,000 American troops converged on the bridge, but Pérez's men drove them back. Time and again, Rincón's troops positioned in the convent repelled waves of American soldiers charging across a wide cornfield. For 90 minutes, Anaya's gun crews outdueled the enemy artillery and forced the Americans to pull back their cannon. When the Americans outflanked the convent, Santa Anna rushed 2,200 of his infantrymen to halt their attack, and he sent 2,000 cavalrymen to harass the American left.

But the Churubusco defenders, running out of ammunition and manpower, had to give ground. Two American infantry regiments took the bridge in vicious hand-to-hand fighting. The troops in the convent, battered beyond all human endurance, could no longer hold out, yet three times the most valiant among them forcibly prevented their comrades from waving a white flag. Finally an American lieutenant mercifully halted the slaughter by waving a white handkerchief himself. Not until then did the Mexican survivors lay down their arms and give themselves up to the Americans.

General Anaya, critically wounded and with his face and hands badly burned, struggled forward to surrender to a huge American general named David Twiggs. Twiggs wanted to confiscate the Mexican ammunition and asked Anaya where it was stored. Anaya replied grimly, "If there was ammunition, you would not be here, general." The Mexican survivors at Churubusco wept with pride at Anaya's remark, and also at the tribute paid them on the spot by the American victors: "The glory is all theirs."

The battles for Mexico City's outer defenses had cost Santa Anna nearly 10,000 dead and wounded. The Americans, too, had been badly gored, losing 1,000 dead and wounded out of the 8,500 troops engaged. So General Scott was more than willing to agree when Santa Anna, cannily bargaining for time to regroup, proposed a truce and the start of peace talks. The guns fell silent on August 21 and remained silent through September 6.

The peace negotiations got nowhere, and on September 7 Scott sent word that he was renewing hostilities. The two armies now stood face to face in long curved lines about three miles below Mexico City: nearly 12,000 Mexicans versus about 9,000 Americans. Blocking the road to the capital were two enormous Mexican citadels. The first of these was a massive stone complex consisting of a mill, Molino del Rey, where cannon and gunpowder were manufactured, and an armament warehouse, Casa Mata. Some 4,000 Mexicans manned the mill and the warehouse; seven guns were emplaced between the two buildings, and 4,000 cavalrymen were poised to ride down the flank of any attacking force.

At dawn on September 8, after a brief artillery bombardment, an American division of 3,250 troops launched a frontal assault on the mill. The Mexican artillery fired with awful effect, scything great gaps in the ranks of a 500-man attack force and killing 11 of its

14 officers. The destruction of this unit was completed by a wild Mexican counterattack. Wrote Alcaraz, "The 3rd Light pursued them, making a vivid fire. Our soldiers, in ecstasies of enthusiasm, made a horrible slaughter among the assailants and actually came to musket range of the enemy's line of battle." Then they withdrew.

Next, an American brigade advanced to within 30 yards of Casa Mata before Mexican cannonading first staggered, then stopped it. Again the defenders counterattacked, tearing at the Americans with their bare hands. The tide of battle surged back and forth between the armies for an hour before the decisive action began at Molino del Rey.

Small groups of Americans worked their way to the walls of the mill and battered down a gate at its southern corner. As the enemy poured in, the Mexicans fought savage little battles for every nook and cranny, retreating room by room, then dividing their decimated forces to fight other Americans who had battered down a door at the northwest corner of the mill.

Every Mexican, great and small, was a battle hero. One defender later wrote that Colonel Lucas Balderas, terribly wounded, "dragged himself with his sword held high to cheer his soldiers until, bleeding copiously, he fell into his son Antonio's arms." And there was Margarito Suazo, formerly a poor craftsman, who had been honored for his soldierly devotion to duty by being named color-bearer: "Margarito was trampled and wounded several times with a bayonet. When he was dying, he took off his clothes and wrapped his bloody body with the flag."

By noon, the Mexicans had been driven out of the mill and the warehouse, leaving nearly 2,000 comrades lying dead or wounded. Still they fought on, retreating slowly in good order, making the Americans pay dearly for the ground they gained. About 800 Americans were killed or wounded in the battle, and still more died in the blazing warehouse when the flames reached the powder magazine and the whole great building blew up.

After the explosion, a deathly calm settled over the battlefield. For four days both the Mexican and American armies regrouped in grim silence in and around the one fortress that still barred the approach to Mexico City. It was an awesome citadel, a tremendous pile of

masonry crowning a 200-foot-high crag that jutted up from the valley floor about 1,000 yards from the ruins of Molino del Rey.

This was Chapultepec, also known simply as "the castle," and it was as much a shrine as a fortress to the Mexicans. Here, more than three hundred years before, the Aztec emperor Moctezuma lolled beside splashing fountains. Here, in 1519, the Spanish conquistador Cortés came with his gold-hungry handful of white-faced soldiers to destroy the palace and the Indian civilization that had built it. Here, in 1783, a Spanish viceroy built a new citadel atop the ruins of Moctezuma's old palace. And some three decades later, at the onset of the Mexican revolutions, the viceroy's building had been abandoned.

But around 1840, the Mexicans had restored and enlarged Chapultepec, and they soon made it the home of the National Military Academy. The young cadets —some of them mere boys of 13—had drilled here, resplendent in their gray uniforms and tasseled blue caps. About 100 cadets were still in Chapultepec on the eve of the last battle of the war. They were ordered to evacuate their school and to go to safe places, but they chose to stay on, proudly guarding this memorial to Mexican history.

The cadets who would fight for Chapultepec along with the remnants of the Mexican army would not be fighting for victory. The war had already been lost at Churubusco, even earlier at Cerro Gordo, and perhaps as far back as the American landing at Veracruz. These young men would be fighting to die with gallantry and thus save the last shreds of Mexican honor and pride in a hopeless cause.

On September 12, both sides completed preparations for the battle. Santa Anna gave General Nicolás Bravo only 800-odd troops to defend Chapultepec; he assumed—erroneously as usual—that the last major struggle for Mexico City would be fought out at the capital's San Cosmé and Belén gates, at the head of two causeways leading up from the marshes. Santa Anna made an elaborate point of inspecting the defenses at those gates. He also wasted a great deal of time exhorting citizens to stay in town, but he could not stop the old and the weak from departing, a steady

221

With Mexico City's cathedral as a backdrop, U.S. troops parade triumphantly through the main plaza in this 1847 lithograph by Carl Nebel. The artist, a German living in Mexico, struck a note of continuing defiance by depicting a civilian *(lower left)* hurling a paving stone at the victors.

223

stream of silent refugees. In a last-ditch attempt to bolster civilian morale, Santa Anna went so far as to put on a pathetic parade in honor of his victory over the Spaniards at Tampico.

At 5:30 a.m. on September 13, the Americans opened their final assault with a heavy bombardment of Chapultepec. About two hours later, the enemy guns shifted their fire to Mexican positions in a grove of cypress trees beneath the fortress, and then American infantrymen began advancing under an umbrella of grapeshot, cannister and explosive shells. It was horrible, Alcaraz recounted. It seemed as though each American cannon "maintained a projectile in the air" at all times, with "the greater part of their discharges taking effect."

With the intensity of the shellfire the battered castle quickly became a charnel house. "In the corridor, converted into a surgical hospital, were found mixed up the putrid bodies, the wounded breathing mournful groans, and the young boys of the college."

The enemy attacks were repulsed and renewed. Always the Americans kept coming. They were, wrote Alcaraz, "a cloud of skirmishers, using rocks, bushes, dead angles and our fortifications for cover, destroying our defenders with their sure shots."

Santa Anna kept maneuvering the bulk of his army aimlessly, not knowing where to assign reinforcements. When he finally sent the famous San Blas Battalion to relieve the fortress, that gallant unit was cut to ribbons, and its brave Indian commander, Colonel D. Santiago Xicontencatl, was killed. Meanwhile, the defense of Chapultepec was crippled by the loss of other key leaders, among them General Pérez, the hero of the bridge at Churubusco.

At 8:30 a.m., American assault troops clambered up the crag and flung scaling ladders against the high castle walls. The defenders toppled many a ladder and shot down many an American soldier at point-blank range. But some ladders stayed up, and the enemy managed to win footholds on the parapets. From these vantage points, they forged outward in vicious hand-to-hand fighting. Alcaraz wrote, "Our defenders, stupefied by the bombardment, fatigued, wanting sleep, and hungry, were hurled down to the rocks by the bayonet or taken prisoner." The Americans, more and more of them, were now sweeping through the fortress, con-

quering it room by room, killing the defenders, killing and mutilating wounded men.

The Mexican soldiers kept up their struggle in dwindling clusters. So did the young cadets. Just before 9:30 a.m., General Bravo tried to stop the slaughter, surrendering the fortress to the nearest American officer, a lowly lieutenant. But the gallant cadets fought on. Alcaraz wrote, "A company of the New York regiment ascended to the top of the building, where some of the students still were firing, the last defenders of that Mexican flag which was to be quickly replaced by the American." One cadet, Agustín Melgar, was wounded twice but still refused to give up. The Americans captured him and then bayoneted him. Melgar was carried down to the hospital, where he died the next day.

After the surrender of Chapultepec, Mexico City fell quickly. Americans swarmed up the two causeways to the capital and battered down the gates. By noon, they had driven through the Belén gate, into the city. Toward nightfall, a surprisingly strong and savage counterattack drove the invaders back to the gate, but there they stayed.

At this point, Mexico's organized resistance ceased. The Mexican army, broken again and this time irreparably, fled the city in small groups under cover of night, and Santa Anna fled too. Next day, diehard patriots began guerrilla actions in and around Mexico City, and they continued their forlorn raids even after the formal negotiations began. Still later, Santa Anna tried to rally Mexicans for an attack on the American rear guard at Puebla, but he could find no followers. The war was really over. All told, in 17 months, more than 25,000 Mexicans had died in combat, as compared to 5,000 Americans.

Negotiations began in earnest on August 27, and the treaty of peace was signed on February 2, 1848, in the palace at Guadalupe-Hidalgo, four miles north of Mexico City. The terms were quite simple: the United States got precisely what it wanted—what it had already taken. Mexico recognized the Rio Grande as its border with Texas. Mexico ceded one third of its territory, California and New Mexico, and received in consolation a payment of $15 million.

The United States threw a second bone to the vanquished Mexicans: it assumed $3,250,000 in debts owed by Mexico to American citizens. To make way for peace, Santa Anna was deposed as president; it was the third time he had lost this office, but he would reclaim it twice more before he hung up his sword for good in 1855.

Soon after the treaty was signed, the American army of occupation began returning home, leaving Mexico to the Mexicans. Ramon Alcaraz and his 14 associates ended their chronicle with a solemn, judicious reprise of the five-month-long evacuation. "The United States troops continued their withdrawing, and finally departed from that ground, the theater of their victories and of our disasters. The war being over, there remained in our hearts a feeling of sadness for the evils it had produced, and in our minds a fruitful lesson of how difficult it is when disorder, asperity and anarchy prevail, to uphold the defense and salvation of a people."

To most Mexicans, this view was just a little short of lily-livered. Mexico had been horribly defeated and ignominiously stripped of the Spanish West—none of which improved the Mexicans' disposition toward their expansionist neighbor. Mexican hatred of the United States still smoldered, and would not burn itself out for a full generation.

There was rancor, too, among the Mexicans in the Spanish West, now the American West. The bitter resentments of many Californios and New Mexicans toward the Americans were eloquently summed up at the time of the treaty by the Mexican diplomat Manuel Crescencio Rejón, who declared, "Our race, our unfortunate people, will have to wander in search of hospitality in a strange land, only to be ejected later. Descendants of the Indians that we are, the North Americans hate us, their spokesmen depreciate us, and they consider us unworthy to form with them one nation and one society."

All too often, ugly episodes proved Rejón right. Many Mexicans suffered prejudice as American settlers crowded in on them and their ancestral lands. For only one egregious example, American hostility toward all Mexicans forced Captain Placido Benavides, who had led a troop of pro-American Mexicans against their own countrymen, to leave the Texas town of Victoria and move his family to a more tolerant, heterogeneous place, Louisiana. In addition, many Mexicans were forced from their land by American squatters and resettled in Mexico. Many more Mexicans emigrated to Mexico because they could not stand the culture shock of American institutions, American ways and the English language, essential now but hard to fit on a Spanish-speaking tongue.

And yet the great majority of Mexican-Americans stuck it out. To a degree, they had been prepared for the change in governments by their long isolation from Mexico, by their latent separatist movements, by their amicable early experiences with American traders. Though they sometimes discovered that an American-run local government was obviously dishonest, it was never irremediably corrupt or downright repressive. Fair-minded Mexicans admitted that the Americans' rough-hewn frontier democracy came closer to the principles on which it was based than did the cynical despotisms that had been forced upon them by their own generals and aristocrats in the name of their good republican constitution.

And with the passage of time, conditions improved for the scattered Mexican-American communities. More and more Americans tolerated Mexicans and even adopted or adapted their fiestas, foods, clothing and architecture. For better and worse, intermarriage was on the increase, and not merely among the aristocrats—the Veramendi clan of Texas, the Chavez of New Mexico and the Vallejos of California—whose wealth made them highly desirable relatives.

Slowly, the life and the opportunities that existed among the Americans in the Spanish West stopped the exodus of Mexicans and began a peaceful re-invasion of people from the homeland. In 1870 more Mexicans—some 23,000 of them—lived in Texas than any other immigrant group but the Germans.

The Mexican-Americans did change, and the Anglo-Americans changed along with them. The Americans learned that the Mexicans' long and patient sufferings were as worthy of respect as their own boisterous victories and flashy successes. Americans learned, too, that their youthful, informal, energetic society need not eliminate the Mexicans' solemn and gracious way of life. And they were beginning to understand that the Mexicans—and their Spanish heritage of culture, courage, dignity and honor—were an indispensable American asset.

The widow of Vicente Lugo presides over her handsome brood on their once-huge Los Angeles ranch, reduced to 400 acres by 1870.

From Mexicans into Mexican-Americans

Mexican courage was severely tested as the Spanish West became United States territory. Many Mexicans began their lives as American citizens by losing their homesteads to squatters, or in fruitless lawsuits over the validity of their old land grants. Don Vicente Lugo, head of a once-influential California family *(below)*, lamented legal judgments that cost him nearly all of his 30,000-acre estate: "I sacrificed even the house in which I lived."

Gradually, the Mexican communi-ties learned how to use the American democratic process to redress grievances. Mexican-Americans around San Antonio became an important political force. Reginaldo del Valle and other young Californians studied law, organized the "Spanish vote" and served their people as state congressmen. By the turn of the century, the Mexican-Americans knew their Spanish heritage, far from being lost in the process of Americanization, had kept them strong through the difficult years of transition.

The middle-class family of Ramon García celebrates the first communion of a daughter in their well-furnished Santa Fe house around 1890. New Mexico, too arid to attract a massive influx of American settlers, survived its change in governments with a minimum of painful disruption.

228

229

White-bearded Jose Policarpo Rodriguez stands with members of his family before their substantial rancho at Privilege Creek in Bandera County, Texas. Born in Mexico, Rodriguez moved to San Antonio as a boy; after annexation, he often served as a guide for the United States Army.

In Ventura, California, the family of state senator Reginaldo del Valle (not present) enjoys a picnic at Rancho Camulos at the turn of the century. The ranch, though reduced in size after the American takeover, became famous as the setting for Helen Hunt Jackson's romantic novel, *Ramona*.

232

TEXT CREDITS

For full reference on specific page credits see bibliography.

Chapter 1: Particularly useful sources for information and quotes in this chapter were: H. E. Bolton, *Coronado*, The Univ. of New Mexico Press, 1964; H. E. Bolton, *The Spanish Borderlands*, Yale Univ. Press, 1921; J. B. Brebner, *The Explorers of North America*, Meridian, 1964; F. W. Hodge and T. H. Lewis, *Spanish Explorers in the Southern United States*, Barnes & Noble, 1907; G. P. Winship, ed. and trans., *The Journey of Coronado*, A. S. Barnes, 1904; 17 — Whitman quotes, Whitman, pp. 402-403; 27 — instructions to Fray Marcos, Day, p. 34; 29 — Fray Marcos reports, Hallenbeck, *Fray Marcos*, p. 34. Chapter 2: Particularly useful sources: H. E. Bolton, *Outpost of Empire*, Alfred A. Knopf, 1939; G. Ashford, *Spanish Texas*, Weybright and Talley, 1970; J. F. Bannon, *The Spanish Borderlands Frontier*, Univ. of New Mexico Press, 1974; C. E. Chapman, *A History of California*, Macmillan, 1921; 49 — Cortés quote, Fehrenbach, *Lone Star*, p. 45; 61 — De León quote, Bolton, *The Spanish Borderlands*, p. 215; 64 — quote from *The Exploits of Esplandian*, Rolle, pp. 33-34; 70 — Anza letter, Bolton, *Anza's California Expeditions*, Vol. 5, p. 3. Chapter 3: Particularly useful sources: H. H. Bancroft, *History of the North Mexican States and Texas*, Arno Press, 1967; W. H. Callcott, *Santa Anna*, Univ. of Oklahoma Press, 1936; C. E. Castañeda, trans., *The Mexican Side of the Texan Revolution*, P. L. Turner, 1928; José Enrique de la Peña, *With Santa Anna in Texas*, trans. and ed. by Carmen Perry, Texas A&M Univ. Press, 1975; 110-112 — Delgado quotes, Sowell, pp. 128-137. Chapter 4: Particularly useful sources: H. H. Bancroft, *History of Arizona and New Mexico*, Horn & Wallace, 1962; Fray F. A. Dominguez, *The Missions of New Mexico, 1776*, ed. by E. B. Adams and Fray A. Chavez, Univ. of New Mexico Press, 1956; E. Fergusson, *New Mexico*, Knopf, 1951; J. Gregg, *Commerce of the Prairies*, ed. by Max Moorhead, Univ. of Oklahoma Press, 1954; L. B. Prince, *Historical Sketches of New Mexico*, Leggat Bros. and Ramset, Millet & Hudson, 1883; A. B. Thomas, *Forgotten Frontiers*, Univ. of Oklahoma Press, 1932; Marc Simmons, *Little Lion of the Southwest*, Swallow Press, 1973; 141 — Rio Grande description, Pike, p. 621; 147 — atrocity description, Kendall, pp. 393-394. Chapter 5: Particularly useful sources: H. H. Bancroft, *History of California*, Arno Press, 1967; C. E. Chapman, *A History of California*, Macmillan, 1921; M. M. McKittrick, *Vallejo*, Binfords & Mort, 1944; N. Van de Grift Sanchez, *Spanish Arcadia*, Powell, 1929; G. Tays, "Mariano Guadalupe Vallejo and Sonoma," *California Historical Society Quarterly*, March 1938; 161-162 — Vancouver quote, Pourade, *Time of the Bells*, pp. 82-83; 170-173 — wedding party description, Davis, p. 51; 174-175 — recipes adapted from Packman; 176 — Dana, quotes, Dana, pp. 90-94; 186 — Senora Vallejo quote, Richman, p. 498; Dana on Vallejo, Dana, pp. 256-257; Vallejo speech, Revere, pp. 28-30. Chapter 6: Particularly useful sources: H. H. Bancroft, *The North Mexican States and Texas*, Arno Press, 1967; José María Roa Bárcena, *Recuerdos de la Invasion Norteamericana*, Editorial Porrua, 1971; N. C. Brooks, *A Complete History of the Mexican War*, Rio Grande Press, 1965; W. H. Callcott, *Santa Anna*, Univ. of Oklahoma Press, 1936; *La Crónica*, Issue 2, Center for Study of Innovative Education, 1975; S. V. Connor and O. B. Faulk, *North America Divided*, Oxford Univ. Press, 1971; J. F. Ramírez, *Mexico During the War with the United States*, W. V. Scholes, ed., Univ. of Missouri Press, 1950; A. C. Ramsey, trans. and ed., *The Other Side* (the Alcaraz chronicles), B. Franklin, 1970.

PICTURE CREDITS

The sources for the illustrations in this book are shown below. Credits from left to right are separated by semicolons, from top to bottom by dashes.

Cover, 40, 69, 162, 163, 187, 191, 192, 193 — The Bancroft Library. 2, 170, 171 — Henry Groskinsky, courtesy Santa Barbara Historical Society. 6, 7 — The Society of Calif. Pioneers. 8, 9 — The Thomas Gilcrease Institute of American History and Art, Tulsa, Okla. 10, 11 — The Society of Calif. Pioneers. 12, 13 — Frank Lerner, courtesy Howard Gray Park III Collection. 14, 15 — John Zern, courtesy San Antonio Museum Assn., Witte Memorial Museum, Texas. 16 — *Portal of the Mission of San Jose, Texas*, Thomas Allen, courtesy Museum of Fine Arts, Boston. 20 — Frank Lerner, courtesy School of American Research, Museum of New Mexico. 21 — Frank Lerner, courtesy Museum of New Mexico Collections — Frank Lerner, courtesy School of American Research, Museum of New Mexico; Frank Lerner, courtesy Spanish Colonial Arts Society, Inc., Museum of New Mexico — Frank Lerner, courtesy Historical Society of New Mexico, Museum of New Mexico. 22 — Henry Groskinsky, courtesy Carmel Mission; Frank Lerner, courtesy San Jose Mission, State and National Historic Site, San Antonio — Henry Groskinsky, courtesy Mission San Juan Capistrano, Calif. 23 — Henry Groskinsky, courtesy Mission San Fernando Rey de España, San Fernando, Calif., except bottom right Henry Groskinsky, courtesy Mission San Juan Capistrano. 24 — Henry Groskinsky, courtesy History Div., Los Angeles County Museum of Natural History — Frank Lerner, courtesy Museum of New Mexico; Paulus Leeser, courtesy The Metropolitan Museum of Art. 25 — Frank Lerner, courtesy Museum of New Mexico — Frank Lerner, courtesy Spanish Colonial Arts Society, Inc., Museum of New Mexico. 28 — The Huntington Library, San Marino, Calif. 31, 32, 33 — Museo de America, Madrid. 36, 37, 65, 201 — Maps by Robert Ritter. 42 — American History Div., The New York Public Library, Astor, Lenox and Tilden Foundations. 45 — Paulus Leeser, courtesy The Metropolitan Museum of Art. 46, 47 — Ernst Haas. 48 — From the collection of Carl Schaefer Dentzel, copied by Roy Robinson. 53 — The Bancroft Library — Manuel Embuena, courtesy Biblioteca Nacional, Madrid. 54 — Benschneider, courtesy Collections of the Historical Society of New Mexico, History Div., Museum of New Mexico. 56, 57 — The Museum of the American Indian, Heye Foundation — Smithsonian Institution, National Anthrop. Archives. 58, 59 — Adam Clark Vroman, courtesy History Div., L.A. County Museum of Natural History — Smithsonian Institution, NAA; Ben Wittick, courtesy Museum of New Mexico — Adam Clark Vroman, courtesy History Div., L.A. County Museum of Natural History. 60, 61 — Smithsonian Institution, NAA. 63 — Benschneider, courtesy History Div., Museum of New Mexico. 66, 67 — Reproduced by permission of the British Library Board. Add. MS. 17662. 68 — © Bradley Smith, courtesy Archivo de Indias, Sevilla. 72, 73 — Yves Debraine, courtesy Dr. Hans von Segesserepp, Luzern. 74, 75 — Manuel Romero de Terreros, Unam. 77 — INAH. Museo Nacional de Historia, Mexico City. 78 through 83 — Milan Havlíček, REFO, Prague, courtesy State Library of the Czech Socialist Republic. MS. XVI B 18. 84, 85 — Frank Lerner, courtesy Peggy Miller, San Antonio, Tex. 86, 87, 90, 91, 92 — Frank Lerner, courtesy D.R.T. Library at the Alamo. 88, 89,

102 — Charles Patteson, courtesy San Antonio Museum Assn., Witte Memorial Museum. 94,95 — Institute of Texan Cultures, San Antonio. 97 — Barker Texas History Center, Univ. of Texas at Austin. 100,202, 203,221 — Frank Lerner, courtesy Latin American Collection, Univ. of Texas at Austin General Libraries. 101 — Prints Div., The New York Public Library, Astor, Lenox and Tilden Foundations — Frank Lerner, courtesy Latin American Collection, Univ. of Texas at Austin General Libraries. 105 — Ed Stewart Photography & Associates, Inc., from the Collections of the San Jacinto Museum of History Assn. 106,107,111 — © Bradley Smith, courtesy INAH. Museo Nacional de Historia. 109 — The Bettmann Archive — Rosenberg Library, Galveston. 112 — The New-York Historical Society. 113 — State Capitol Building, Austin, Texas. 115 — Reyes Valerio Constantino; Ed Stewart Photography & Associates, Inc., from the Collections of The San Jacinto Museum of History Assn. 116,117,120,121 — Frank Lerner, courtesy Collections in the Museum of New Mexico. 118,144,145,228,229 — Museum of New Mexico. 122 — Nebraska State Historical Society. 125,143 — Frank Lerner, courtesy History Div., Museum of New Mexico. 127 — Science and Technology Research Center, The New York Public Library, Astor, Lenox and Tilden Foundations. 128,129 — C. E. Watkins, courtesy The Bancroft Library. 132 — Frank Lerner, from the collection of Mr. and Mrs. Larry Frank — Frank Lerner, courtesy Holy Cross Church, Santa Cruz, N. Mex. 133 — Frank Lerner, from the collection of Mr. and Mrs. Larry Frank — Frank Lerner, courtesy Archdiocese of Santa Fe, Museum of New Mexico; Frank Lerner, courtesy Fred Harvey Foundation, Museum of New Mexico. 134 — Frank Lerner, courtesy Fred Harvey Foundation, Museum of New Mexico; Frank Lerner, from the collection of Mr. and Mrs. Larry Frank. 135 — Frank Lerner, courtesy Historical Society of New Mexico, Museum of New Mexico; Frank Lerner, from the collection of Mr. and Mrs. Larry Frank — Frank Lerner, courtesy Spanish Colonial Arts Society, Inc., Museum of New Mexico. 137 — Western History Dept., Denver Public Library. 138,139 — Rare Book Div., The New York Public Library, Astor, Lenox and Tilden Foundations. 140,141 — General Research and Humanities Div., The New York Public Library, Astor, Lenox and Tilden Foundations. 148,149 — Inset, Henry Groskinsky, courtesy Franciscan Friars of California — C. E. Watkins, courtesy The Huntington Library. 150,151 — Inset, Henry Groskinsky, courtesy San Gabriel Mission Parish — C. E. Watkins, courtesy The Huntington Library. 152,153 — Inset, Henry Groskinsky, courtesy Mission San Francisco de Asis — Calif. Historical Society Library. 154,155 — Inset, Henry Groskinsky, courtesy Old Mission Santa Ines — C. C. Pierce Collection in The Huntington Library. 156,157 — Inset, Henry Groskinsky, courtesy Mission San Luis Rey — C. E. Watkins, courtesy The Huntington Library. 158 — Bowers Museum, City of Santa Ana, Calif. 165 — Henry Groskinsky, courtesy Santa Barbara Mission Archive Library. 166,167 — Drawings by Russell A. Ruiz, courtesy Santa Barbara Mission Archive Library, copied by Dean Austin (2) — Drawing by Don Bolognese. 168,169 — Henry Groskinsky, courtesy San Gabriel Mission Parish. 172 — Stearns-Gaffey Collection in The Huntington Library. 174,226,227 — Henry Groskinsky, courtesy History Div., L.A. County Museum of Natural History. 178,179 — Henry Groskinsky, courtesy Mr. and Mrs. W. Edwin Gledhill. 182 — The Bancroft Library; Henry Groskinsky, courtesy Santa Barbara Historical Society. 183 — The Bancroft Library — Mary Stewart, LaJolla, Calif., and Dr. Ben Ely Grant III, Loma Linda Univ.; The Bancroft Library. 184, 185 — Historical Collection, Title Insurance & Trust Company, San Diego, except top right C. C. Pierce Collection in The Huntington Library. 190 — Henry Groskinsky, courtesy Calif. State Dept. of Parks & Recreation. 194,195 — Henry Groskinsky, courtesy Calif. State Dept. of Parks & Recreation (5); The Bancroft Library. 196,197 — Albert Moldvay. 198 — Samuel Chamberlain painting © Time Inc., copied by Paulus Leeser, courtesy U.S. Military Academy Museum, West Point. 204 — Burt Franklin Publishers, New York, copied by Herb Orth. 206,207 — The Franklin D. Roosevelt Library. 208,209,222,223 — Frank Lerner, courtesy of the Texas State Archives. 212,213 — Library of Congress. 217 — Carlos Alcazar, courtesy INAH. Museo Nacional de Historia. 230,231 — D.R.T. Library at the Alamo. 232,233 — Title Insurance & Trust Company, Los Angeles.

ACKNOWLEDGMENTS

The index for this book was prepared by Gale L. Partoyan. The editors give special thanks to the following persons: David Nevin and Keith Wheeler, who wrote portions of the book; Dr. Félix Almaráz, Univ. of Texas, San Antonio, who read portions of the text. The editors also thank Rev. Roger Anderson, O.F.M., Old Mission Santa Ines; Sylvia Arden, Wayne M. Fabert, San Diego Historical Society; Mary Beebe, Mission Nuestra Señora de la Soledad; Deborah Beevor, Weidenfeld and Nicolson, London; Gene Brack, New Mexico State Univ.; John Cahoon, John Dewar, William M. Mason, Los Angeles County Museum of Natural History; Jean Carefoot, Texas State Library; Maud D. Cole, Rare Book Div., New York Public Library; Michael Cox, Christine Mather, Arthur Olivas, Fred Vigil, Michael Webber, Museum of New Mexico; Dr. Carl S. Dentzel, Ruth M. Christensen, Ronald Kinsey, The Southwest Museum; Mrs. Madie Brown Emparan, Sonoma, Calif.; Larry Frank, Arroyo Hondo, N.M.; Suzanne H. Gallup, Lawrence Dinnean, The Bancroft Library; Jane Garner, Univ. of Texas General Libraries; Rev. Maynard Geiger, O.F.M., Old Mission Santa Barbara; Campbell Grant, Carpenteria, Calif.; Mrs. Sylvia Griffiths, Robert Gates, Santa Barbara Historical Society; Dr. Lewis Hieb, Washington State Univ.; Alan Jutzi, Mary Wright, Barbara Quinn, Winifred Popp, The Huntington Library; Dr. Chester Kielman, Barker Texas History Center, Univ. of Texas; Dorothy Knepper, San Jacinto Museum of History Assn.; Russ Leadabrand, South Pasadena, Calif.; Irene Lichens, Society of Calif. Pioneers; Moira Lucey, Madrid; Rev. Leo Mattecheck, Mission San Gabriel; Rev. Reginald McDonough, O.F.M., Mission San Miguel; Catherine McDowell, Maria Watson, D.R.T. Library at the Alamo; Mrs. Myrtle McKittrick, Oakland, Calif.; R. L. Menefee, William Getchy, Calif. Dept. of Parks and Recreation; Robert Miller, La Crónica, Center for the Study of Innovative Education, Pomona, Calif.; Samuel Nesmith, Laura Simmons, Institute of Texan Cultures; Dr. Helmut Nickel, The Metropolitan Museum of Art; Elvi Ogard, Fine Arts Museum, Santa Fe; Wendell Ott, Roswell Museum and Art Center; Robert Pettit, Nebraska State Historical Society; Miss Frederica D. Poett, Santa Barbara; Rev. Francis Paul Prucha, S. J., Marquette Univ.; Paula Richardson, NAA, Smithsonian Institution; Polly Schaafsma, Arroyo Hondo; Carlos Sandoval, New York; Dick Smith, Santa Barbara News-Press; Cecilia Steinfeldt, Witte Memorial Museum; Mrs. Mary Stewart, LaJolla, Calif.; Lydia Modi Vitale, Univ. of Santa Clara; D. Weber, San Diego State Univ.

Ahlborn, Richard Eigne, *The Sculpted Saints of a Borderland Mission.* Southwestern Mission Research Center, 1974.

Aiton, Arthur S., "Coronado's Muster Role." *The American Historical Review,* Vol. 44, No. 3, April 1939.

Ashford, Gerald, *Spanish Texas.* Jenkins Publ. Co., 1971.

Baker, Patricia, "The Bandini Family." *The Journal of San Diego History,* Vol. 15, No. 1, Winter 1969.

Bancroft, Hubert Howe:

History of Arizona and New Mexico. Horn & Wallace, 1962.

History of California. Arno Press in cooperation with McGraw-Hill, 1967.

History of Mexico. Arno Press in cooperation with McGraw-Hill, 1967.

History of the North Mexican States and Texas. Arno Press in cooperation with McGraw-Hill, 1967.

Bannon, John Francis, *The Spanish Borderlands Frontier 1513-1821.* Univ. of New Mexico Press, 1974.

Bauer, K. Jack, *The Mexican War.* Macmillan, 1974.

Bean, W., *California: An Interpretive History.* McGraw-Hill, 1968.

Beck, Warren A., *New Mexico.* Univ. of Oklahoma Press, 1962.

Beck, Warren A., and Ynez D. Haase, *Historical Atlas of California.* Univ. of Oklahoma Press, 1974.

Beck, W. A., and D. A. Williams, *California.* Doubleday, 1972.

Bell, Douglas, *Elizabethan Seamen.* J. B. Lippincott, 1936.

Bolton, Herbert E.:

Coronado: Knight of Pueblos and Plains. Whittlesey House, McGraw-Hill and the Univ. of New Mexico Press, 1949.

Outpost of Empire. Alfred A. Knopf, 1939.

Boyd, E.:

Popular Arts of Colonial New Mexico. Museum of International Folk Art, Santa Fe, 1959.

Popular Arts of Spanish New Mexico. Museum of New Mexico Press, 1974.

Brack, Gene M., *Mexico Views Manifest Destiny, 1821-1846.* Univ. of New Mexico Press, 1975.

Brebner, John Bartlet, *The Explorers of North America, 1492-1806.* Meridian Books, The World Publishing Co., 1964.

Brooks, Nathan C., *A Complete History of the Mexican War: Its Causes and Consequences.* The Rio Grande Press, 1965.

Callcott, W. H., *Santa Anna.* Univ. of Oklahoma Press, 1936.

Castañeda, Carlos E., trans., *The Mexican Side of the Texas Revolution.* P. L. Turner Co., 1928.

Chamberlain, Samuel, *My Confession.* Harper, 1956.

Chapman, Charles E.:

The Founding of Spanish California. Macmillan, 1916.

A History of California: The Spanish Period. Macmillan, 1921.

Chavez, Fray Angelico, *My Penitente Land.* Univ. of New Mexico Press, 1974.

Clayton, Merle, "The Bandinis, Grandees in an Era of Grandeur." *San Diego Magazine,* Vol. 21, Nos. 6-8, April, May, June, 1969.

Connor, Seymour V., and Odie B. Faulk, *North America Divided.* Oxford Univ. Press, 1971.

Dana, Richard Henry, *Two Years before the Mast.* World, 1946.

Davis, W. H., *Seventy-five Years in California.* John Howell, 1967.

Day, A. Grove, *Coronado's Quest.* Univ. of California Press, 1940.

De la Peña, José Enrique, *With Santa Anna in Texas,* trans. and ed. by Carmen Perry. Texas A&M Univ. Press, 1975.

Domínguez, Fray Francisco A., *The Missions of New Mexico,* ed. by E. B. Adams and Fray A. Chavez. Univ. of New Mexico Press, 1956.

Dozier, Edward P., *The Pueblo Indians of North America.* Holt, Rinehart and Winston, 1970.

Dunn, William E., *Spanish and French Rivalry in the Gulf Region of the U.S., 1678-1702.* Books for Libraries Press, 1971.

The Editorial Staff of Sunset Books, *The California Missions, A Pictorial History.* The Lane Book Co., 1964.

Farnham, Thomas J., *Life, Travels and Adventures in California and Scenes in the Pacific Ocean.* Wm. H. Graham, 1847.

Faulk, Odie B.:

Arizona, a Short History. Univ. of Oklahoma Press, 1970.

The Last Years of Spanish Texas, 1778-1821. Mouton, 1964.

Fehrenbach, T. R., *Lone Star: A History of Texas and the Texans.* Macmillan, 1968.

Fergusson, E., *New Mexico: Pageant of Three Peoples.* Knopf, 1951.

Frémont, John C., *Memoirs of My Life.* Belford, Clarke, 1887.

Geiger, Maynard J., O.F.M.:

Father Junipero Serra Paintings. Franciscan Fathers, 1958.

Franciscan Missionaries in Hispanic California, 1769-1848. The Huntington Library, 1969.

The Letters of Alfred Robinson. The Zamorano Club, Los Angeles, 1972.

Goetzmann, W. H., *Exploration and Empire.* Knopf, 1971.

Grant, Campbell, *Rock Art of the American Indian.* T. Y. Crowell, 1967.

Gregg, Andrew K., *New Mexico in the Nineteenth Century.* Univ. of New Mexico Press, 1968.

Gregg, Josiah, *Commerce of the Prairies,* ed. by Max Moorhead. Univ. of Oklahoma Press, 1954.

Hackett, C. W., "The Revolt of the Pueblo Indians of New Mexico in 1680." *Texas State Historical Association Quarterly,* Vol. 15, No. 2, October 1911.

Hallenback, Cleve:

Alvar Nunez Cabeza de Vaca. The Arthur H. Clark Co., 1940.

The Journey of Fray Marcos de Niza. Univ. Press, Dallas, 1949.

Hammond, George P., and Agapito Rey. *Don Juan de Onate: Colonizer of New Mexico 1595-1628.* Univ. of New Mexico Press, 1953.

Hittell, Theodore H., *History of California.* Pacific Press Publishing House and Occidental Publishing Co., 1885.

Hodge, F. W., and T. H. Lewis, *Spanish Explorers in the Southern United States, 1528-1543.* Barnes and Noble, 1907 (1954).

Hollon, W. Eugene, *The Lost Pathfinder: Zebulon Montgomery Pike.* Univ. of Oklahoma Press, 1949.

Horgan, Paul, *The Centuries of Santa Fe.* E. P. Dutton, 1956.

Hubbard, Harry D., *Vallejo,* Meador Publishing Co., 1941.

Innes, Hammond, *The Conquistadors.* Alfred A. Knopf, 1967.

Institute of Texan Cultures, *The Mexican Texans.* Univ. of Texas at San Antonio, 1975.

Jenkins, Myra Ellen, et al., *The Historic Preservation Program for New Mexico,* Vol. 1, State Planning Office, Santa Fe, 1974.

John, Elizabeth A. H., *Storms Brewed in Other Men's Worlds.* Texas A&M Univ. Press, 1975.

Johns, Sally C., "Viva los Californios: The Battle of San Pasqual." *The Journal of San Diego History,* Vol. 19, Fall 1973.

Jones, Oakah L., Jr., *Pueblo Warriors & Spanish Conquest.* Univ. of Oklahoma Press, 1966.

Kendall, George Wilkins, *The Texan Santa Fe Expedition.* The Lakeside Press, 1929.

A Kingdom of Saints: The Larry Frank Collection of New Mexico Spanish Colonial Art Works. Roswell Museum and Art Center, Nov. 1975 through May 1976.

Laughlin, Ruth, *Caballeros.* D. Appleton & Co., 1931.

Letter from Father Eusebio Francisco Kino to the Duchess d'Aveiro, 15th December 1683. Huntington Library, Manuscript #HM 9994.

Lummis, Charles F.:
  The Land of Poco Tiempo. Charles Scribner's Sons, 1893.
  A New Mexican David. Charles Scribner's Sons, 1905.

McGann, Thomas F., "The Ordeal of Cabeza de Vaca." *American Heritage,* December 1960.

McGinty, B., "The Carrillos of San Diego." *Historical Society of Southern California Quarterly,* Vol. 49, Nos. 1-2, March and June 1957.

McKittrick, Myrtle M., *Vallejo, Son of California.* Binfords and Mort, 1944.

Meyer, Larry L., "A State of Less than Enchantment." *The American West,* Vol. 12, No. 5, September 1975.

Miller, R. L., "A California Romance in Perspective: The Elopement, Marriage and Ecclesiastical Trial of Henry D. Fitch and Josefa Carrillo." *Journal of San Diego History,* Vol. 19, No. 2, Spring 1973.

Moorhead, Max L., *The Presidio.* Univ. of Oklahoma Press, 1975.

Moquin, Wayne, ed., *A Documentary History of the Mexican Americans.* Praeger Publishers, 1971.

Nelson, Edna Deu Pree, *The California Dons.* Appleton-Century-Crofts, 1962.

Nunis, Doyce B., Jr., *The Drawings of Ignacio Tirsch.* Dawson's Book Shop, Los Angeles, 1972.

Packman, Ana Bégné, *Early California Hospitality.* The Arthur H. Clark Co., 1938.

Parkes, Henry B., *A History of Mexico.* Houghton Mifflin, 1938.

Parry, J. H., *The Age of Reconnaissance.* World, 1963.

Pike, Zebulon Montgomery, *The Expeditions of Zebulon Montgomery Pike,* ed. by Elliott Covers. Ross & Haines, 1965.

Pitt, Leonard, *The Decline of the Californios.* Univ. of California Press, 1971.

Polzer, Charles, S. J., *A Kino Guide.* Southwestern Mission Research Center, 1972.

Ponton, Brownie and Bates H. M'Farland, "Alvar Nunez Cabeza de Vaca." *Texas Historical Association Quarterly,* Vol. 1.

Pourade, Richard F.:
  The Explorers. Union-Tribune Publishing Co., 1960.
  Time of the Bells. Union-Tribune Publishing Co., 1961.

Prince, L. Bradford, *Historical Sketches of New Mexico.* Leggat Brothers and Ramsey, Millet & Hudson, 1883.

Ramsey, Albert C., *The Other Side, or Notes for the History of the War Between Mexico and the United States.* Burt Franklin, 1970.

Reese, James V., and Lorrin Kennamer, *Texas, Land of Contrast.* W. S. Benson & Co., 1972.

Repplier, Agnes, *Junípero Serra.* Doubleday Doran & Co., 1933.

Revere, Joseph Warren, *A Tour of Duty in California.* C. S. Francis & Co., 1849.

Richman, Irving Berdine, *California Under Spain and Mexico, 1535-1847.* Houghton Mifflin, 1911.

Rittenhouse, Jack D., *The Santa Fe Trail: A Historical Bibliography.* Univ. of New Mexico Press, 1971.

Robinson, Alfred, *Life in California During a Residence of Several Years in That Territory.* Da Capo Press, 1969.

Robinson, W. W., *Los Angeles from the Days of the Pueblo.* California Historical Society, 1959.

Rolle, Andrew F., *California: A History.* AHM Publ. Corp., 1969.

Sanchez Lamego, Miguel A., *El Colegio Militar y la Defensa de Chapultepec en Septiembre 1847.* Mexico City, 1947.

Sanchez, Nellie Van de Grift, *Spanish Arcadia.* Powell, 1929.

Santa Barbara, Tierra Adorada. Security First National Bank of Los Angeles, 1930.

Scherer, Joanna Cohan, *Indians.* The Ridge Press and Crown Pub., 1973.

Shalkop, R. L., *Wooden Saints: The Santos of New Mexico.* Taylor Museum, Colorado Springs Fine Arts Center, 1967.

Silverberg, R., *The Pueblo Revolt.* Weybright and Talley, 1970.

Simmons, Marc, *The Little Lion of the Southwest.* Swallow Press, 1973.

Simpson, Sir George, *An Overland Journey round the World during the Years 1841 and 1842.* Lee and Blanchard, 1847.

Smith, Bradley, *Spain: A History in Art.* Simon and Schuster, 1966.

Smith, Justin H., *The War with Mexico,* 2 vols., Macmillan, 1919.

Sowell, A. J., *History of Fort Bend County.* W. J. Coyle, 1904.

Spicer, E. H., *Cycles of Conquest.* Univ. of Arizona Press, 1962.

Supplee, Charles, and Douglas and Barbara Anderson, *Canyon de Chelly.* KC Publications, 1974.

Tanner, Clara Lee, *Southwest Indian Painting.* Univ. of Arizona Press, 1957.

Tays, George, "Mariano Guadalupe Vallejo and Sonoma." *California Historical Society Quarterly,* Vol. 16, No. 2, June 1937.

Terrell, John U., *Journey into Darkness.* William Morrow, 1962.

Thomas, Alfred Barnaby:
  After Coronado. Univ. of Oklahoma Press, 1935.
  The Plains Indians and New Mexico, 1751-1778. Univ. of New Mexico Press, 1940.

Treutlein, Theodore E., "The Portolá Expedition of 1769-1770." *California Historical Society Quarterly,* Vol. 42.

Twitchell, Ralph Emerson, *The Leading Facts of New Mexican History.* Torch Press, 1911-1912.

Tyler, Ronnie C., *The Mexican War: A Lithographic Record.* Texas State Historical Assn., 1973.

Van Nostrand, Joanne, *A Pictorial and Narrative History of Monterey.* California Historical Society, 1968.

Villagrá, Gaspar Pérez de, *History of New Mexico.* Quivira Society Publications, Vol. 4, 1933.

Waters, Frank, *Book of the Hopi.* The Viking Press, 1963.

Watkins, T. H., *California, an Illustrated History.* American West Publishing Co., 1973.

Webb, Walter Prescott, ed.-in-chief, *The Handbook of Texas.* Texas State Historical Assn., 1952.

Weems, John Edward, *To Conquer a Peace: The War between the United States and Mexico.* Doubleday, 1974.

Whitman, Walt, *The Complete Poetry and Prose of Walt Whitman.* With an intro. by Malcolm Cowley. Pellegrini & Cudahy, 1948.

Williams, Neville, *The Sea Dogs.* Macmillan, 1975.

Williams, Stanley T., *The Spanish Background of American Literature.* Yale Univ. Press, 1955.

Williamson, James A., *Sir Francis Drake.* Collins, London, 1951.

Winship, George Parker, ed. and trans., *The Journey of Coronado.* A. S. Barnes, 1904.

Printed in U.S.A.